# Life Coaching Skills

# Life Coaching Skills

## How to Develop Skilled Clients

Richard Nelson-Jones

 SAGE Publications

London • Thousand Oaks • New Delhi

SAGE Publications Ltd
1 Oliver's Yard
55 City Road
London EC1Y 1SP

SAGE Publications Inc.
2455 Teller Road
Thousand Oaks, California 91320

SAGE Publications India Pvt Ltd
B-42, Panchsheel Enclave
Post Box 4109
New Delhi 110 017

**British Library Cataloguing in Publication data**

A catalogue record for this book is available
from the British Library

ISBN-10 1-4129-3393-5          ISBN-13 978-1-4129-3393-3
ISBN-10 1-4129-3394-3 (pbk)    ISBN-13 978-1-4129-3394-0 (pbk)

**Library of Congress control number available**

Typeset by C&M Digitals (P) Ltd., Chennai, India
Printed on paper from sustainable resources.
Printed and bound in Great Britain by TJ International Ltd, Padstow, Cornwall

# Contents

# List of Activities

# List of Activities

# Preface

Welcome to *Life Coaching Skills: How to Develop Skilled Clients*. The following are answers to some questions you may have about the book.

## What is the Book's Purpose?

This is a practical 'how to' book on the skills of being a life coach. Life coaching is a rapidly growing area. It is based on the assumption that possessing good psychological skills can help everyone, not just disturbed people, to lead more satisfactory lives. Life coaching may be seen as having two main areas: coaching for business and coaching for personal life. This book mainly focuses on how to coach clients to lead their personal lives more successfully, though it includes a chapter on occupation skills coaching.

## For Whom is this Book Intended?

The life coaching market is still in the process of formation. Coaching does not carry the connotations of disturbance attached to counselling and psychotherapy, since just about everyone can improve their life skills. Here are some markets for which the book is suitable:

- coach training courses – an emerging area in a number of academic departments;
- coaching units on other professional courses – for instance, counselling and psychotherapy, school and sports psychology and health-related courses;
- coaching modules on undergraduate courses, such as behavioural science courses; and
- coaching courses for those wanting to develop their life skills.

In addition the book can be of interest to:

- coaches and others undergoing supervision as part of continuing training and development; and
- helping service professionals – for skills development and for reference purposes.

## What are the Book's Contents?

The first chapter introduces the idea of life coaching and discusses some dimensions of it, including how it differs from counselling and psychotherapy. Chapter 2 looks at lifeskills as consisting of communication/action skills and mind skills, with a comment on feelings and physical reactions. Chapter 3 presents a four-stage life coaching model, the stages being relating, understanding, changing and client self-coaching. In Chapters 4 to 8 some central skills of being a lifeskills coach are presented: namely, coaching relationship; assessment and goal setting; presentation; demonstration; and consolidation. Chapter 9 provides an introduction to life coaching in groups and includes material on preparing groups and leading sessions. Chapters 10 to 12 discuss life coaching in three important areas: relationships, occupation and health. Chapter 13 looks at ethical issues and dilemmas in life coaching and in life coach training. The book's final chapter addresses the issue of how to help clients to develop self-coaching skills. Throughout the book there are practical activities whereby coaching trainees can improve their skills.

## What Features Does the Book Possess?

*Textbook Format*   This book is intended as an introductory textbook. To date there is very little textbook literature in the area of life coaching.

*Comprehensiveness*   The book contains a description of the present status of life coaching, presents the skills of life coaching and shows the application of life coaching in a number of different areas.

*Recency*   The book incorporates the latest literature about life coaching.

*Practical Activities*   The book includes numerous practical activities to help readers develop their knowledge and skills.

*Practical Examples*    The book contains numerous case studies and vignettes.

*Anglo-Australian Emphasis*    The book emphasizes British and Australian books, articles and research findings as well as some American sources.

*Readability*    I have endeavoured to write the book in clear, simple English.

## A Final Word

I hope the book helps you to develop your coaching skills and that working with it contributes to making life happier and more fulfilled for you and many others.

Richard Nelson-Jones

# 1
# *What is Life Coaching?*

Life coaching is coaching that focuses on improving people's personal lives as well as their working lives. Though a relatively recent phenomenon, it is undoubtedly here to stay. In the USA, since the mid-1990s, there has been a huge increase in attention to life coaching. In 1996 the International Coach Federation (ICF), founded in 1992, had its first convention in the USA. Life coaching is spreading worldwide, including to Britain and Australia. For instance, in 2002, the Association for Coaching was established in Britain and in 2005 the British Psychological Society set up a Coaching Psychology Section. Also in 2002, the Interest Group Coaching Psychology (IGCP) was established in the Australian Psychological Society.

## *Defining Life Coaching*

Even in the USA, the profession of coaching is not known clearly by the public. Prior (2003), who was co-Chair of the ICF Ethics and Standards Committee, writes that, more often than not, coaching is incorrectly understood by an unknowing public to be a virtual version of modern therapy. Currently the profession of life coaching is in its early days. Thus, while there are definitions of life coaching, none has become firmly established as a widely accepted definition of the field. Dictionary definitions of coaching emphasize words like instruction and training. Thus, a coach instructs or trains another person, whom I shall call the client, about how to lead their life.

Ways of defining life coaching include the following. Grant and Palmer (2002) state that coaching psychology is for enhancing well-being and performance in personal life and work domains with normal, non-clinical populations. The IGCP (2005: 2) of the Australian Psychological Society states that coaching psychology is 'the systematic application of behavioural science to the enhancement of life experience, work performance and well-being for individuals, groups and organizations who do not have significant mental health issues or abnormal levels of stress'. Downey (2003: 21) states that, 'Coaching is the art of facilitating the performance, learning and development of another'. Finally, Auerbach (2001: 10) states, 'Personal coaching involves helping generally well-functioning people create and achieve goals, maximize personal development, and navigate transitions on the path to realizing their ideal vision for the current and emerging chapters of their lives'. A definition of life coaching as used in this book is provided at the end of the chapter when the reasons for it should be clearer to the reader.

## Dimensions of Life

Let's look at some of the elements of defining life coaching. First, take the word 'life'. This leads into the area of *whose* life. As may be gleaned from the preceding paragraph, the main focus of life coaching is on the lives of ordinary people of all ages. Life coaching can also include a focus on superior functioning. However, even though some therapeutic approaches contain coaching, words like 'therapy' and 'counselling' best describe the services that such less well-functioning clients need.

Another area of meaning for 'life', in terms of our definition, is that coaching can go on for life. This is a position advocated by some life coaches, for instance Williams and Davis (2002). The coach is available on an ongoing basis to assist clients to lead the most satisfying, significant and successful lives that they can. Another way of looking at life is that coaching can take place at various stages of it. For instance, relationship coaching can strengthen people's ability to have good relationships at different stages, such as the initial learning of relationship skills, pre-marital coaching, marital and family coaching, and living a retired life.

Still another way of looking at life in terms of life coaching is that coaching can concern different aspects of it. Williams and Davis (2002) propose that what they term 'total life coaching' covers all areas of life. These areas are career/life purpose, family and friends, finances, romance/intimacy, health/self care, social/fun, personal/spiritual development and physical environment.

Mulligan (1999) lists seven major areas: health, spiritual/religious life, work and career, finances, personal relationships, family/extended family and friends/social life. Though there is some overlap between the areas, coaching of clients may take place in any or all of them. Other areas for coaching include coaching tailored to women or men, creativity coaching, and retirement coaching (Wigman, 2005).

Related to coaching for different aspects of life is the notion of coaching for skills or for life skills. For instance, health skills can cover keeping fit skills, managing weight skills and managing stress skills, among others. Career skills can include those for choosing a career, handling various aspects of the work environment, changing jobs or even areas of work, as well as pre-retirement and retirement skills. Furthermore, maximizing enjoyment of leisure can also be included. There are numerous personal relationship skills including listening and showing understanding skills, assertiveness skills, managing anger and conflict skills, and sexual relationship skills. Each of the broad areas of skills cited by Williams and Davis and Mulligan above can be broken down into different life skills.

Yet another way of looking at life in this context is to consider what constitutes a life skill. There are two main areas of sub-skill for every life skill, namely mind skills, and communication/action skills. For example, being assertive is a skill that is useful in numerous situations. However assertiveness consists of mind skills, such as the ability to perceive accurately, to have realistic personal rules and to engage in appropriate self-talk. Assertiveness also involves sending overt messages of appropriate verbal, vocal and bodily communication. The position taken in this book is that, while it is possible to coach people without overtly using the concept of skills, it is often of great advantage to get people thinking in terms of the mind skills and communication/action skills that make up the life skills they require both for specific situations and for life in general.

The reader may be wondering about feelings and physical reactions. These are regarded as part of genetic human nature. As such, they are not skills but are capable of being influenced by how well a person uses mind skills and communication/action skills. For instance, when being assertive such skills can be used to experience feelings fully and to manage them appropriately.

## Dimensions of Life Coaching

What does coaching a person to lead a more fulfilled life involve? To put it simply there is a coach, a client , the process of coaching and then what the client does on her or his own when not in contact with, or after contact with, the coach. To date in Britain and Australia, there is no widely recognized professional qualification for life coaches. Consequently, people with varying backgrounds are offering coaching: psychologists, social workers, nurses, teachers, people in industry and lay people, to name but a few. The level of skill of such people varies widely from the highly competent to the incompetent. Probably it is just a matter of time before coaching becomes more professionalized, where those accredited as life coaches will have to undergo training and practice under supervision before they are allowed to coach on their own. In the British and Australian Psychological Societies it is likely that the current interest groups in coaching will develop into professional groups with standards for training and accreditation. Other professions, such as social work and personnel management, may also train and accredit coaches in the future. Inevitably much life coaching will continue to be done informally, by parents, teachers, bosses and so on.

Life coaching clients can be just about anyone. Coaching can take place at virtually all life stages, from the very young to the old preparing for death. At the moment, life coaching tends to be for the relatively affluent few who can afford the fees charged by private coaches. Wigman (2005: 2) writes: 'The hottest propositions for personal coaching seem to be among the cash-rich and time-poor professionals, and among the retired and parents of teenagers.' As more becomes known regarding how to live most effectively at each age, it is likely that there will be an increase in people wanting to improve their lives by being coached.

Ways of offering coaching to the less wealthy will also likely be developed, though how fast this takes place remains an open question. It is possible that educational institutions will provide more life coaching. Offering coaching to young people partly helps society avoid the personal and financial costs of the breakdown of families through people never having learned good life skills. A contributing reason to the likely spread of coaching is that having a life coach does not have the stigma of having psychological problems that is frequently attached to seeing counsellors and psychotherapists.

Questions about the processes of life coaching are difficult to answer from the viewpoint of how life coaching is currently being practised. Coaches come from a range of theoretical backgrounds and some even have little such background. Much of the coaching literature indicates that the writers practise on the basis of what seems to work for them rather than from clear theoretical positions. The approach to coaching taken in this book is based on a combination of cognitive-behavioural and humanistic theory. Behaviour consists of how people think as well as how they act. Cognitive-behaviourism holds that behaviour is learned from a mixture of instruction, reward or reinforcement, demonstration or modelling and practise. The consequences of these experiences are that fortunate people are helped to develop the mind skills and the communication skills to lead life effectively whereas less fortunate people are not. Humanistic theory emphasizes the importance of the relationship between coach and client. In many instances, a sound coaching relationship can assist clients by helping them to have the confidence to exhibit and improve behaviours that are already in their repertoires. Coaches need to treat clients as individuals who need different amounts of a warm, non-controlling relationship and a focus on specific skills, depending on their circumstances.

Life coaching can involve helping a person learn a skill for the first time, helping them maintain and improve existing skills and assisting them to weaken and, if possible, stop exhibiting unwanted skills. Coaching can last from a single session to a lifetime. However, those who have regular contact with coaches throughout their lives, partly for financial reasons, are likely to be very much a minority. Many people come to coaching because they are not getting as much out of life as they would like. Often coaching starts by providing them with assistance for a problem and then broadens into helping them live more effectively in other areas. Another approach to coaching is to have it when one feels it necessary. For instance, there may be a major decision or change in one's life with which one would like assistance. Still another approach, especially in business, is to be coached at the request of another person. For instance, a reason that business people get sent for coaching is to help them learn the skills they will require to take up a new position. Another reason is to help them to remedy any skills weaknesses they may have that stop them from making their best contribution to a firm's profitability.

Life coaching can be performed in numerous ways and combinations of ways. A face-to-face meeting has much to recommend it at the start of coaching. This can help build the coach–client relationship as well as give the coach experience of the client's body communication. Other considerations favouring face-to-face meetings are when coaches and clients prefer to work that way, when there is a focus on demonstrating and rehearsing bodily communication, and when clients need personal contact to maintain the relationship – as with some teenage clients, for instance.

The other main method of life coaching is by phone contact. For instance, a coach may initially meet face-to-face with a client and then engage in a phone relationship in which the client phones the coach at a fixed time for a fixed period, commonly 30 minutes. For busy clients, this has the advantage of saving them time. Some skills, for instance mind skills, may be taught nearly or just as well over the phone as in person. Furthermore, certain clients appreciate the opportunity to talk by phone over current and emerging issues with skilled coaches on an ongoing basis. E-mail messages are also used, though they have the disadvantage of not being as immediate as face-to-face or phone conversations. In time, with advances in communication technology, it is likely that coaching sessions can be held with coaches and clients seeing one another on screens in their separate locations.

Life coaching can be can be conducted with individuals, couples, groups and in classrooms. This book focuses mainly on working with individuals, though a chapter on working with groups is included. Life coaching is also a self-help or self-coaching process. A major reason why this book focuses on a life-skills approach to coaching is that, ultimately, clients have to become their own coaches if they are to lead their lives soundly. The aim of all good coaching is effective self-coaching. Where possible, clients should be coached in such a way that they understand the skills well enough that they can monitor their performance and, where necessary, make corrections in how they are thinking and communicating. Life coaching can also take place through reading and working with self-help books and watching self-help videos and CDs. Such self-coaching can take place in conjunction with, or independently of, personal or phone sessions with coaches.

# Differences between Counselling, Psychotherapy and Life Coaching

Before suggesting some differences between counselling or psychotherapy and life coaching, I stress that there are many similarities. Both counselling and life coaching aim to help clients lead fulfilled lives. In addition, they leave the client with the right to choose what sort of life they want to lead. Some counselling approaches, in particular the cognitive and cognitive-behavioural approaches, contain a large coaching element within them. Though they do not emphasize the word skills, approaches like rational emotive behaviour therapy and cognitive therapy aim to teach and coach clients in key mind skills and, to a lesser extent, in communication skills so that they can deal better with the problems for which they came to counselling. Life coaches can gain much from being familiar with theories of counselling and therapy (Corsini and Wedding, 2005; Nelson-Jones, 2006a).

Now let's look at some ways that life coaching differs from conventional counselling and therapy. The goals of life coaching are both positive and stated in the positive. There is an assumption of seeking mental wellness rather than overcoming mental illness. Though an exaggeration, there is some truth in Peltier's comment: 'High performance athletes are coached; sick, weak or crazy people get therapy' (Peltier, 2001: *xix*). Life coaching is not geared towards those whose problems are best described by the latest version of the American Psychiatric Association's *Diagnostic and Statistical Manual of Mental Disorders*. Such people require psychotherapy. Coaching clients are not worked with in psychiatric hospitals. Often very competent people seek life coaching; they want to be even more effective in leading their lives. Normal people also seek life coaching to maximize aspects of their potential and get more out of life. Life coaching does this by bringing psychological knowledge to address everyday issues and problems such as relationships, health, career, finances and spiritual concerns, among others.

Though there is some overlap, the clients for life coaching differ from those for counselling and therapy. Clients come for counselling very often because they are suffering and in psychological pain. They want to feel, think and act at a level that they regard as normal for the society of which they are a part. At the very least, they want to stop continually feeling very low. Approximately 10 per cent of the population will need counselling at some stage of their lives. However, even normal people can feel unfulfilled. Clients seek life coaching to gain ways of or skills for becoming even more successful and happier than they already are. Rather than being motivated by pain, they are motivated by gain. Their problems are often more to do with achieving their positive potential than dealing with negative issues. They may realize that, during their upbringing, they were not systematically trained in many of the skills for leading a successful life. In addition, they may want coaching to face new challenges in their lives. There is a vast potential market for life coaching in the 90 per cent or so of people who do not need counselling. In addition, many who have been counselled may later want life coaching to become even happier and more skilled at living.

There are many broader reasons why there is a need for disciplined life coaching. With the increase in economic affluence in the Western world, there does not appear to have been a corresponding increase in overall happiness. For example, the divorce rate in countries like Britain, Australia and the USA is about 50 per cent of first marriages, with many also failing at subsequent marriages. In addition, the increased mobility and time spent at work by both sexes has contributed to a breakdown in traditional support systems, such as the extended family and local church. People are bombarded every day by information that often causes them to question how they are living. Arguably, this is a more challenging time in which to live. Not only are the former sources of support in decline, but there is a whole new range of problems with the rapid increase in changes brought about by technological invention. However, there is also a whole new range of opportunities with the increase in psychological knowledge and the possibility of using this knowledge to help not just therapy clients but also the rest of the population to lead happier lives.

Alongside the difference of life coaching goals to those of counselling and therapy, the ways of attaining them also differ. With its main emphasis on working with non-disturbed people, life coaching is less likely to be conducted with a psychodynamic approach. Mutual goals are established quite quickly in life coaching. If anything, life coaching directly encourages and trains clients in how to deal with and improve their present and their futures, rather than to understand their past.

The nature of coaches' relationships with clients also differs from that in counselling. Already I have mentioned that life coaching may be conducted over the phone as well as in person. With coaching clients in general being less disturbed than counselling clients, coaches need spend less time in helping clients listen to themselves. Though good active listening skills are still vital for effective coaching, and though clients are regarded as the main sources of information regarding how to lead their lives, coaches can be more active in making suggestions about areas that require work and what skills clients need to attain in them. The assumption is that so long as the coach is not overbearing, clients are well enough to discuss issues with coaches rather than automatically agree. Though some clients may want to be coached in a person-centred way, many clients are prepared for the coach to take a more active coaching role than that in traditional counselling. Once client and coach settle on objectives, they agree on ways to attain them as quickly as possible. While many counsellors work within an educational approach, coaches can often be seen as emphasizing the training of clients in skills even more than in counselling. Thus the coaching relationship is both facilitative and didactic, the exact mixture between the two depending on the needs of the client at any given moment.

Another issue is that of the language of coaching. Some counselling approaches, such as the person-centred approach, have counsellors conceptualizing clients in a different language to that in which counselling is conducted. Counselling is conducted mainly using the clients' language, and clients do not use person-centred terms like 'self-actualizing' and 'conditions of worth'. Psychodynamic counsellors also do not fully share their language or their approach with clients. In life coaching, coaches use everyday language to describe and train clients in how to become more effective.

This is a similar attitude to that taken in cognitive-behavioural therapy. However, cognitive-behavioural approaches like rational emotive behaviour therapy and cognitive therapy tend not to focus on a full range of mind skills, and also tend not to use the word skills. As mentioned previously, I think it advantageous to use skills language and to identify the mind skills and communication/action skills that the client requires.

One of the ways coaching can differ from counselling and therapy is that often clients do not mind other people knowing that they are being coached. Many life coaching clients see their coaching as something positive to share with others rather than as a sign of weakness. Sometimes coaches meet with clients in public places, such as cafes or restaurants. Indeed some coaches ask former and sometimes current clients to recommend their services. In the business world, being coached is frequently viewed as a normal activity rather than something unusual or demeaning. Nevertheless, though in some ways the ethics of life coaching differ from counselling, coaches need to be very careful how they behave, for instance in making sure to gain permission before revealing a client's identity.

## Life Coaching Defined for this Book

Life coaching has numerous facets and is conducted in many different ways. The definition of life coaching on which the remainder of this book is based is the following:

> Life coaching involves coaches using their skills to help generally adequately functioning people learn to improve and maintain their mind skills and communication/action skills and so lead happier, more productive and fulfilled lives. The ultimate aim of life coaching is to help clients become skilled at self-coaching.

This book is primarily about life coaching for individuals in their personal lives rather than about executive, business or performance coaching.

# 2
# *What are Lifeskills?*

This chapter discusses the concept of lifeskills that was only briefly mentioned in the Chapter 1. One of the most valuable insights that can come from the psychotherapy literature is the emphasis on thoughts or cognitions that mediate behaviour. In addition to their extensive writing of therapy books, leading cognitive psychotherapists such as Albert Ellis and Aaron Beck have written self-help books (Beck, 1988; Ellis, 1999, 2001). However, they have failed to write books directly about how to coach normal people. This is despite the fact that their work has much to offer coaching.

As a coach, it is possible to help a person or client handle a specific situation better. The coaching focuses on getting the person to behave in ways so that they can cope with the situation but has no emphasis on assisting them to retain what they have learned. Nevertheless, if they are successful, they will likely repeat some of their newly coached behaviour to help them cope with future similar situations.

Life coaching goes beyond this form of coaching oriented to a problem situation in some important ways. Life coaching is about coaching people in skills to give them a better chance not only in handling immediate situations but also subsequent situations throughout their lives. As such, it does not leave the longer-term outcomes of coaching to chance. Furthermore, life coaching is positive in helping people lead happier and more fulfilled lives by being more skillful in how they live. In life coaching people can be helped to develop skills to fulfill their potential and not just to make up for past deprivations, which tends to be the main focus of counselling and psychotherapy. The following are some examples of people in the early stages of life coaching.

Anne, 27, is getting to the stage in her life where she wants to get married. She has had a number of relationships but now wants one with real commitment on both sides. She sees Denis, 42, a life coach to help her develop her skills of knowing herself, knowing the sort of person she wants to marry, having the confidence to be her real self as she looks for a mate, and developing the skills of dropping her facade and letting herself be truly known when she finds someone who might be suitable. Anne also works with Denis on other areas in her life, for instance her skills at managing a sales team where she is employed.

Tom, 32, sees life coach Emily, 37, to discuss ways of making the transition from working for an accounting firm to establishing his own accountancy practice. Tom wants to look at the reasons why he is so afraid of becoming independent and to work on becoming more rational over the decision. Tom also wants Emily's assistance in identifying the skills he already possesses and those where he might be stronger if he were to become his own boss: for example, he decides he needs to work on his marketing skills.

Joan, 67, sees life coach Brett, 46, because she has recently been widowed and wants to review her life to make the most of her remaining years. Joan sees herself as a successful person but one with a major adjustment to make. Skills areas on which Joan works with Brett are dealing with grief, keeping in touch with her children and grandchildren yet not being swamped by them, looking for new activities, managing finances, and ultimately the skills of finding another mate and/or living happily on her own.

Jen, 18, agrees with her parents that she should see life coach Trish, 38, because they are afraid that she might remain overweight. Trish encourages Jen to talk about her life, her generally satisfactory relationship with her parents, her other relationships, her hobbies and what she wants to make of herself. What Jen really wants is a good career in management and ultimately a happy family life. Trish helps Jen to develop a plan to acquire the skills that would make her more likely to achieve her goals. As part of the plan, Jen agrees to work on the mind skills and action skills for becoming and staying fit.

## *What is a Lifeskill?*

One aspect of the word 'skills' pertains to *areas* of skill: for instance, listening skills or disclosing skills. Another aspect refers to *level of competence*; whether one is skilled or unskilled in an area of skill. However, competence in a skill is best viewed not as an either/or matter in which people either possess or do not possess a skill. Rather, within a skills area, it is preferable to think of people as possessing *good skills* or *poor skills,* or a mixture of the two. In all skills areas they are likely to possess mixtures of strengths and deficiencies. For instance, in the skills area of listening, they may be good at understanding others but poor at showing understanding. In just about all areas of their functioning both coaches and clients will, in varying degrees, possess a mixture of poor and good skills. A third aspect of skill relates to the *knowledge and sequence of choices* entailed in implementing the skill. The essential element of any skill is the ability to implement sequences of choices to achieve objectives. For example, if coaches are to be good at listening deeply and accurately to clients, they have to make and implement effective choices in this coaching and human being skills area. As mentioned in Chapter 1, a lifeskill can consist of communication/action sub-skills and mind sub-skills, both of which can influence feelings and physical reactions. Often in future, for the sake of simplicity, they will be referred to as skills rather than as sub-skills.

## Communication and Action Skills

There are five main ways that coaches and clients can send messages by creating communication and taking action. *Verbal* communication consists of messages sent with words: for example, by saying 'I understand what you are saying' or 'I don't understand'. *Vocal* communication consists of messages sent through one's voice: for instance, through volume, articulation, pitch, emphasis and speech rate. *Bodily* communication consists of messages sent by the body, such as through gaze, eye contact, facial expression, posture, gestures, physical proximity, and clothes and grooming. *Touch* communication is a special category of bodily communication. Messages sent by touch include: what part of the body one uses; what part of another's body gets touched; and how gentle or firm is the touching. *Taking action* communication consists of messages sent when not face-to-face with others: for example, sending a follow-up note to a client who has missed an appointment. Though not emphasized in the following discussion, it is extremely important to acknowledge cultural differences in communication.

### Verbal Communication Skills

Let's look at some skills of verbal communication or talk.

*Language*　Language consists of many elements other than which language they speak. For instance, there may be a formal language (words either BBC or ABC news readers might use), as well as an informal or colloquial language (words one might use with mates in the pub).

*Content*　Content may refer to topic area, problem area or the task being undertaken, such as learning coaching skills. In addition, content refers to the focus of talk, whether it be about oneself, others or the environment. Furthermore, content can refer to the evaluative dimension of talk: for example, happy clients may say many positive things about themselves such as 'I'm successful' and 'I'm optimistic'.

*Amount of Speech*　In coaching, the coach may talk more than the counsellor in counselling, though always making sure that clients have sufficient space to say what they want.

*Ownership of Speech*　Thomas Gordon (1970), in his book *Parent Effectiveness Training*, makes a useful distinction between 'You' messages and 'I' messages. 'You' messages focus on the other person and can be judgmental: for example, 'You don't appreciate what I'm doing for you' or 'You're not listening to me properly'. 'I' messages use the word 'I' and are centred in a person as the sender: for instance, 'I feel appreciated' or 'I'm not experiencing being heard correctly'.

## Vocal Communication Skills

A person's vocal messages can speak volumes about what they truly feel and how emotionally responsive they are to others' feelings. Following are five dimensions of vocal messages. They form the acronym VAPER – volume, articulation, pitch, emphasis and rate.

*Volume*　Volume refers to loudness or softness. Coaching trainees need to disclose at a level of audibility that is comfortable and easy for clients to hear. Though a booming voice overwhelms, speaking too quietly may communicate that one is a 'wimp'. A firm and confident voice is a good starting point from which to make variations as appropriate, for instance by speaking more gently or more loudly.

*Articulation*　Articulation refers to the clarity of speech. Coaches and clients who enunciate words well are easier to understand than those not doing so.

*Pitch*   Pitch refers to the height or depth of one's voice. An optimum pitch range includes all the levels at which a pleasing voice can be produced without strain. Errors of pitch include either being too high pitched or too low pitched.

*Emphasis*   A coach's voice uses emphasis when responding to clients' feelings and nuances, and when sharing feelings. Coaching trainees may use either too much emphasis and seem melodramatic or too little emphasis and come across as wooden. In addition, they may use emphasis in the wrong places.

*Rate*   Often speech rate is measured by words per minute. Speech rate depends not only on how quickly words are spoken but on the frequency and duration of pauses between them. If speaking very quickly, coaching trainees appear anxious and clients may have difficulty understanding them. On the other hand, too ponderous a speech rate can be boring or pompous. Pausing and being silent at the right times is another important aspect of speech rate.

## Bodily Communication Skills

When both speaking and listening coaches, trainees and clients disclose themselves through how they create their bodily communication. One of the main reasons for having some face-to-face contact in coaching is so that the coach can actually see and experience how the client communicates. Following are some of the main kinds of bodily communication skills.

*Facial Expressions*   Facial expressions are perhaps the main vehicle for sending body messages. Ekman, Friesen and Ellsworth (1972) have found that there are seven main facial expressions of emotion: happiness, interest, surprise, fear, sadness, anger and disgust or contempt. A person's mouth and eyebrows can convey much information: for instance, if they are 'down in the mouth' or have 'raised eyebrows'.

*Gaze*   Gaze, or looking at other people in the area of their faces, is both a way of showing interest and a way of collecting facial information. Speakers look at listeners about 40 per cent of the time and listeners look at speakers about 70–75 per cent of the time. Gaze is useful for coordinating speech: for example, speakers look just before the end of utterances to collect feedback about their listener's reactions. Women are generally more visually attentive than men in all measures of gaze (Argyle, 1999).

*Eye Contact*   Eye contact is a more direct way than gaze of sending messages, be they of interest, anger or sexual attraction.

*Gestures*   Gestures are physical movements that can frame or illustrate words coming before, during or after what is being said. An example of using a gesture to display and emphasize an emotion is clenching one's fist to show aggression. Gestures may also illustrate shapes, sizes or movements, particularly when these are difficult to describe in words. How people gesture can vary according to their sex. Sometimes men's gestures are larger, more sweeping and forceful, while women's gestures are smaller and more inhibited. Gestures can also take the place of words: for example, nodding one's head either up and down or sideways for saying 'yes' or 'no', respectively.

*Posture*   A coaching trainee's posture may convey various messages. Turning one's body towards the client is more encouraging than turning away from them. In addition, whether the trainee leans forwards or backwards may indicate interest or disinterest. Height tends to be associated with status, such as when one 'talks down to' or 'talks up to' someone. Women may be at a disadvantage unless another's body posture is changed: for instance, by sitting down.

   Posture may also communicate how anxious a person is: for instance, sitting with arms and legs tightly crossed suggests being emotionally as well as literally uptight. However, for women, it is possible to appear too relaxed: some men may mistakenly perceive uncrossed and open legs as a sign of sexual availability whether a skirt, trousers or jeans is worn. Such perceptions manifest confusing standards in how people decode body messages.

*Physical Closeness*   The degree of physical closeness that is comfortable for Britons and Antipodeans is generally the same (Hall, 1966). The zones vary according to the nature of the relationship. As Hall observes, in the *intimate zone* (between 6 to 18 inches) it is easy to touch and be touched. This zone is reserved for spouses, lovers, close friends and relatives. The *personal zone* (between 18 and 48 inches) is appropriate for less close friends and for parties and other social gatherings. The *social zone* (between 4 to 12 feet) is comfortable for people not known at all well. The *public zone* (over 12 feet) is the distance for addressing public gatherings.

*Clothes*   If clothes do not make the coach, they certainly send many messages that can influence how much and in which areas clients reveal themselves. These messages include social and occupational standing, sex-role identity, ethnicity, conformity to peer group norms, rebelliousness and how outgoing they are. While maintaining their individuality, coaching trainees need to dress appropriately for their clientele and, often, this may be dressing rather more formally than for counselling.

*Grooming* Personal grooming also provides important information about how well people take care of themselves; for instance, clean or dirty, neat or tidy. In addition, the length and styling of hair sends messages about what sort of person one is. Here, again, coaches may need to be more formal than counsellors.

## Activity 2.1    Assessing My Communication Skills for Coaching

Where possible do this activity with a partner.

1.  Each of you, to the best of your ability, assesses your own verbal communication skills as a coach, for instance in the areas of:

    *   language;
    *   content;
    *   amount of speech; and
    *   ownership of speech.

Then partner A reveals her/his answers to partner B and gets feedback. Afterwards, partner B reveals her/his answers to partner A and gets feedback.

2.  Each of you, to the best of your ability, assesses your own vocal communication skills as a coach, for instance in the areas of:

    *   volume;
    *   articulation;
    *   pitch;
    *   emphasis; and
    *   rate.

Then partner A reveals her/his answers to partner B and gets feedback. Afterwards, partner B reveals her/his answers to partner A and gets feedback.

3.  Each of you, to the best of your ability, assesses your own bodily communication skills as a coach, for instance in the areas of:

    *   facial expressions;
    *   gaze;

- eye contact;
- gestures;
- posture;
- physical closeness;
- clothes; and
- grooming.

Then partner A reveals her/his answers to partner B and gets feedback. Afterwards, partner B reveals her/his answers to partner A and gets feedback.

4. If you are considering coaching in ways other than face-to-face, by phone for example, discuss how this might affect the ways in which you communicate.

# Mind Skills

Probably most readers are unused to thinking about how they think in lifeskills or skills terms. However, it can be helpful to break down how we think into component skills that one can address in one's own life and also in clients' lives. Coaching trainees can learn coaching skills and assist clients much more effectively if they harness their mind's potential. Below are descriptions of some central mental processes, or mind skills. There is no 'magic' to thinking in terms of mind skills as the following passages show.

## Creating Rules Skills

Rules are the 'dos' and 'don'ts' by which people lead their lives. Influences from the past and present have helped to create and to sustain everyone's rules: for example, family, religion, gender, culture, race, peer group, age, exposure to the media and so on.

Ellis, the founder of rational emotive behaviour therapy, uses the term *beliefs* rather than rules. His work is highly relevant to coaching and living. Ellis considers that people create and maintain much of their distress and unhappiness through demanding and absolutistic thinking and making demands, rather than through preferential thinking and having prefer-ences (Ellis, 2001; 2003; 2005). He asserts that people can possess healthy, productive and adaptive, and rational beliefs that are consistent with social reality and generally consist of preferences, desires and wants. When thinking rationally about situations that either block or sabotage their goals, people who have rational beliefs are engaging in preferential thinking. Preferential, as contrasted with demanding, thinking involves explicitly and/or tacitly reacting with beliefs in realistic ways and experiencing appropriate emotional and behavioural consequences. Irrational or unrealistic beliefs are rigid and dogmatic, mostly get in the way of people's efforts to achieve their goals, and consist of 'musts', 'oughts' and 'shoulds'. When thinking irrationally about activating events or adversities that sabotage their goals, people engage in demanding thinking.

Box 2.1 emphasizes the distinction between demanding and preferring. Notice that each of the demanding or unrealistic rules has been reworded to become a preferential or realistic rule.

---

### Box 2.1   Creating Demanding and Preferential Rules

#### Demanding Rules

- I must be the perfect trainee.
- I must be liked by everyone.
- I must always be in control of my family.

#### Preferential Rules

- I'd prefer to be a highly competent trainee but I'm learning and am bound to make some mistakes.
- I'd prefer to be liked but it's also even more important to be true to myself.
- I'd prefer to influence my family in ways to attain important goals but total control is both undesirable and unrealistic.

---

### Creating Perceptions Skills

One of the most influential approaches to cognitive psychotherapy is that of American psychiatrist, Aaron Beck (Beck, 1976; Beck and Weishaar, 2005). Whereas Ellis emphasizes preferential thinking, based on realistic rules, Beck emphasizes propositional thinking, based on testing the reality of perceptions about oneself, others and the environment. Propositional thinking is a useful mind skill to which coaches can attend. This section focuses on how accurately one perceives oneself rather than on how accurately one perceives others.

The self-concept is one's picture of oneself; what one thinks of as 'I' or 'Me'. It consists of a series of different perceptions of varying degrees of accuracy. Areas of one's self-concept include perceptions regarding family of origin, current relationships, body image, age, gender, sexual orientation, culture, race, social class, religious beliefs, health, work, study activities, leisure pursuits, tastes and preferences, among others.

Centrality is one dimension of self-concept: 'What is really important to me?' For instance, a committed Christian's faith is fundamental to their self-concept. Another dimension of self-concept is that of positive and negative evaluations of personal characteristics: 'What do I like and dislike about myself?' A further important dimension of self-concept is that of how confident one is. A person may accurately perceive their level of confidence or may over- or underestimate it.

A principal skill of learning to perceive more accurately is being able to distinguish fact from inference. Take the statement 'All Aborigines walk in single file, at least the one I saw did'. That you saw one Aborigine is fact, that all Aborigines walk in single file is inference or factually unsupported supposition. Coaches, trainees and clients need to guard against tendencies to jump to unwarranted conclusions. Furthermore, they need to be prepared to change or modify their conclusions in the light of emerging information.

Box 2.2 depicts Damien, 28, a coaching client, who initially jumps to an unduly negative conclusion about his level of performance, and then reality tests the perception to see how accurately it fits the available facts.

---

### Box 2.2    Reality-Testing a Perception

#### Situation

Damien, aged 28, assesses his performance at work.

#### Initial Unrealistic Perception

I'm not very good at my job.

*(Continued)*

---

---

## Box 2.2    (Continued)

### Reality-Testing the Initial Perception

Where is the evidence that I'm doing poorly? I've been at my job for one month. It's a challenging job. I started off not doing particularly well but even that perception may be unrealistic. I have had to learn a lot of new things and I have found it a struggle. Denise and Geoff, who started off the same time as me, are learning the job at about the same rate as I am. The boss criticizes all three of us and is sparing with praise. However, he does recognize that all three of us have made progress. When I step back, I can see that I have made reasonable progress in the time available and I am not helping by being so hard on myself.

### Revised Realistic Perception

My progress is satisfactory for this stage, I am improving and should definitely continue with the job.

---

### Creating Self-Talk Skills

Self-talk goes by numerous other names, including: inner monologue, inner dialogue, inner speech, self-verbalizing, self-instructing and talking to oneself. In any relationship of more than one person, there are at least three conversations going on: the public conversation and each person's private self-talk.

All verbal thinking can be regarded as self-talk. However, here the focus is on a specific area of self-talk, namely coaching clients in instructing themselves in order to handle specific situations better. Coping self-talk, which is the opposite of negative or destructive self-talk, can perform various functions. It can alert a person that they need to take something into account. The basic alerting self-instruction is 'STOP … THINK'. Self-talk can also perform a calming function. Sample calming self-statements include 'Keep calm', 'Slow down', 'Relax' and 'Breath slowly and regularly'. Coaching self-talk is no substitute for possessing the skills to perform a task but it can assist performance. The first step in coaching self-talk is to break a task down. Then one can instruct oneself through the steps of implementing it. Affirming self-talk, which focuses on reminding oneself of realistic factors in one's favour, is another self-talk skill. Clients can be coached to tell themselves that they can cope, to acknowledge their strengths, and, where appropriate, to acknowledge their support factors.

Coping self-talk may be used before, during and after specific situations. Often choosing alerting, calming, coaching and affirming self-talk are combined, though not necessarily all at the same time: for example 'STOP … THINK, I can choose how to act. Calm down. Just take one step at a time. I have some skills for managing this situation.' Coaches need to help clients discover and practice the self-talk that works well for them.

## Creating Visual Images Skills

When experiencing any significant feeling or sensation, people are likely to think in pictures as well as words. Those whose most highly valued representational system is visual tend to respond to the world and organize it in terms of mental images (Lazarus, 1984, 2005). Coaches, trainees and clients can use mental images or pictorial images to support or oppress themselves, both now and later. For example, not only are others seen face to face but pictures are stored about them in the mind.

People differ not only in how much they visualize but also in how vividly. Vividness incorporates the degree to which all relevant senses – sight, smell, sound, taste and touch – are conjured up by the visual image. Another possible aspect of vividness is the extent to which visual images either elicit or are accompanied by feelings – for instance, hope, sadness or anger.

As with self-talk, visual images can be alerting, calming, coaching and affirming. Often appropriate self-talk can be combined with appropriate visual images. For example, a client could imagine a large advertising billboard with the words 'STOP … THINK' prominently displayed. Each client probably can visualize one or more special scenes where they feel calm and relaxed, for instance looking at a valley with lush green meadows or sitting in a favorite chair at home. With regard to using coaching imagery, clients have virtually unlimited opportunities to visualize themselves as they practise using desired skills. Clients can accompany their affirming self-talk with affirming visual images. They can tell themselves they can cope and can picture themselves performing competently in specific situations. Many sports people, such as Tiger Woods, use affirming visual images to enhance performance (Woods, 1997).

## Creating Explanations Skills

Explanations of cause are the reasons that people give to themselves for what happens. These explanations can influence how they think about their past, present and future. Also, explanations of cause influence how they feel, physically react and act. Frequently, people make explanatory errors that interfere with their motivation and effectiveness. Let's take the example of the women's movement. When women explained their lack of status as due to male dominance, they were relatively powerless. However, when women also attributed their lack of status to their own insufficient assertion, they empowered themselves.

Clients can stay stuck in personal, work and other problems through wholly or partially explaining their causes inaccurately. Possible faulty explanations for the causes of problems include: 'It's my genes'; 'It's my unfortunate past'; 'It's my bad luck'; 'It's my poor environment'; 'It's all their fault'; or 'It's all my fault'. Sometimes clients succumb to the temptation of externalizing problems: they are the victims of others' inconsiderate and aggressive behaviours. Such clients explain cause from outside to inside. However, change usually requires explaining cause from inside to outside.

A client can strengthen or weaken their motivation to attain higher skills levels by how they explain the causes of their successes and failures. For instance, they may rightly or wrongly assign the causes for their good or poor performance to such factors as prior experience, ability, effort, anxiety, task difficulty, adequacy of environment, opportunities to practise skills, competing demands, financial worries, external work pressures, external relationship pressures, supportive home environment, supportive work environment, or luck, to mention but some. Assuming personal responsibility for performance levels involves the ability or skill of explaining cause accurately and, where possible, addressing relevant considerations constructively. Box 2.3 illustrates how a trainee, Hannah, creates helpful explanations for what happens in her life and in her coaching skills training group.

---

### Box 2.3   Creating Helpful Explanations

Hannah, 23, realizes that her parents were not always able to show their love as she would have liked. Though she missed having as much affection as she wanted, rather than blame her parents Hannah assumes responsibility for making the most of her life. With regard to coaching skills training, Hannah tries to make the most of the opportunities that are either provided in the group or that she can create. She works really hard to keep her side of the skills training contract by giving and getting as much as she can from the trainer and from the other group members. Hannah considers that it is ultimately up to her own ability and effort whether or not she becomes a really skilled coach.

---

## *Creating Expectations Skills*

Humans seek to predict their futures so that they can influence and control them. Consequential thinking entails creating expectations about the consequences of human behaviour. For good or ill, people can create and influence their consequences, including their own and others' feelings, physical reactions, thoughts and communications.

Though expectations about positive and negative consequences tend to be interrelated, here I treat them separately. Clients can make the mistake of inaccurately expecting negative consequences by underestimating loss and by overestimating loss. Both entail inaccurately estimating the 'downside' of their communication and actions. Clients can also inaccurately expect positive consequences by overestimating gain and by underestimating gain. Optimists may overestimate gain, while pessimists may overestimate loss.

Clients create expectations, to varying degrees of accuracy, about their competence and coping ability. Such expectations influence how confident they feel and how they communicate and act. Communicating and acting skillfully is not simply a matter of knowing what to do; clients need the confidence to use their skills. Expectations about competence differ from expectations about outcomes. Expectations about competence involve predictions about one's ability to accomplish a certain level of performance, for instance in listening. Outcome expectations involve predictions about the likely consequences of one's performance, for instance that if a client listens skillfully then she or he will probably experience better home and work relationships.

Expectations about one's level of competence also influence how much effort to expend and how long to persist in the face of setbacks and difficulties. Unlike self-doubt, firm expectations of competence can strengthen clients' resilience when engaging in difficult tasks. In addition, expectations about level of competence influence how one thinks and feels. Many clients who judge themselves to be insufficiently competent in dealing with, say, the demands of their work group, may tend to exaggerate their personal deficiencies, become disheartened more easily and give up in face of difficulties. On the other hand, those clients with a strong sense of personal competence, though possibly temporarily demoralized by setbacks, are more likely to stay task-oriented and to intensify their efforts when their performance falls short of their goals.

Related to expectations about one's level of competence are expectations about one's ability to cope with difficult situations and people. In life a client's lack of confidence about their ability to cope with difficulties, crises and critical incidents can affect adversely how they handle them, if and when they occur. Ironically, at the times when they need to be most realistic and rational, their emotional brain can take over and strong feelings can overcome reason.

Box 2.4 illustrates how Olivia, a trainee on a coaching course, possesses realistic expectations that support her interviewing.

---

### Box 2.4   Creating Helpful Expectations

#### Situation

Olivia, 31, a trainee, is about to interview a client, Ellie, 24, as part of her supervised coaching practise.

#### Helpful Expectations

Okay, I am feeling nervous about interviewing Ellie. I can expect to feel a bit nervous since I still have had very little experience at working with clients. However, let's look at the reality of the situation. First, I am learning coaching skills and should not expect to be really competent from the start. Second, Ellie knows that she is seeing a trainee rather than a fully qualified coach. Consequently, Ellie will not be expecting a professional performance. Third, if I do experience difficulty I can discuss it with my supervisor and try not to make the same mistakes again. I am glad that we have moved on to the part of the course where we see real clients. I am looking forward to the challenge both of possibly helping Ellie and of learning to become a better coach.

---

## Other mind skills

In the preceding sections, the reader was introduced to six key mind skills. This number of skills was considered sufficient as an introduction to thinking about mind skills. However, the mind is much more complicated than the six skills illustrated. Two additional mind areas are now briefly mentioned.

## Creating Realistic Goals Skills

Some clients have difficulty articulating goals and consequently relinquish much opportunity to create their futures. Goals can be short, medium or long term and in various areas: for instance, relationships, study, work, recreation, health and finances. When in close relationships, goals may need to be negotiated so that they become shared goals. Apart from not possessing goals, errors in goal setting include not reflecting values, insufficient realism, inadequate specificity and unclear time frames. Clients' goals in relation to problem areas may suffer from not being expressed in skills language. Furthermore, they may not focus on how to think as well as on how to communicate or act.

## Creating Realistic Decision-Making Skills

Clients may possess decision-making styles that lessen their effectiveness. For instance, they may be hyper-vigilant and try too hard by taking every possible consideration into account. Conversely, they may be impulsive and rush into both major and minor decisions. Some may do their best to avoid decisions altogether. Sometimes decisions are best made in collaboration with others; in such instances, decision errors include being overly competitive or compliant. Realistic decision-making can be viewed as taking place in two main stages: first, confronting and making decisions; second, implementing and evaluating them. Clients may have skills weaknesses in either or both stages. An illustrative weakness when making decisions is failure to generate sufficient decision options. An illustrative weakness when implementing decisions is poor planning.

### Activity 2.2    Assessing My Mind Skills for Coaching

Where possible do this activity with a partner. Each of you, to the best of your ability, assesses your own mind skills as a coach, for instance in the areas of:

*   creating rules;
*   creating perceptions;
*   creating self-talk;
*   creating visual images;
*   creating explanations; and
*   creating expectations.

Then partner A reveals her/his answers to partner B and gets feedback. Afterwards, partner B reveals her/his answers to partner A and gets feedback.

## *Feelings and Physical Reactions*

To a large extent, people are what they feel. Important feelings include: happiness, interest, surprise, fear, sadness, anger and disgust or contempt. Dictionary definitions of feelings tend to use words like 'physical sensation', 'emotions' and 'awareness'. All three of these illustrate a dimension of feelings. Feelings as *physical sensations* or as *physical reactions* represent people's underlying biological nature. People are biological beings first, persons second. As such they need to learn to value and live with their underlying biological nature. The word *emotions* implies movement. Feelings are processes. People are subject to a continuous flow of biological experiencing. *Awareness* implies that people can be conscious of their feelings. However, at varying levels and in different ways, they may also be out of touch with them.

Physical reactions both represent and accompany feelings and, in a sense, are indistinguishable. For example, bodily changes associated with anxiety can include: galvanic skin response (detectable electrical changes taking place in the skin), raised blood pressure, a pounding heart and a rapid pulse, shallow and rapid breathing, muscular tension, drying of the mouth, stomach problems (such as ulcers), speech difficulties (such as stammering), sleep difficulties and sexual problems (such as complete or partial loss of desire). Other physical reactions include a slowing down of body movements when depressed, a smile when happy, and dilated eye pupils in moments of anger or sexual attraction.

Feelings and physical reactions are central to coaching but, as mentioned in the previous chapter, are not skills in themselves. Coaching trainees require the capacity to experience and understand both their own and their clients' feelings. However, just because feelings represent people's biological nature, this does not mean that trainees and their clients can do nothing about them. In coaching, three somewhat overlapping areas where feelings and accompanying physical reactions are important include experiencing feelings, expressing feelings and managing feelings. In each of these three areas, coaches and coaching skills trainees can work with clients' communications/actions, thoughts and mental processes to influence how they feel and physically react.

# 3
# A Skills Model for Life Coaching

Models of how to conduct personal and executive coaching exist, for instance those of Auerbach (2001) and Hudson (1999). However, such models are insufficiently articulate both about the fact that they are building skills and that they do not clearly distinguish mind skills from communication/action skills. The life coaching model presented in Box 3.1 provides a systematic framework to guide coaches in working with clients. Its purpose differs from a model designed for therapy in that it focuses on building skills strengths as much as, if not more so than, overcoming weaknesses. Life coaching clients are at varying stages of development, with the assumption being that they are at least functioning at normal levels for our society. However, some clients are functioning even better than this at the start of coaching and still want to improve.

Thus all life coaching clients can be seen as having some skills strengths with some already functioning very well. Coaches need be sensitive in how they use language with clients. As Williams and Thomas ask: 'Improve your weaknesses or build on your strengths, which would you rather do?' (2005: 74). At the very least, clients want to improve their weaker areas into strengths within the context of their already having strengths in other areas of life.

The life coaching model assumes that, in most instances, clients will be working with coaches for limited periods of time. The model can be adapted for coaches and clients who decide on and can afford ongoing long-term relationships. With its emphasis on coaching clients so that they can coach themselves afterwards, the model aims to make long-term coaching less necessary, though it may still be useful for some clients. If desirable, clients can go back for refresher sessions on previously addressed skills or, when needed, have more coaching to strengthen different skills. In as much as it is possible coaching skills are used to progressively augment and build clients' skills so that they become skilled self-coaches.

---

### Box 3.1    The Life Coaching Model

## Stage 1 Relating

**Main task: Form a collaborative working relationship.**

### Phase 1 Starting the Initial Session
Communicating with and providing information for clients prior to the first session. Meeting, greeting and seating, making opening remarks and encouraging clients to say what they want from coaching.

### Phase 2 Facilitating Client Disclosure
Allowing clients space to reveal more about their lives, goals, strengths and problem(s) from their own perspective.

## Stage 2 Understanding

**Main task: Assess and agree on a shared analysis of one or more of the client's life goals and the skills they need to attain them.**

### Phase 1 Reconnaissance, Detecting and Deciding
As necessary, conducting a broad review in each goals area the client wants, so as to collect information to understand her/him better. Collecting specific evidence to test ideas about skills in one or more areas and then reviewing available information to suggest which skills might require improving.

### Phase 2 Agreeing on a Shared Analysis of How to Achieve the Client's Life Goal(s)
Negotiating a preliminary analysis of how to achieve one or more life goals, involving agreeing on mind skills and communication/action skills for improvement.

## Stage 3 Changing

*Main task: Assist the client to change.*

---

---

## Box 3.1    (Continued)

### *Phase 1 Intervening*
Helping clients to develop and implement strategies for achieving goals and improving relevant mind skills and communication/action skills for now and later.

### *Phase 2 Ending*
Assisting clients to consolidate their skills for use afterwards and to plan how to maintain them when coaching ends or becomes less frequent.

## Stage 4 Client Self-Coaching

**Main task: Client enacts and improves skills on her/his own.**

### *Phase 1 Maintenance and Improvement*
Clients, largely on their own, monitor their progress, where necessary retrieve lapses, and keep on using and improving their skills.

### *Phase 2 Self-Directed Growth*
Clients adopt a life skills approach to living. They extend their work on skills for areas in which they have received coaching to coach themselves in a range of other areas.

---

The presentation of a life coaching model in four stages, each with two phases, may make the coaching process seem more rigid than is often the case. Often the stages and phases overlap and coaches and clients require flexibility in moving among them. Furthermore, clients come to coaching with different goals, strengths and areas they want to improve. Their motivation for change can also differ, though good coaches can help them address this if it is a problem. Sometimes what clients need is more a relationship to help them release skills that they already have in their repertoires. Other clients may require more direct assistance in learning to improve their skills. A brief overview of the life coaching model is now provided, with the first three stages looked at both from the coach's and the client's perspective.

# Stages and Phases of the Life Coaching Model

## Stage 1 Relating

The main goal of the relating stage is for coach and client to start establishing a good collaborative working relationship. Other goals are to find out why they have come for coaching and to gain an initial understanding of their skills strengths and the areas in which they think they require coaching.

## Phase 1 Starting the Initial Session

*The Coach in the Process* The initial session really starts from the moment the client first hears about the coach. Coaches can gain or lose clients from how they advertise, how easy they are to contact, the kind of messages they leave on their answerphone, and how friendly they sound on the phone. If the coach works for an agency, how pleasantly and tactfully the office staff behave towards potential and first-time clients is very important.

In order to meet with the first client in a session, arriving early gives coaches time to relax and prepare the room and, if necessary, the recording equipment. They can check the client's name and other details about them, such as who referred them.

Coaches need to develop good skills for meeting, greeting and seating clients. They should be warm and friendly but not effusive. When clients are in reception areas coaches can go to meet them, call them by name and introduce themselves. Then coaches can show clients into the coaching room and indicate where they should sit. Most coaches are relatively sparing with small talk during this process.

When both parties are seated coaches can make an opening statement that indicates the time boundaries of the session by saying something like, 'We have about __ minutes together.' Initial coaching sessions can be as short as 45 minutes, but often are longer, say 60 or 90 minutes, to give time for coaches and clients to get a better picture of the skills the client wants to or needs to improve. During this initial stage coaches may need to clarify the degree of confidentiality they can offer. For example, if a client works for an organization that commissioned the coaching, the coach may have some basic reporting back to do. Coaches may also suggest that they record the session on cassette and that the client plays it back as homework.

Coaches then give clients permission to talk. Examples of this are: 'Please tell me why you've come' and 'What skills would you like us to try to improve?' Though coaches should try to create an emotional climate of warmth, respect and interest, they need to remain mindful that coaching tends to be more directly focused on strengthening skills than is the case with therapy. At the start of initial sessions, this means that they may need to screen out some moderately disturbed or very disturbed clients and refer them for therapy. Even where this is unnecessary, they frequently need to clarify their role so that clients understand more of the nature of the coaching process. Coaches should be prepared to answer questions, but avoid long-winded replies.

At some stage during the start of sessions, coaches can give clients an initial understanding of how they work. For instance, a coach might say:

> I see my role as helping you to develop skills that can improve how you function in the areas that we decide on. First, I would like us both to get a clearer picture of what you want and how you are functioning. Then I would like to discuss with you some mind skills and communication skills that might assist you to function better. I would rather leave a discussion of mind skills until I can illustrate the idea from what you tell me.

*The Client in the Process*   Clients come to coaching for a number of reasons. Some are referred by people such as friends and bosses to assist them to function well in taking on new tasks. Such tasks can include starting a relationship with someone of real interest or a change of job. Clients may also come for assistance in overcoming problems that are not serious enough for them to enter therapy. Some clients seek coaching to improve already existing strengths. Clients who enter coaching to work on a problem may continue being coached to improve their strengths.

From the start many coaching clients view the process in positive terms. They are enthused about the possibility of working on goals that are important to them. This is unlike many counselling clients, for whom it may be a huge step to seek assistance in easing their suffering. Nevertheless, from the moment they set eyes on their coaches, clients start summing them up. Coaches' vocal and bodily communication can speak to clients just as loudly as their words. Questions running through clients' minds include: 'Can I trust this coach?', 'How much am I prepared to reveal?' and 'Can this person be of real assistance to me?' Inevitably coaching clients have some unfinished business that may interfere with the coaching relationship, though hopefully coaches can behave in ways that calm these fears.

## Phase 2 Facilitating Client Disclosure

*The Coach in the Process*   Even where clients either decide to come to coaching or have been referred for a specific purpose, if time allows it is a good idea to encourage them to talk about their lives, goals, strengths and problems from their own perspective. The main purpose of the early part of initial coaching sessions is to build good relationships with clients. Helping clients to feel accurately understood as they share their inner worlds is a good way of achieving this objective. Allowing clients to talk about their strengths as well as areas in which they want to improve is another way of enhancing the coach – client relationship.

In addition, as a coach I want to get clients to be actively involved in the coaching process and not just responding to me. One reason is that coaches cannot always be certain where clients are going to take them. By getting too focused too soon, coaches may stay on the surface rather than help clients to access material that is more important to work on for them. As clients reveal themselves, coaches start the process of making their own hypotheses about the overall skills on which the client needs to work. In addition, they can get some early impressions of clients' mind skills and communication/action skills. During this process of client disclosure, coaches require good relationship enhancement skills: for instance, active listening, summarizing and asking some (but not too many at this stage) questions.

In life coaching, it is advisable for coaches to take notes as discretely as is reasonable. They can explain that they take notes to remember relevant information for when they later suggest ways of attaining clients' goals. When agreeing on a shared analysis of one or more of the clients' life goals and the skills they need to attain them, it is very useful for coaches to do this from actual material that clients have provided, including quoting back pertinent statements that clients have made. Most coaching clients have little difficulty with their coaches' taking notes since they see it as part of the process of helping them.

*The Client in the Process*   Clients have different needs in wanting to discuss their lives. Some may come with a very specific agenda for coaching and be reluctant to spend much time in a broader exploration of how they function. Many are glad to talk about themselves, though in varying degrees can be selective about what they say. Some clients require assistance in finding out what their real goals are and in stating them clearly. Clients may not be used to examining their strengths and can require assistance in doing so. Clients can also talk about what they see as their problems. Some rationing of disclosure is likely, though this should be less than in counselling since coaching clients are generally less disturbed than many counselling clients. Coaching clients are often positive about the process and eager to reveal various aspects of their lives. They usually appreciate starting by having an open-ended discussion of their perceptions of their goals, strengths and areas in need of improvement before they get down to focusing on specific skills.

## Stage 2 Understanding

The main objective of the understanding stage is for coaches to work with clients to assess and agree on a shared analysis of one or more of the client's life goals and on the skills that they might need to attain them. Coaches and clients move from discussing areas for improvement in everyday terms to assessing how clients could be functioning better. Ultimately, coaches and clients have a discussion of the mind skills and communication/action skills the client needs to work on. Throughout coaches respect clients as intelligent co-workers, who are ultimately responsible for providing the material for, and deciding on, which skills they need to address.

### Phase 1 Reconnaisance, Detecting and Deciding

*The Coach in the Process*   In Stage 2 of the life coaching model, coaches perform a more active role than in Stage 1. Sometimes in coaching it is useful to conduct a broader reconnaissance before deciding on the areas in which to work. This is not always possible or wanted. For instance, a coach may have been hired by a travel agency to work on improving a staff member's listening skills and may be reluctant to get into other areas. The nature of the exploration in such instances would focus on understanding the situations in which the client uses listening skills and exploring what skills the client has and needs in these situations.

Other clients appreciate the coach conducting a broad reconnaissance. They may come to coaching with one area in which they want to work but be interested in finding out how they can function better in other areas as well. Coach skills for conducting a reconnaissance include helping clients to see that its purpose is to help them understand themselves better and set realistic goals for coaching. Some coaches use questionnaires to explore clients' goals and how they are getting on in different areas of their life. Such questionnaires may be provided either prior to or after initial sessions.

When conducting a reconnaissance, coaches can ask clients in which areas they want them to focus. Alternatively, they can tactfully move the focus of the interview from area to area. The reconnaissance may briefly deal with clients' pasts, though this tends not to be a major focus in coaching. Coaching reconnaisances tend to be oriented towards the future and cover what clients want to get from different areas of life: for instance, how does the client view success in specific areas, such as personal relations and work? It is important to look out for clients' strengths, and skills in need of improvement in areas such as: friendship, family and intimate relationships; work, study and leisure activities; and physical fitness and health care. For some coaches and clients it can also be important to collect information relevant to culture, social class and gender issues. Spiritual and existential issues is another area of importance to some clients.

Coaches need to end the broad reconnaisance by confirming with clients the areas they want to work on. They can ask clients this question but should not be shy about tactfully suggesting other areas as well. Then, coaches may still collect more information to test ideas about possible mind skills and communication/action skills in need of improvement in at least the first skills area they have agreed to work on. When this process is over, coaches should pull together their conclusions for discussing with clients. Coaches can ask clients to give them a few minutes to look over their notes and any other information so that they can offer them specific suggestions about how they might work together. When making notes, I highlight information that may be important. For example, I place a 'T' by any thoughts that appear to be particularly relevant for justifying work on improving a mind skill.

*The Client in the Process*   Clients need to perceive that a reconnaissance is of some potential benefit to them. When they come to coaching with specific goals, they may only respond positively to questions in or around the area of their objectives. Often clients willingly collaborate in sensitively conducted attempts to understand them, their strengths and their areas in need of improvement more fully. When helped to review different aspects of their lives, they feel affirmed and can gain useful insights.

Clients can be very cooperative in providing additional information that helps them understand how they may be blocking the attainment of one or more of their goals. For instance, in the example of improving a client's job interview skills, coaches are likely to ask follow-up questions that elicit thoughts and feelings that may occur before, during and even after a specific interview. The client can also help the coach understand how their use of skills may differ according to different variables in the job interview situation; for instance, when answering aggressive questions. Furthermore, the client can show the coach their actual verbal, vocal and bodily communication during the various phases of a job interview.

I find that clients understand when I politely ask them to allow me some time to pull together the information they have provided so that I can discuss with them some specific suggestions concerning the skills they might improve and how they might do this. What is damaging is a confusing and ill-considered assessment of how they might improve their lives in specific ways rather than one carefully crafted from what they have said.

### *Phase 2 Agreeing on a Shared Analysis of How to Achieve the Client's Life Goal(s)*

*The Coach in the Process*    After making preliminary assessments, coaches attempt to agree with clients on a shared analysis of the mind skills and communication/action skills that the client needs to attain a goal. To avoid confusion, coaches should only analyse one goal at a time. This goal should be identified in the previous phase so that the coach can collect information concerning it. Coaches offer suggestions of skills requiring improvement for discussion with clients. Furthermore, where necessary, they illustrate how they have come to their conclusions with the material that clients have provided earlier.

Good coach suggestions of skills that clients might improve follow logically from information revealed to date. As appropriate coaches work with clients to explain, modify or even discard suggestions with which clients are unhappy. It is vitally important that clients agree on where best to improve their skills since they are the ones who need to work hard to change.

Coaching sessions can be conducted with a small whiteboard to one side that the client and coach can turn to when wanted. I do not favour using the whiteboard before agreeing on a shared analysis part of an initial session. Premature use of the whiteboard risks slowing down and even confusing the assessment process.

Using visual as well as verbal presentation to define how to attain a goal has many advantages. Visual as well as verbal communication can stimulate interest. In addition, clients' memories are fallible and by the time coaches move on to the next topic clients may have started forgetting what has already happened without a record of it. Furthermore, coaches can use the whiteboard to modify suggestions of skills to work on in line with client feedback. By the time coaches finish the analysis, clients should have a good visual overview of the mind skills and communication/action skills they might improve to attain their stated goal.

Once agreement is reached on the skills that clients need to improve, both parties can record this as a basis for their future work. However, as coaching progresses, coaches may require flexibility in modifying their shared analyses of problems and the skills clients need to improve. An illustrative example of a visual analysis in skills terms is provided in Box 3.2.

---

### Box 3.2  Example of a Shared Analysis of How to Achieve a Goal

#### Clients' Goal

To improve my job interview skills.

#### Shared Analysis of How to Improve My Job Interview Skills

| Mind skills goals | Communication/action skills goals |
|---|---|
| To improve my: | To improve my: |
| *Creating rules skills* | *Preparation skills* |
| 'I don't have to give the perfect answer.' | Finding out more about the job. |
| *Creating perceptions skills* | *Meeting and greeting skills* |
| 'I have much relevant background.' | Say 'hello' directly to panel members. |
| *Creating self-talk skills* | *Answering questions skills* |
| 'Tell myself to stay calm and to listen carefully to the questions.' | Verbal skills: be brief. Vocal skills: speak clearly. Body skills: look alert. |

---

*The Client in the Process*   Many clients come for coaching because they are unclear about what their goals are and/or about how to achieve them. Some clients come for help with specific problems. Such clients may be successful but still want to improve their lives and how they perform in specific areas. Other clients have larger and broader objectives and want psychological knowledge and skills to gain more happiness and satisfaction in life.

Whatever their motivation for seeking coaching, clients genuinely appreciate coaches who help them to define their goals and then, in easily understood language, show them how they can make progress in attaining them. Clients need to be active participants in the process of agreeing upon a shared analysis of problems. If necessary, they should be helped to understand how important it is for them to question anything that is unclear. They should feel free to seek modifications of, or abandonment of, any of the coach's suggestions about skills requiring improvement.

Clients generally like to be invited to contribute feedback. They like illustrations of how coaches have arrived at their suggestions based on material that they have shared previously. Clients appreciate seeing the attainment of their goals broken down into specific skills that they need to improve. Often, by the end of this process, they understand that situations previously viewed as overwhelming, and goals that seemed unattainable, are now within their grasp.

## Stage 3 Changing

The main goal of the changing stage is for coaches to work with clients to bring about improvements in their behaviour.

### Phase 1 Intervening

*The Coach in the Process*   To intervene effectively coaches require good relationship skills and good training skills. Skilled coaches adjust the balance between relationship orientations and task orientations, depending on the client and what is needed at the time. For instance, some clients already have a good idea of what to do but need the coaching relationship to support them in using their skills. With other clients, coaches may need to put more emphasis on helping them to learn one or more skills or, at the very least, learn how to be more skilled.

Coaches work much of the time with the three coaching or training methods of 'tell', 'show' and 'do', the topics of Chapters 6, 7 and 8 of this book. 'Tell' entails providing clients with clear instructions concerning the skills they wish to develop. 'Show' means providing demonstrations of how to use the skills in practice. 'Do' means arranging for clients to perform structured activities in coaching sessions and homework tasks.

Within collaborative working relationships, coaches help clients apply specific mind skills and communication/action skills interventions. In the context of this book, these interventions are predominantly cognitive-behavioural and humanistic. To the extent possible, coaches pay particular attention to helping clients acquire the skills for self-coaching both now and when they are on their own. Coaches help clients become clear about the fact that they are learning and using skills that they can work to improve. Just like a football coach in the Premier League, life coaches see their role as helping clients to build their skills for future use. Frequently, coaches ask clients to fill out homework or 'take away' sheets in which they record skills written on the whiteboard during sessions. They may also ask clients to prepare for a session by thinking about issues that the client wants to work on in the next session.

*The Client in the Process*   Clients are encouraged to participate actively during the intervening stage. In a sense, their role is that of learners or participants who are acquiring greater levels of skills from user-friendly coaches. They collaborate with coaches in setting session agendas, sharing their thoughts and feelings, and participating in in-session learning activities to build their knowledge and skills. Clients also participate actively in the process by doing homework and keeping their own records of work covered during coaching.

Coaching clients tend to be well motivated to negotiate and carry out homework assignments. They can be helped to see such assignments as laying the groundwork not just for work conducted during coaching but for future self-coaching. Some such assignments prepare for the next session: for instance, paying attention to the kind of self-talk they are using about future public speaking assignments. Carrying out this preparation can save time during the next session and make it more useful too. Other assignments involve implementing and monitoring their use of skills learned during previous sessions: for example, learning to replace self-defeating perceptions with more realistic ones or trying to improve their verbal, vocal and bodily communication in specific situations.

## Phase 2 Ending

*The Coach in the Process*   Sometimes the ending of coaching is agreed in advance: for example, coaching will end after six sessions. Very often such an arrangement will mean that the client has agreed to work on, or been sent to be coached for, only one or two skills. With short-term coaching there is more of a risk that clients may not have improved as much as they might, and may lose some or all of their improvement. At the other extreme, some coaches work on an ongoing basis with clients to improve and maintain their skills across a number of areas – relationships, health, career and so on. Such really long-term coaching relationships are rare and usually only for the wealthy. More often, coaches work with clients in one or more skills areas and end by mutual agreement. Some of these coaching relationships may go on longer than clients originally intended if they find the coaching really useful. In addition, there is crisis coaching where clients may require coaching in getting skills very quickly. Also, on occasion, coaching may end prematurely; for instance when the client is dissatisfied or moves location unexpectedly.

If coaching is not already for a fixed term, most often coaches and clients discuss the topic of ending before they reach the final session. Relationship issues tend to be less prominent when ending coaching than when ending counselling, partly because coaching clients tend to be less disturbed than counselling clients and also the coaching agenda tends to be clearer. As with counselling, a useful option with some clients is to reduce contact by spacing out the final few sessions. This practice can give clients more time to integrate coached skills into their repertoires. Certain clients may appreciate the opportunity for booster sessions, say three or six months later. Some coaches check on clients' progress after a fixed period of time. Coaches may also discuss client access to them, say by phone or email, when official coaching ends.

The life coaching model seeks to avoid the 'coach and hope' approach. Coaches encourage acquisition and maintenance of skills by: coaching the skills so clearly that clients become their own coaches; working with real-life situations during coaching; and using time between sessions productively to perform homework assignments and to practise skills. Coaches also often encourage clients to record sessions and, in a final session, coach and client can go over how to implement skills and how to deal with setbacks after coaching ends. Coaches and clients can develop and rehearse coping strategies for preventing and managing lapses and relapses. Sometimes clients require assistance in identifying people to support their efforts to maintain skills. Coaches can also provide information about further skills building opportunities.

*The Client in the Process*  Hopefully, towards the ending phase of coaching, clients are satisfied that they have made real progress in improving the targeted skills. Nevertheless, questions that clients can ask towards the end of coaching include: 'How can I get my coaching gains to last?', 'What difficulties do I anticipate?' and 'How do I deal with lapses and mistakes?'

Clients can help their coaching gains to last if they have learned the mind skills and communication/action skills components of overall skills clearly and thoroughly. They require time to practise, practise and practise their skills. As part of their practise, they may experience difficulty in various situations. Sometimes they can handle these difficult situations adequately but on other occasions it is advisable for them to discuss the difficulties with their coaches. Where necessary, clients can get their coaches to role-play these situations with them and make suggestions for handling them skillfully. Clients also need to learn that having lapses and making mistakes are signals telling them to get back on track rather than signs that they are losing their skills. They can discuss with their coaches where they think they are vulnerable to losing their skills and get support and practise in how best to maintain them.

Clients can ensure that ending is handled as beneficially as possible for them. They can actively participate in discussions about how they can maintain and improve their skills once coaching ends. Clients should implicitly and, if necessary, explicitly receive the consistent message that they possess the resources to become happier and more effective people.

## Stage 4 Client Self-Coaching

### Phase 1 Maintenance and Improvement

In the life coaching model, coaches prepare clients for using the targeted skills on their own. Clients should be clear about the mind skills and communication/action skills they have worked on. When formal coaching ends, they should already have had the opportunity to check on how well they use the skills. Nevertheless, there is a risk that, without knowing that the coach is still checking on them, clients may be less diligent about applying their skills, including correcting themselves when they go wrong. Coaches can emphasize the importance of clients continuing to use and monitor their targeted skills. If necessary, they can get clients to list the advantages of continuing to use their skills.

If coaching has been thorough, clients should have a good idea of how to use and maintain targeted skills on their own. If necessary, they can rehearse the mind skills and communication/action skills required for upcoming situations until they reach a satisfactory standard. When they find that they have not used a skill well, clients should be prepared to analyse what they failed to do rather than let themselves get discouraged. Former clients are more likely to keep using their skills if they understand that making mistakes is often part of life and that they have the knowledge and skills to correct mistakes and get back on track.

### Phase 2 Self-Directed Growth

If possible, clients should see their coaching as contributing to self-directed growth. During coaching, they will have broken down at least one area into mind skills and communication/action skills in need of improvement. Life coaches can prepare clients for self-directed growth after coaching ends. Some former clients do this anyway, even if coaches have not mentioned it. On their own, former clients can take areas in which they want to improve and break them down into mind skills and communication/action skills for improvement. They can plan how they will improve the various skills they target, implement their plans, and make modifications and corrections as needed. Where appropriate, former clients can identify people who can support them in improving their skills.

When working with their mind skills, former clients will realize that the knowledge and skills they learned and applied during coaching can be readily adapted to being skilled at dealing with other situations and challenges in their lives. For instance, the skills of challenging and replacing a demanding rule in one area are the same as needed for other areas. Though communication/action skills tend to vary according to different areas, former clients can still break them down into the verbal, vocal and bodily components required for managing situations, which gives them a start in knowing where to change.

Where possible, former clients should adopt a life coaching approach to living. Coaches may have helped them get so far but they should then use their knowledge and skills in any other area of their life that requires their assistance. Former clients can not only become their own best coaches, they can also make for a more skilled world by helping others.

### Activity 3.1   The Life Coaching Model

1.  Describe some coach skills and client behaviours for the following stages and phases of the life coaching model.

## Stage 1 Relating

### Phase 1 Starting the Initial Session

- Coach skills.
- Client behaviours.

### Phase 2 Facilitating Client Disclosure

- Coach skills.
- Client behaviours.

## Stage 2 Understanding

### Phase 1 Reconnaisance, Detecting and Deciding

- Coach skills.
- Client behaviours.

### Phase 2 Agreeing on a Shared Analysis of How to Achieve the Client's Life Goal(s)

- Coach skills.
- Client behaviours.

## Stage 3 Changing

### Phase 1 Intervening

- Coach skills.
- Client behaviours.

### Phase 2 Ending

- Coach skills.
- Client behaviours.

2. How can coaches help clients to become effective self-coaches for when coaching ends?

# 4
# *The Coaching Relationship*

The coaching relationship consists of the coach's and the client's relationship to each other both when they are together and apart. It also consists of the client's relationship to the coach, albeit often unawares, when coaching ends; inasmuch as the client is still influenced by the coach, the relationship continues.

## *Listening and Showing Understanding Skills*

### *Active Listening*

Active listening is a central skill in developing and maintaining coaching relationships. Hearing involves the capacity to be aware of and receive sound. Listening involves not only receiving sound but understanding its meaning as far as possible. Thus it not only involves hearing words but also being sensitive to vocal and bodily cues, and to the social context of communication. Active listening goes one stage further; it entails, in addition to understanding accurately a speaker's communications, being able to show them that you have understood. Important consequences of active listening include establishing rapport and trust, gaining greater understanding in both speaker and listener, helping clients to experience feelings and gathering information.

Clients who are listened to attentively are more likely to assume responsibility for working to improve their skills than those who are not. One reason is that active listening may reduce defensiveness. Another reason is that active listening provides a base for offering well-timed challenges that encourage clients to assume rather than to avoid responsibility. Active listening provides a climate in which clients can assume greater personal agency for constructing their communication, action and meanings.

## Respect and Acceptance

An important component of active listening is the ability to possess an attitude of respect and acceptance. Such an attitude involves respecting clients as separate human beings with rights to their own thoughts and feelings, and withholding judgment on their goodness or badness. This does not mean that you agree with everything they say but rather you are secure enough to respect what they say as their version of reality. There are many barriers and filters that act as sources of interference to receiving another's communication loud and clear. For instance, coaches may be threatened by certain clients' feelings, such as anger. Coaches may also have varying degrees of prejudice. You may tune out to people who differ from you because of age, sex, sexual orientation, culture, race, social class, intelligence level or physical disability, among other possible differences. Coaches too concerned with maintaining a smooth professional façade may also be too busy listening to their own needs to accept clients fully.

## Tuning In to the Client's Internal Viewpoint

The skill of listening to and understanding clients is based on choosing to acknowledge the separateness between 'me' and 'you' by getting inside the internal viewpoint of the other, rather than remaining in one's own external viewpoint. If coaches respond to what clients say in ways that show accurate understanding of the clients' perspectives, they respond as if inside the client's internal viewpoint. However, if coaches choose not to show understanding of their clients' perspectives or lack the skills to understand them, they respond from an external viewpoint. Box 4.1 provides examples of coach responses from external and internal viewpoints.

## Box 4.1    Coach Responses from Internal and External Viewpoints

### External Viewpoint Responses

Well, there were other ways you could have responded to your boss.
There are lots of ways of handling situations like that.
Everyone boasts sometimes.
You should not let that sort of thing happen.
You're a very good person.

### Internal Viewpoint Responses

You're basically satisfied with your life but still think there are some areas to address.
You have very mixed feelings about staying in the relationship.
You're pleased to have made some friends at work.
You want to work on becoming more fit.
You're feeling scared about giving a presentation with your manager present.

Often coaching trainees can show that they are working from within their client's internal viewpoint by starting their response with 'You'. However, as the statement 'You should show you can speak up to her' indicates, trainees can make responses starting with the word 'You' that are clearly coming from the external viewpoint and are manifestly directive.

Trainees should always consciously choose whether or not to respond as if inside their clients' internal viewpoint. Think of a three-link chain: client statement/coach response/client statement. Trainees who respond from clients' internal viewpoints allow them to choose either to continue on the same path or to change direction. However, if trainees respond from their external viewpoints, they can influence clients in such a way as to divert or block those trains of thoughts, feelings and experiences that they might otherwise have chosen.

### Opening Remarks, Small Rewards and Open-Ended Questions

Opening remarks, small rewards and open-ended questions tend to require a few verbal messages as well as good vocal and body messages. They make it easier for clients to talk.

## *Opening Remarks*

Life coaching always starts with you as the coach acknowledging the client's name, saying who you are and checking 'where the client is at'. Opening remarks, openers or permissions to talk are brief statements indicating that coaches are prepared to listen. Coaches start initial sessions with opening remarks that build rapport and encourage clients to share why they have come. Coaches can leave until later a statement about how they work. Opening remarks are 'door openers' that give clients the message 'I'm interested and prepared to listen. Please share with me your internal viewpoint.'

Examples of opening remarks that might be used in initial life coaching sessions include:

When meeting the client outside your office:
'Hello (state client's name), I'm (state your name). Please come in.'

*When the client is seated:*
'Please tell me why you've come.'
'Please tell me why you're here.'
'Please tell me what you want from these sessions.'
'Please tell me what are your goals?'
'Please put me in the picture.'
'You've been referred by _____. Now, what do you want to achieve from these sessions?'

## *Small Rewards*

Small rewards are brief verbal and non-verbal expressions of interest designed to encourage clients to continue speaking. The message they convey is 'I'm with you. Please go on.' Wrongly used, small rewards can encourage clients to respond to coach agendas rather than to their own. For instance, coaching trainees may say 'Tell me more' whenever clients talk about topics of interest to them. Many small rewards can be body rather than verbal messages: for example, facial expressions, head nods and good eye contact. Box 4.2 provides examples of verbal small rewards, though perhaps the most frequently used 'Uh-hmm' is more a vocal than a verbal message.

---

### *Box 4.2    Examples of Small Rewards*

| | |
|---|---|
| Uh-hmm | Sure |
| Please continue | Indeed |

---

---

### Box 4.2 (Continued)

| | |
|---|---|
| Tell me more | And... |
| Go on | So... |
| I see | Really |
| Oh? | Right |
| Then... | Yes |
| I hear you | You're not kidding |

Another kind of small reward is to repeat the last word a client has said:

| | |
|---|---|
| **Client:** | I'm feeling excited. |
| **Coach:** | Excited. |

---

### Open-Ended Questions

Coaches and coaching trainees may use questions in ways that either help clients to elaborate their internal viewpoints or lead them out of their viewpoints, possibly into the coach's own. Open-ended questions allow clients to share their internal viewpoints without curtailing their options. A good use of open-ended questions is when, in the initial session, trainees wish to assist clients to explore their goals. In subsequent sessions too, trainees are likely to find open-ended questions useful. Open-ended questions include: 'Tell me about it?'; 'Please can you elaborate?'; and, slightly less open-ended, 'How do you feel about that?'

Open-ended questions may be contrasted with closed questions that curtail speakers' options: indeed they often give only two options, 'yes' or 'no'.

| | |
|---|---|
| *Open-ended question:* | How do you feel about your job? |
| *Closed question:* | Is your job good or bad? |

Open-ended questions may also be contrasted with leading questions that put answers into clients' mouths:

| | |
|---|---|
| *Open-ended question*: | What do you think about him? |
| *Leading question:* | He's a great person, isn't he? |

Closed and leading questions may have various negative outcomes. Trainees may be perceived as controlling the conversation. They may block clients from getting in touch with and listening to themselves and responding from their internal viewpoint. They may set the stage for an interrogation. Since closed and leading questions can be disincentives to talking, they can create silences in which the stage is set for further closed questions.

It should not be implied that coaching trainees should never use closed questions since this depends on the goals of their listening. Closed questions can be useful for collecting information. However, they should be used sparingly when trainees wish to help others share their worlds. Trainees may also need to use even open-ended questions with some discretion.

## *Reflecting Feelings*

Skilled coaches are very sharp at picking up on clients' feelings. Reflecting clients' feelings at the start of initial sessions is important to show them that one is tuned in to them as persons. Reflecting feelings is both similar to yet different from paraphrasing. Both reflecting feelings and paraphrasing involve mirroring. In addition, reflecting feelings usually involves paraphrasing. However, the language of feelings is not words. Feelings are bodily sensations to which word labels can be attached. Consequently, paraphrasing alone has distinct limitations. For example, clients may send voice and body messages that qualify or negate verbal messages; Ellie says 'I'm Okay' yet speaks softly and has tearful eyes. A good reflection of feelings picks up these other messages as well. Reflecting feelings entails responding to clients' music and not just to their words. To do this, coaching trainee responses need to incorporate appropriate vocal and body messages.

Reflecting feelings involves feeling with a client's flow of emotions and experiencing and communicating this back. Often trainees have trouble in reflecting feelings. They may just talk about feelings rather than offer an expressive emotional companionship. Inadequately distinguishing between thoughts and feelings can be another problem for both clients and coaches. For example, 'I feel that equality between the sexes is essential' describes a thought rather than a feeling. On the other hand, 'I feel angry when I see sexual discrimination' labels a feeling. This distinction between thoughts and feelings is important both in reflecting feelings and also when helping clients to influence how they feel by altering how they think. Constant reflections of feelings run the risk of encouraging clients to wallow in feelings rather than to move on to how best to deal with them.

Reflecting feelings involves both receiver and sender skills:

### Receiver skills

Understanding clients' body messages.
Understanding clients' vocal messages.
Understanding clients' verbal messages.

Tuning in to the flow of one's own emotional reactions.
Taking into account the context of clients' messages.
Sensing the surface and underlying meanings of clients' messages.

**Sender skills**

Responding in ways that pick up on clients' feelings words and phrases.
Rewording feelings appropriately, using expressive rather than wooden language.
Using vocal and body messages that neither add to nor subtract from the emotions conveyed.
Checking the accuracy of one's understanding.

## Picking Up On Feelings Words and Phrases

Let's start with the obvious. A good but not infallible way to understand what clients feel is to listen to their feelings words and phrases. Feelings phrases are colloquial expressions used to describe feelings words. For example, 'I'm over the moon' is a feelings phrase describing the word delight. Picking up feelings words and phrases is similar to paraphrasing but with a heightened focus on feelings rather than informational content. Sometimes coaching trainees ask, 'Well, what did you feel?' after clients have just told them. They need to discipline their listening more. On occasion feelings words are not the central message. For instance, Samuel may say 'It's just great' that, after the break-up of a relationship, he is living on his own again while at the same time his voice chokes, his face looks sad and the corners of his mouth are turned down.

The following are some dimensions of reflecting feelings words and phrases:

*Strength of Feelings*     Mirror the strength of clients' feelings words in reflections. For example, Lucy has just had a negative experience about which she might feel either 'devastated' (strong intensity), 'upset' (moderate intensity) or 'slightly upset' (weak intensity). Corresponding mirroring words might be either 'sent reeling' (strong intensity), or 'distressed' (moderate intensity), or 'a little distressed' (weak intensity). Trainees may err on the side of either adding or subtracting intensity.

*Multiple and Mixed Feelings*     Sometimes clients use many words to describe their feelings. The words may form a cluster around the same theme, in which case a trainee may choose only to reword the crux of the feeling. Alternatively, clients may have varying degrees of mixed feelings ranging from simple opposites, for instance happy/sad to more complex combinations such as hurt/angry. Good reflections pick up on all key elements of feelings messages. For instance:

> *Client:* I'm happy but scared at what is involved in getting promoted.
>
> *Coaching trainee:* You're glad but frightened about the extra responsibility in the promotion.

*Assisting Labelling of Feelings*    Sometimes coaches and trainees assist clients in finding the right feelings words. Here reflecting feelings extends to helping the client choose feelings words that resonate for them.

> *Client:* I don't quite know how to express my reaction to finding a job at last ... possibly pleased ... a weight off my mind ... unsure of myself ...
>
> *Coach:* Glad, relieved, uncertain…
>
> *Client:* Relieved, that's what I really feel above all.

## Picking Up On Vocal and Body Messages

Much information about clients' feelings does not come from what they say but from how they say it. Sometimes clients' verbal, vocal and body messages are consistent. In such instances, it is relatively easy to label feelings and their intensity accurately. On other occasions, clients' messages are encoded. Clients may struggle to express what they *truly* feel in face of their conditioning about what they *should* feel. Furthermore, it takes time for clients to trust coaches and coaching trainees. Consequently many emotional messages 'come out sideways' rather than loud and clear. Effective coaches are skilled at listening with the 'third ear' to clients' vocal and body messages, and to what is left unsaid or camouflaged.

Coaching trainees unclear about clients' real or underlying feelings can check with them. For instance, they can make comments like 'I think I hear you saying (state feelings tentatively) ... Am I right?' or 'I would like to understand what you're feeling but I'm still not altogether clear. Can you help me?' Another option is to say: 'I'm getting a mixed message from you. On the one hand you are saying you do not mind. On the other hand you seem tense?' After a pause, they might add: 'I'm wondering if you are putting on a brave face?' A further consideration in picking up on feelings is to understand whether and to what extent clients possess insight into their feelings.

## *Sender Skills of Reflecting Feelings*

When reflecting feelings a coaching trainee may wonder how best to respond to the numerous verbal, vocal and body messages that they have received. There are no simple answers. What they should try to do is to (1) decode the overall message accurately, and (2) formulate an emotionally expressive response that communicates back the crux of the client's feelings. Here are a few guidelines for sending reflecting feelings messages:

*Send Back the Crux of the Client's Message* Where possible, trainees should show that they have understood the client's main message or messages. Whatever else they do, they should try to communicate back the core feeling.

| | |
|---|---|
| *Client:* | At work Hannah and I keep disagreeing and don't seem to get anywhere. I don't know what to do. It's so upsetting. I wish I knew the answer. |
| *Coaching trainee:* | You're extremely frustrated with constant unproductive arguments and not knowing how to improve matters. |

*When responding, state the client's main feeling first* Even though the clients may not start with their main feeling, they may feel better understood by trainees who reflect their main feeling at the front of their response than if they reflect information first.

| | |
|---|---|
| *Client:* | My suggestion on decorating the living room was agreed to. I'm really glad. |
| *Coaching trainee:* | You're extremely pleased that your idea was accepted. |

In the above example, the trainee has tuned in to feelings immediately. However, imagine the trainee had replied: 'Your suggestion about decorating the living room was accepted and you're extremely pleased.' The trainee has started by responding from the head to the client's head. By the time the trainee reflects the feeling of pleasure, it may be too late for the client to experience being fully emotionally understood.

*Keep Your Response Appropriately Simple* Use simple and clear language. Avoid unnecessary words and qualifications. However, be prepared to state different parts of multiple and mixed messages.

*Use Vocal and Body Messages to Add Expressiveness to Verbal Message(s)* Coaching trainees are not just talking about feelings, they are reflecting feelings. For instance, if a bereaved client says 'I feel so sad', they can adjust their vocal and facial expression to mirror, to some extent, a sense of sorrow. Consistency between their verbal, voice and body messages is important. If they send mixed messages, clients may perceive them as insincere.

*Check Understanding*　　Trainees respond to client statements with different degrees of tentativeness depending on how clearly the messages were communicated and how confident they are about having received them accurately. However, all reflections should contain an element of checking whether they accurately understand clients' internal viewpoints. Sometimes they can check by slight voice inflections. On other occasions they can check more explicitly.

*Reflect Feelings and Reasons*　　A useful variation in active listening is to reflect both feelings and the reasons for them. Reflecting back reasons does not mean that a coaching trainee makes an interpretation or offers an explanation from their external viewpoint. Instead, where clients have already provided reasons for a feeling, they reflect these feelings back in a 'You feel … because …' statement that mirrors the internal viewpoint. Here is an example:

| | |
|---|---|
| *William:* | Ever since she left, I'm afraid that I will find no one new for a relationship. |
| *Coaching trainee:* | You're scared because you fear not meeting another girlfriend. |
| *William:* | Yes. I get anxious just thinking of how difficult it may be. |

Here the trainee's 'You feel … because … ' response showed more understanding of William's predicament than if the response had stopped after 'You're scared'. Put another way, the 'because' part of the trainee's response identified the thinking contributing to William's feeling. Thus, 'You feel … because … ' reflections are useful not only for helping clients tell their stories but also for assessing how clients' thinking contributes to unwanted feelings.

## Activity 4.1　Reflecting Feelings Skills

As appropriate, complete each part of this exercise on your own, with a partner or in a group. Suggested answers to Parts A and B are provided at the end of this chapter.

## Part A   Identify and Reflect Feelings Words and Phrases

For each of the following statements: (a) identify the words and phrases the client has used to describe how she or he feels; and (b) reflect the client's feelings, starting your response with either 'You feel' or 'You're'.

### Example
*Jim to coach*: 'I'm really pleased that they've hired me and am certain it's the right job.'

(a)   Jim's feelings words and phrases: really pleased, certain.
(b)   Reflection of feeling: 'You feel pleased at getting the job which you're sure is right.'

### Your Responses
1.   *Chloe to coach*: 'I'm very concerned about my weight.'

    (a)   Chloe's feelings words and phrases.
    (b)   Your reflection of feeling.

2.   *John to coach*: 'I'm delighted at the promotion but I'm also anxious about how I will do.'

    (a)   John's feelings words and phrases.
    (b)   Your reflection of feeling.

## Part B   Reflect Feelings and Reasons

For each of the following client statements formulate a reflective response that uses the 'You feel…because…' format.

### Example
*Julia*:    'I've struggled so hard to get to where I am and now I have to face getting on with a new boss.'

*Coach*:    'You feel worried because after all that effort you need to relate with a new boss.'

### Your Responses
1.   *Aaron to coach*: 'I think she is just great but worry about holding her interest.'

    (a)   You feel
    (b)   because

2.   *Liz to coach*: 'I'm really happy that Pete and I don't fight so much. I feel much better about our relationship.'

    (a)   You feel
    (b)   because

# Using Mind Skills

Many if not all coaching trainees' minds interfere with their listening. However, you can use your minds to guide you in listening well. Here it is briefly illustrated how the mind skills mentioned in Chapter 2 can be used either to support or to sabotage good listening skills.

## Creating Rules

Two major listening mistakes are being too judgmental and giving gratuitous advice. As a coaching trainee your rules and personal agendas may intrude on your capacity to care for and nurture the growth and happiness of clients. For instance, if you are inwardly or outwardly critical of aspects of clients' thoughts, feelings and experiences then there is a good chance that you possess one or more unrealistic rules that 'drive' unhelpful communication. If this is the case, you can detect, challenge and restate the unrealistic rules so that they become realistic rules that enhance rather than erode your ability to listen.

## Creating Perceptions

Humility is always in order when contemplating how good a listener you are. Without knowing it, coaching trainees can easily distort clients' experiences by passing them through a filter of their own experiencing and life histories. There may be certain topics and situations where anxiety interferes with their ability to perceive clients' communications accurately. For instance, some trainees become anxious when the topic turns to sexuality. Trainees, and experienced coaches too, can also feel threatened by certain categories of clients: for example, highly successful clients, very intelligent clients and clients who hold strong views with which they disagree. Furthermore, when anxious, trainees' mind tricks and self-protective habits can interfere with the accuracy of their perceptions. In a coaching situation you may become defensive when clients provide feedback that differs from your picture of yourself: for instance, that you do not always listen well.

As a trainee coach you can use skills for testing the reality of your perceptions so that your own experiencing, defensiveness and agendas do not distort how you perceive clients. Furthermore, you can strive to create compassionate rather than judgmental perceptions of clients and of their human strengths and frailties.

### Creating Self-Talk

As a coaching trainee you can create goal setting self-talk that disciplines you to focus on listening: for example 'STOP ... THINK ... I can show my respect for my client by listening well to her/him'. When you feel yourself getting emotionally aroused, such as anxious or angry, you can create cooling and calming self-talk statements such as: 'Calm down ... my anxiety is a signal that I need to listen carefully.' Trainees can also create coaching self-talk statements for the skills of listening well: for instance, 'Let's make the effort to understand her/his perspective.' Furthermore, as shown in Box 4.3, you can create corrective self-talk once you realize that you are prone to making mistakes that interfere with listening.

---

### Box 4.3   Examples of Corrective Self-Talk

**For interrupting:** Remember to hear her/him out.
**For being too controlling:** Coaching involves respecting clients as separate individuals and freeing them to develop their unique potentials.
**For being too judgmental:** Clients are more likely to disclose if feeling safe.
**For giving too much advice:** I am more helpful if I let clients own their problems.

---

### Creating Visual Images

Coaching trainees can use visual images to enter into clients' internal viewpoints. For instance, when clients describe past or current experiences, you can create imaginary pictures that may help you to understand these experiences. Furthermore, when clients describe visual images or fantasies, you can try to picture them visually too. However, as a trainee you should remember that your visual images can contain errors. Your imagination may be heavily coloured by your own personal experiences, developmental history and current social and cultural environment. Asking clients to describe their experiences and visual images more graphically is one skill trainees can use to guard against the potential to distort images.

### Creating Explanations

Coaching trainees must assume responsibility for how well they listen. Even if you consider that clients behave unreasonably in their private lives, you still need to assume responsibility for listening accurately, so that you may help them as much as possible. Being critical/defensive, dominant/controlling and withdrawn/submissive are three styles of interacting that may interfere with listening. If as a coaching trainee you possess any of these three styles, you need to assume more responsibility for disciplining your listening. If your tendency is critical/defensive or dominant/controlling, your outward communication shows that you do not listen properly. However, the effects of being withdrawn/submissive on listening may be outwardly less obvious. If you allow clients to be rude and inconsiderate, your irritation with them may cause you inwardly to tune out to them.

## Creating Expectations

An important skill for coaching trainees is to avoid mind reading, or responding on the basis of unnecessary expectations concerning what clients think or are about to say. For example, if you rush in to finish off clients' sentences, your responses can get clients' trains of thought wrong. Furthermore, even when the clients provides correction, trainees may still erroneously think that their version is best. One skill for creating accurate expectations about what clients may say next is to listen carefully to what has already been said. Ways of testing the reality of expectations about what clients think or will say include holding back and waiting for them to speak again and using active listening skills so that they can disclose further. It is even possible to tactfully ask them what they are thinking.

## Structuring Skills

Structuring is a term used to describe how coaches let clients know their respective roles at different stages of coaching. Here the focus is on structuring skills in the early part of coaching, which may only last for the first 10 to 15 minutes of initial sessions.

Effective structuring both leads to positive outcomes and prevents or minimizes the chances of negative outcomes. The functions of structuring in initial sessions include clarifying roles, explaining the purpose of coaching and providing an introductory rationale for working within the life coaching model. When structuring in initial sessions, coaching trainees are, in fact, assisting clients to assume responsibility for developing their skills. Trainees can establish cooperative alliances with clients as partners in developing their skills rather than doing things either to or for them.

At the start of initial sessions a choice that coaching trainees face is that of how much to structure. It is often best to do initial structuring in two statements, an opening statement and a follow-up statement, rather than to do it all at the beginning. In two-part structuring, trainees' opening statements provide the first occasion for structuring. Here they can establish time boundaries and give clients permission to talk. After trainees have used their active listening skills to assist clients to say why they want coaching they may summarize the main points for clients and check the accuracy of their summaries. Then trainees can briefly and simply explain the remainder of the coaching process to clients. Box 4.4 presents two possible second structuring statements providing a framework for the life coaching model presented in Chapter 3. The first statement is where the client clearly has only one main area to work on and the second statement is where the client has presented more than one area. If a specific situation has not already emerged then a trainee's follow-up statement may request the client to identify a situation within a main area for their work together.

---

### Box 4.4    Examples of Structuring Statements

## Opening or First Structuring Statement

We have about 45 minutes together, please tell me why you want coaching.

## Possible Second Structuring Statements

### a) Single Area
You've given me some idea why you'd like to be coached. Now what I'd like to do is to ask some more questions to help us understand more fully the area in which you want coaching (specify). Then depending on what we find, I will review with you some skills to help you perform better. Once we agree on what skills might be useful, then we can look at ways to develop them. Does this way of proceeding sound all right?

### b) More than One Area
After summarizing the different areas, the coaching trainee says:

For which of these areas would you like coaching first? (The client states her or his choice). Good. Now I wonder if we can identify a particular situation within this area that it is important for you to manage better. Then we can explore this situation more fully and perhaps come up with some useful skills for dealing with it. Is that all right with you?

---

Structuring can strengthen collaborative working relationships by establishing agendas or goals for the coaching process as well as obtaining agreement on how to proceed. Trainees may need to help clients choose a particular situation to work on that is important for them. Trainees may also need to respond to questions. However, trainees should not allow themselves to be lured into an intellectual discussion of the coaching process. If they make structuring statements in a comfortable and confident way, most clients will be happy to work within the suggested framework.

## *Answers to Activity 4.1*

## Part A    Identify and Reflect Feelings Words and Phrases

1(a).   Chloe's feelings words and phrases: 'very concerned'.
1(b).   Reflection of feeling: 'You feel very worried about how heavy you are.'
2(a).   John's feelings words and phrases: 'delighted', 'anxious'.
2(b).   Reflection of feeling: 'You feel really happy at getting promoted but also worried about performing well.'

## Part B    Reflect Feelings and Reasons

1.   'You *feel* concerned *because* you wonder about your ability to keep such a wonderful person interested.'
2.   'You *feel* really pleased *because* you and Pete are getting on better and you are now much more optimistic about your relationship.'

# 5
# Skills for Assessment and Setting Goals

## Purposes of Assessment

This chapter addresses the coaching skills required for Stage 2 (Understanding) of the life coaching model, the main task of which is to assess and agree on a shared analysis of one or more of the client's life goals and the skills they need to attain them. Clients come to life coaching with numerous different agendas. In the area of relationships, some clients are sent by others to improve a single skill, say the ability to handle a difficult customer assertively. Other clients, though self-referred, also want a narrow focus in coaching – for instance, how they can listen better or resolve a conflict with a specific person. Still other clients want a broader focus – for example, how they can improve the way they relate in general so that they can become happier and more successful. Such clients may already be relating quite well but want to relate even better.

Assessment in life coaching is an ongoing process that starts with initial assessment by coaches in conjunction with clients. Assessment can be achieved in ways that are helpful or harmful. The coach's role in initial assessment is to help clients to find out the area or areas in which they want to work, and then to identify the specific mind skills and communication/action skills for so doing. Coaches and coaching trainees require high levels of the listening skills and expanding understanding skills described in the last chapter to do this well. They need to work closely with clients to discover what specific skills they need to work on. However, if clients are serious about learning skills for life, the process of coaching must include helping them learn to coach themselves on their own once coaching ends.

Assessment lays the base for building clients' skills strengths. Unlike in counselling and psychotherapy, it is not assumed that there are problems on which they need to work that are caused by them possessing distinct skills weaknesses. Once clients say why they have come for coaching and have had a chance to reveal something about themselves, coaching trainees can structure the session in ways that facilitate assessment and setting goals. They may let clients know that they want to conduct a broad review in each goals area the client wants, so as to understand them better. Here they collect specific evidence to test ideas about the client's skills in these areas and then review available information to suggest which skills might require improving.

Coaching trainees may then say that they want to move beyond using ordinary language to help the client improve one or more skills. Most people do not think of how they function in terms of skills but trainees can point out that, just like in every other area of life, they can relate in skilled or unskilled ways. Furthermore how they think is made up of mind skills or thinking skills and how they act is made up of communication skills and action skills. Some clients may take time adjusting to a skills framework, but most experience little difficulty with it and find that it helps them to break down how they function in useful ways. It can also be pointed out that feelings and physical reactions are not skills in themselves but that clients can influence them by how they think and act. The aim of an initial assessment is to negotiate a preliminary analysis of how to achieve one or more life goals involving agreeing on the mind skills and communication/action skills for improvement.

# Skills for Assessment

Chapter 4 introduced the reader to some listening and showing understanding skills and to the skill of structuring. All of these skills are highly relevant to assessment. Though much of the time during initial assessment coaches and coaching trainees are searching for information, it is essential that this is done in a way that builds on what clients say and that they feel they are being helped to better understand themselves.

## Questioning Skills

Judicious questioning can help clients better explore, clarify and understand their internal viewpoints. Questions can also assist coaching trainees to collect relevant information for understanding and breaking down the areas in which clients want to improve. Once this is done both client and trainee possess more information for developing hypotheses about how weaknesses in skills are sustained. In the life coaching's understanding stage, coaches and coaching trainees act rather like detectives. They cooperate with clients first to ask questions that clarify and break down their areas of concern and then to ask further questions that can lead to agreement on the analysis of at least one area in skills terms.

Coaching trainees have numerous choices when questioning. Though focusing on clients' presents and futures, information about the past can also be relevant and should not be totally excluded. How detailed should be the inquiries into each topic area? Through intuition, experience and reasoning, effective practitioners assess when areas may continue to yield valuable information and when to move on. Trainees need to be sensitive to the intimacy and threat level of questions. However, they will still tactfully ask intimate questions, if appropriate. Trainees require caution regarding the timing and ordering of questions. They may defer some intimate or probing questions pending the establishment of greater trust, though this is less of a problem with coaching clients than with counselling clients. Trainees also need to be careful not to conduct interrogations that may lead to either defensiveness or dependence, or both.

## *Types of Questions*

Coaching trainees need to choose among different types of questions, including the following. Already in the previous chapter I have dealt with the difference between open-ended versus closed questions.

*Clarification questions* seek information about and clarify the coaching trainee's perception of clients' words and phrases. Examples include:

> When you say ——, what do you mean?
> It sounds to me like you're saying ——?

*Elaboration questions* are open questions that give clients the opportunity to expand on what they have already started taking about. Examples include:

> Would you care to elaborate?
> Is there anything more you wish to add?

*Specific detail questions* aim to collect concrete information about clients' areas of concern and problematic skills patterns. Specific detail questions focus on how, what, when, and where. How questions are particularly useful for eliciting details of how clients act, and include:

How do/did you think, feel or act (or a combination of these)?

What questions include:

What happened?
What are the likely consequences of doing that?

When questions include:

When did it start?
When is your next public speech?

Where questions include:

Where does it happen?

*'Show me' questions* ask clients to show the coaching trainee how they communicated in a particular situation. Sometimes trainees act the other person in a role play. Examples include:

Show me how you actually spoke to ——?
Imagine I am your ——, show me how you behaved to me?

*Eliciting personal meaning questions*: the information clients provide often has personal or symbolic meaning for them and questions can be asked to elicit these meanings. For example, if whenever a husband would come home late without having called her, his wife would think he did not care about her (Beck, 1988). Eliciting personal meanings questions should be open and tentative since the client should in principle know the answer better than anyone else but may turn out not to realize it. Illustrative questions include:

I'm wondering what the meaning of —— is for you?
What do you make of that?
Why is it so important for you?

*Searching for strengths questions*: Ivey and Ivey (2003) use the term positive asset search to describe searching for clients' strengths. They observe that, since people grow from their strengths, the positive asset search is a useful method to ensure a more optimistic and directed interview. Illustrative questions include:

What do you see as your strengths?
What are your assets?
Was there anything good in the way you behaved?
What skills do you bring to this problem?

*Solution-focused questions* ask clients to provide information concerning the extent to which they have tried or are trying to do something about their issues, for example:

What have you attempted to do to date to achieve your goal?
What are your options?
What are you planning to do?
How can you change your behaviour?

Once coaching trainees agree with clients on a specific concern to address, there are a number of areas in which they can ask questions. These areas include a brief history of the concern; the client's feelings, physical reactions; thoughts; and how they communicate. Throughout this process of asking questions, the trainee should take brief notes. Some trainees dislike taking notes since they fear it blocks their relationships with clients. The following are three reasons for discreetly taking notes. First, note-taking can enable trainees to be more, not less, psychologically present to clients – it relieves the pressure on them to memorize information. Second, when later they come to redefine clients' areas of concern in skills terms, they can draw evidence for their suggestions from their records of what clients have said. Third, trainees have a record to which they can refer back, if necessary, for use in subsequent sessions.

## Work in Partnership With Clients

In life coaching questions aim to provide information as much for clients as for coaches. Coaching trainees should try to avoid questioning in ways that create dependency, passivity and resistance. For instance, coaches can ask questions for establishing agendas and transition questions that have the advantage of getting clients involved in the detective work of identifying and clarifying problems. Clients are invited to participate in working in areas important for them. Illustrative questions include:

You've mentioned three areas (specify), which one would you like to focus on first?
Is there anything you would like to add before we move on to ——?

Coaching trainees should remember to intersperse active listening with questions. Clients feel interrogated when trainees ask a series of questions in quick succession. Trainees can greatly soften their questioning if they pause to see if clients wish to continue responding and then reflect each response. Interspersing active listening has the added advantage of ensuring that trainees check the accuracy of their understanding. Here is an example:

| *James*: | I'm getting anxious over my upcoming presentation to the Board. |
| *Coaching trainee*: | You're worried about your presentation. Would you care to say more about this? |
| *James*: | Yes. It is in three week's time and I feel overwhelmed. |
| *Coaching trainee*: | So you experience the giving of the presentation as overpowering. |
| *James*: | I feel my whole future depends on it. |
| *Coaching trainee*: | You think it is make-or-break. Can you explain this further? |

Though only a short excerpt, the coaching trainee facilitates James's description of his internal viewpoint. The trainee asks questions in ways that encourage the expression of feelings as well as of thoughts.

## *Activity 5.1   Questioning Skills*

## Part A   Formulating Questions

Provide two examples of each of the following types of questions:

(a)  clarification;
(b)  elaboration;
(c)  specific detail, including a

  –  how question
  –  what question
  –  when question
  –  where question;

(d)  'show me';
(e)  eliciting personal meaning;
(f)  searching for strengths; and
(g)  solution focused.

## Part B    Practising in Pairs or in a Group

Coach each other for sessions consisting of:

- initial structuring;
- facilitating the client who responds to the initial structuring by sharing her or his reasons for wanting coaching;
- a second statement to establish the structure for asking questions to identify and clarify the client's need for coaching; and then,
- interspersed with active listening, ask appropriate questions for your client and you to get greater understanding of the area for coaching.

At the end of each session, the 'client' gives the 'coach' feedback on her/his questioning skills. It can help to play back audio or video recordings of your work.

## *Giving Feedback*

Before discussing coaches and trainee coaches *giving* feedback, along with Williams and Thomas (2005) I mention that *requesting* feedback can be a very useful skill for coaching. They should listen carefully to client feedback and, unless absolutely necessary, avoid interrupting. Coaching trainees can learn how they are coming across to clients. Feedback can be about their relationship or it can also be about the client's reaction to how a coach is approaching training them in a particular skill. If you consider the feedback helpful, you should be willing to thank clients for it.

Effective coaches understand that often the best feedback clients can have is the ability to assess and learn from their own experience. Coaching trainees can assist clients to develop skills at evaluating not only how they behave but also their behaviour's consequences for other people. Trainees can also encourage clients to be open to relevant feedback from others. Clients inevitably receive much feedback from people with whom they interact and they can become more aware of such feedback, including its accuracy.

Coaching trainees can also provide feedback themselves. Box 5.1 summarizes some guidelines for coach feedback, though trainees should vary which guidelines they follow according to circumstances.

---

## Box 5.1   Guidelines for Giving Feedback

### Use 'I' Messages Rather than 'You' Messages

*'You' message*
'You did ...'
*'I' message*
'I thought you ...'

### Be Specific and, Where Possible, State Feedback in the Positive

*Non-specific and negative*
'You spoke poorly.'
*Specific and positive*
'I thought you could use more eye contact and speak in a louder voice.'

### Use Confirmatory as well as Corrective Feedback

'I thought your use of eye contact was good but that you could still speak in a louder voice.'

### Consider Emotional as well as Behavioural Feedback

'When you made very direct eye contact and spoke in a loud voice, I felt overpowered by you.'

### Consider Demonstrating your Feedback

'I would like to show you how your eye contact came over to me (then demonstrate)'.

### Consider Cultural Sensitivity Feedback

'I wonder whether there was a cultural issue (specify which) operating in the speaking session.'

### Provide an Opportunity for the Receiver to Respond to Your Feedback

'Would you like to respond to my feedback?'

---

In addition to the items mentioned in Box 5.1, coaching trainees can consider audio-visual feedback. Audio cassette feedback is especially useful when focusing on verbal and vocal messages. Videotape feedback is especially useful for focusing on body messages. Audio-visual feedback lends itself to self-assessment by clients. It provides facts rather than perceptions and inferences. Playing and discussing audio-visual feedback of role-plays can provide valuable learning experiences for clients.

## Feedback or Confrontation

How can feedback be distinguished from confrontation? Much feedback is either in line with or reasonably close to clients' existing perceptions. Such feedback does not provide any major challenge to how they see themselves. Confrontation is a category of feedback where clients' self-concepts are challenged. Confrontations may focus either on inconsistencies, for instance between words and actions, on distortions of reality, such as selecting out inconvenient feedback, or on not owning responsibility for the consequences of one's behaviour. How as well as what coaches confront is important. Given the right trusting atmosphere, constructive confrontations have their place in coaching. However, where possible, help clients to confront themselves: for example, by asking them to search for evidence to back their statements. Trainees should also use a minimum amount of 'muscle'. Although sometimes desirable, strong confrontations are generally to be avoided.

## *Activity 5.2   Feedback Skills*

1. Refer to the guidelines for offering feedback in Box 5.1 and formulate statements for illustrating each of the different guidelines.
2. Work in a pair with Partner A as 'client' and Partner B as 'coach'.

   - Partner A selects a situation involving another person where she/he thinks she/he might communicate better.
   - Partners A and B conduct a mini role-play in which Partner B plays the other person and Partner A demonstrates how she/he currently communicates in the situation.
   - Afterwards, Partner B invites Partner A to comment on her/his verbal, vocal and body messages in the situation. Then Partner B gives feedback to Partner A.
   - Next, hold a sharing and discussion session about Partner A's skills in offering feedback.
   - Then, if appropriate, reverse roles.

## Role-Playing

Especially where relationship skills are involved, valuable information may be provided when coaches conduct assessment role plays with clients. Lifeskills involve sending vocal and body as well as verbal messages. Coaches are limited in their ability to assess if they restrict themselves to verbal description and behaviour. At it simplest, an assessment role play might entail asking a client to imagine you are someone with whom they experience difficulty. They are then instructed to speak to you with the vocal and body as well as the verbal messages that they would use in real life. Elaborations of this can include more effort in setting the scene and in telling you how to respond. You can also mirror clients' behaviour and reverse roles to help them assess how they communicate. Some clients may require encouragement to overcome their anxiety about engaging in role-playing. You can explain to them that you are more likely to be able to help them if you observe how they actually behave rather than just hear their descriptions. You can let them know that you understand that they may feel uncomfortable at first but this should pass.

## Observation in Natural Settings

Assessment information can be obtained about clients through coaches and coaching trainees observing them in their natural environments. Often clients come for life coaching on the recommendation of others – for instance, managers by senior managers, pupils by teachers and some clients by friends. Sometimes either verbal or written reports are sent to coaches explaining the reasons for the referral. All such reports, while potentially valuable, are also open to the referees' personal needs and biases. Observing clients in natural settings can give first-hand information about some of their skills. Writing about executive coaching, Peltier observes: 'Direct observation is so important and powerful that coaches must forcefully advocate for its use.' (Peltier, 2001: 12).

Take the example of clients who badly want – and may have been instructed by their superiors – to improve their skills of speaking in public. Coaching trainees can find out about how they perform through self-report and by role-playing. However, they are likely to get even more accurate information by observing clients in real situations. The client and the relevant people in the setting need to give permission for this to happen. Some clients are perfectly willing to give permission since they see coaching as a legitimate way of building their strengths. The relevant people in some settings, where the idea is to help clients to perform better, are also very willing to allow coaches to observe how clients perform.

Observational assessment information about behaviour in natural settings can come from people other than coaches and coaching trainees. Teachers, spouses, friends, bosses and colleagues can each be sources of such information. Again, the permission of the client is essential. Furthermore it can be important to train the third-party observers in what to look for and how to record it. Throughout coaching, collecting information in natural settings may take place. Such information may be especially useful in assessing the extent to which coached skills are transferred to everyday life.

### Behaviour Rating Forms

Systematic collection of observational information involves the use of behaviour rating forms. Box 5.2 gives an example of a behaviour rating form that might be used to assess conversational skills, say talking to friends or interacting with family members at dinner. If the form is being used to collect baseline information, the client should be asked to behave as closely as possible to normal.

| Box 5.2   A Sample Behaviour Rating Form for Verbal Conversation Skills | |
|---|---|
| Initiates topic | |
| Reveals personal information | |
| Asks for personal information | |
| Gives opinion | |
| Asks opinion | |
| Shows understanding | |
| Agrees | |
| Disagrees | |
| Interrupts | |
| Shows aggression | |
| Shows support | |
| Shows appreciation | |
| Uses humour | |

The behaviour rating form can be filled out quantitatively by marking each time the client engages in a behaviour. A way of filling in the form qualitatively is to use a five-point scale of appropriateness for each behaviour, ranging from one for very inappropriate to five for very appropriate. Behaviour rating forms can include vocal and body as well as verbal messages. Because there are many issues connected with what actually is a unit of behaviour and what each category measures, coaches and coaching trainees have to think carefully before using such forms. If correctly used, behaviour rating forms filled out in natural settings can provide a useful record of both initial baseline behaviour and of transfer of training and change over time.

## The Situation–Thoughts–Consequences (STC) Framework

Though sometimes people react automatically, most of the time how they think mediates how they behave. Though Ellis does not state it quite as simplistically as this, he provides an ABC framework for making this point (Ellis, 2003, 2005). Here A stands for the activating event and C for the feelings and action consequences of the activating event. His Rational Emotive Behaviour Therapy focuses on addressing B (for the person's beliefs about the activating event), which can be either rational beliefs (rB) or irrational beliefs (iB), or frequently a mixture of the two. Consequences (C) are most often influenced by what people think at B, their beliefs, rather than being a direct reaction to the activating event (A).

While agreeing with Ellis about the influence of how people think, I consider that his ABC model is too restricted, in particular in its focus on beliefs. People's thinking is much more complicated than the beliefs or rules they have. As described in Chapter 2, a person's thinking also includes their perceptions, self-talk, visual images, explanations and expectations, among other mental processes. Consequently, I have widened Ellis's Activating Event–Beliefs–Consequences (ABC) framework into a Situation–Thoughts–Consequences (STC) framework. The simple STC framework provides the first step in understanding the relationship between what happens to a person and how they react:

S = The situation.
T = A person's thoughts and mind skills relating to the situation, including their visual images.
C = Their feelings, physical reactions, communication and actions that are the consequences of both S and T.

The idea is that people do not go automatically from the situation (S) to the consequences of the situation (C). Instead the consequences of the situation are mediated by what and how they think (T). Their feelings, physical reactions, communication and actions, for good or ill, are mediated by their thoughts and mental processes.

Box 5.3 provides an STC worksheet that clients can use at the start of coaching, during coaching sessions and between sessions to monitor and analyse their thoughts in situations. Coaches and coaching trainees can show clients how to complete the worksheet during a session, possibly using a whiteboard as an aid. The worksheet in Box 5.3 has been filled out for Ken, a 35-year-old sales manager who is very anxious about an upcoming conference presentation and thinks in negative ways. The worksheet goes beyond identifying the client's thoughts to identify also the mind skills that these thoughts represent. Note that the first person singular has been used throughout the worksheet, even though it may have been filled out in a coaching session. This is because clients tend to think in the first person singular.

---

### Box 5.3 STC (Situation–Thoughts–Consequences) Worksheet

## Situation

*State my problem situation clearly and succinctly.*
In two week's time I have to make a presentation at a conference.

## Thoughts

*Record my thoughts about the situation.*
'I must do very well.' (creating rules)
'I'm no good at public speaking.' (creating perceptions)
'I am afraid that I will make a mess of the talk.' (creating expectations)

## Consequences

*What are the consequences of my thoughts about the situation?*
*My feelings and physical reactions*
Feelings: very anxious.

*(Continued)*

---

---

### Box 5.3    (Continued)

Physical reactions: tension in my stomach, not sleeping properly.
*My communications and actions*
In the past I have avoided speaking at conferences whenever possible.
I have started withdrawing from my friends.

---

## Form Hypotheses About Mind Skills to Improve

For some people all roads lead to Rome and they focus on one important mind skill. For example, rational emotive behaviour therapists focus on altering irrational beliefs or rules, and cognitive therapists focus on improving clients' ability to test the reality of their perceptions.

Clients rarely, if ever, tell coaching trainees: 'Look, I've got this poor mind skill I need to improve! [and then proceed to name it]'. Trainees who think that many clients need to improve more than one mind skill have to make inferences and form hypotheses about possible poor skills. Inferences about thinking may stem from clients' words, feelings and actions. Trainees may obtain clues from how clients use language. For example, use of words like 'should', 'ought' or 'must' may indicate unrealistically rigid rules. Use of verbs like 'I can't' and expressions like 'I had no choice' may indicate insufficient ownership of personal responsibility in explaining cause. Use of terms such as 'What will people think of me?' and 'I wonder if I look as stupid as I feel' represent both negative self-talk and also indicate an unrealistic rule about needing others' approval.

Coaching trainees can identify and collect evidence that helps them form hypotheses about clients' poor mind skills. As part of the process of assessing thinking, trainees may collect further information that either supports or negates their hypotheses. Conversely, they may choose not to collect further information about some hypotheses.

## Activity 5.3    Using the Situation–Thoughts–Consequences (STC) Framework

Make up a worksheet similar to that in Box 5.3. Coach a partner who acts as a client and presents you with a situation in which he or she has experienced and still is experiencing unwanted feelings. With the aim of assisting your client to learn how to do this for themselves, assist her/him to fill out the STC worksheet in which they describe the situation, list their main thoughts and images in relation to it, where appropriate identify relevant mind skills, and identify the feelings/physical reactions consequences and the communication/action consequences of these thoughts and images.

Afterwards, discuss and reverse roles.

## *Psychological Tests and Skills Inventories*

Numerous psychological tests and skills inventories are available for those engaged in coaching to choose from though, from the client's viewpoint, taking any psychometric measure should be voluntary. Psychological tests are essentially objective, standardized measures of a sample of behaviour. Objective means that the test has been constructed to measure and score the behaviour under consideration without interpretation by the tester. Standardized means that the test will be administered in the same way to all who take it, and scored so that an individual's score can be compared with the scores of a group of similar people. Sometimes psychological tests are designed to be self-administered rather than administered by a professional person – for example, Holland's Self-Directed Search (Holland, 1987). Although they overlap, a distinction is made here between psychological tests and skills inventories. Skills inventories are self-reporting measures designed to elicit participants' perceptions of their behaviours and cognitions in different skills areas, for example assertiveness. Information about tests and measures that are available may be found in sourcebooks, publishers' catalogues, and in research articles and books.

Coaches need to be competent in the three major aspects of using tests and skills inventories: selection, administration and scoring, and interpreting results. Test publishers and distributors may apply user-qualification criteria before making tests and inventories available. In all events, there is an ethical obligation for coaches to be trained and competent in the use of any test or skills inventory they select (Rogers, 2004).

# *Encouraging Clients to Set Personal Goals*

Having worked with clients to collect assessment information, how do coaches then use it to help them to improve their effectiveness? A theme of this chapter is the importance of building client self-assessment skills. However self-assessment is not an end in itself; rather it is the stepping stone to setting personal goals. It can help clients to have overall goals that they wish to attain by the end of coaching, as well as sub-goals that involve acquiring the specific skills that will enable them to attain their overall goals.

## State Overall Goals

As suggested in the following incomplete sentences clients can set overall personal goals at any stage of skills coaching.

By the end of coaching, my goal is to be able to …
By the end of the month, my goal is to be able to …
By the end of this week, my goal is to be able to …
In the three months after my skills coaching ends, my goal is to …

Clients may require assistance in stating overall goals. The following are considerations for good statements of overall goals.

*Realism*   Clients' goals are realistic when they adequately acknowledge the constraints of their emotional resources and personal skills. These constraints should be neither overestimated nor underestimated. Goals should reflect realistic and potentially attainable standards.

*Specificity*   Clients should state their goals specifically. Ideally goals should be stated so that clients can easily measure the success of their attempts to attain them. For instance, 'My goal is to make more friends' is not as good as, 'My goal is to make at least two new friends by the end of the month.'

*A Time Frame*   Clients should state the time frame in which they want to accomplish each goal. Vague statements of intention are insufficient.

Coaches and trainees should encourage clients to keep written records of their personal goals. These goals can be placed in prominent positions at home and possibly at work too. At the end of a stipulated time frame, written statements of goals provide a yardstick for participants to measure how well they have progressed. A more formal approach to written statements of goals is to make them constitute all or part of the learning contracts that clients make either with themselves or those coaching them.

## State Sub-Goals

At the start of coaching, clients may have insufficient insight into the skills on which they need to work to be able to state sub-goals. For instance, a client in coaching for public speaking may have an overall goal, 'By the end of coaching I want to address my fellow sales representatives in a calm and relaxed way, yet make all my points clearly and cogently.' At the start of initial assessment this client is likely only to have a vague idea of the specific mind skills and possibly also of the specific communication skills needed to attain this overall goal. By the end of initial assessment, the client is likely to have been helped to a statement of her or his specific sub-goals. The following is a format that coaches and clients can use to state goals and sub-goals. As mentioned in Chapter 2, for the sake of simplicity, mind skills sub-goals and communication skills sub-goals are frequently referred to just as goals rather than sub-goals.

> By the end of … [stipulate period], my goal is to be able to … [stipulate overall goal].
> To attain my goal(s), the specific mind skills I need to develop are: [list specific mind skills].
> To attain my goal(s), the specific communication skills I need to develop are [list specific communication skills].

---

### Box 5.4    Goals for Becoming More Outgoing

Jenny, 21, had always been slightly shy. In the past this had not been a major problem since she got on well with people when forced into close contact. On leaving university and going to work in London, Jenny had to become more active in making social contacts. She saw a coach, Helen, and together they assessed her situation and identified some skills on which Jenny needed to work.

### Jenny's Overall Goal.

To become more outgoing and to make two new friends in the next month.

### Jenny's Sub-Goals

These sub-goals are illustrative and the mind skills include some thoughts that she needs to change.

*(Continued)*

---

---

### Box 5.4    (Continued)

| Mind skills | Communication skills |
|---|---|
| *Creating rules skills*<br>'I must be liked immediately.'<br>*Creating perceptions skills*<br>'Other people are not interested in me.'<br>*Creating self-talk skills*<br>Not using enough calming and coaching self-talk. | *Making contact skills*<br>Taking the initiative in introducing myself.<br>*Self-disclosure skills*<br>Revealing more of myself. |

---

## Activity 5.4    Assessing and Agreeing on Life Goals

Work as a coach with a partner who presents an area in her/his life in which she/he wants to perform better.

1.  Together you perform Stage 1 of the life coaching model, the main task of which is to establish a collaborative working relationship.

    Phase 1:  Start the initial session.
    Phase 2:  Facilitate client disclosure.

2.  Together you perform Stage 2 of the life coaching model, the main task of which is to assess and agree on a shared analysis of one (or more) of the client's life goals and the skills they need to attain them.

    Phase 1:  Reconnaisance, detecting and deciding.
    Phase 2:  Agreeing on a shared analysis of how to achieve the client's life goal(s).

Make sure to identify at least one mind skill and one communication/action skill each for improvement.

Afterwards discuss and, if you have the time, reverse roles.

# 6
# *Presentation Skills*

Skilled coaching, based on a cognitive-behavioural framework with a humanistic face, uses a mixture of facilitation skills and training skills. The cognitive-behavioural approach to coaching differs from many other approaches in several ways. Unlike the humanistic approach, there is no assumption that the client potentially knows it all. For instance, most clients have a very vague idea about the mind skills on which they need to work. Furthermore, humanistic approaches tend not to favour direct training, a feature of the cognitive-behavioural approach, albeit alongside good use of facilitation skills. Coaches should know more about the skills of living and working effectively than the client and be prepared to pass this knowledge on. Some coaches use little or no face-to-face contact. Coaching often requires face-to-face contact and it cannot be done so adequately on the phone; imagine a football or tennis coach only coaching their client on the phone. Life skills, like sports skills, contain distinct behaviours that are improved by the coach watching and helping the client to understand and change them. In short, though some coaching can be done by facilitation alone and by indirect contact, the approach to coaching taken here focuses on both the facilitation and training skills most often used on a face-to-face basis.

The next three chapters address some of the skills required for Stage 3 (Assisting the client to change) of the life coaching model. If anything, the chapters focus more on the training than the facilitative role of coaches. In this role coaches tell, show and do. Correspondingly clients are assisted in acquiring and building skills by hearing, observing and doing, though they learn from introspection and discussion as well. Box 6.1 shows the coaching and learning modes employed in skills coaching. The notion of consolidation has been incorporated into Box 6.1 to highlight the importance of coaches and coaching trainees focusing throughout on issues of transfer, maintenance and developing skills once formal coaching ends.

---

### Box 6.1 Models of Coaching and Learning

| Coaching mode | Learning mode |
|---|---|
| Assessment | Learning from self-evaluation and self-monitoring |
| Facilitation | Learning from introspection and discussion |
| Telling | Learning from hearing and explanation |
| Showing | Learning from observing and participation in demonstrations |
| Doing | Learning from activities and homework tasks |
| Consolidation | Learning from developing self-caching skills in all the above modes |

---

This chapter reviews presentation skills, the 'telling' mode. Following are examples of coaches with varying degrees of skills in presenting information:

Julia is coaching Kevin in how to say no to unreasonable requests. Julia has not mastered the skill herself and consequently only focuses on telling Kevin how to communicate and pays no attention to the anxiety generated by his poor mind skills.

José is coaching Marianne on how to identify leisure interests. His preparation has been poor and he has failed to identify some important sources of information. In addition he confuses Marianne by using some unclear and rambling sentences.

Rachel is coaching Alison in how to reduce parent–child conflict. Rachel is thoroughly prepared and contributes material on managing conflict in short and easily comprehensible sentences. She makes sure that Alison can share her ideas and comments as she learns to use better skills.

There is no magic about presentation skills. However, often coaches are trained well in facilitation skills but are inadequately trained in presentation, demonstration and managing activities skills. In coaching sessions there is a tension between using didactic and facilitative skills. A balance is required depending on the client, the coach and the objectives of particular sessions.

## *Preparing Clear Content*

Coaching trainees and experienced coaches too need to be clear about the skills they are trying to impart. Coaching trainees may especially need to take time to prepare for working with specific clients. This entails making sure that they understand the skill or skills to be focused on clearly and that they can communicate their knowledge well.

## *Keeping Manageable Goals*

Some life coaching goes nowhere because coaches have inadequately worked out with clients the skills on which they need to work. Muddled thinking leads to muddled presentations. Assuming that at least one mind skill and at least one communication skill has been stated for an overall skill that the client is trying to obtain or improve, the coach then needs to know how to present them to the client in a way that is likely to enhance the client's willingness to work on them.

For example in Box 5.4 of the previous chapter, the client Jenny had an overall goal of becoming more outgoing and making two new friends in the next month. The mind skills she wanted to focus on included creating rules, creating perceptions and creating self-talk, and the communication skills were making contact skills and self-disclosure skills. A coaching trainee may need to focus on just one mind skill and one communication skill as they learn coaching skills. By trying to do too much, they risk not coaching thoroughly. Say, with the agreement of the client, the coaching trainee decides to focus on the mind skill of creating rules and the communication skill of taking the initiative in introducing oneself. Now, just focusing on the mind skill goal, this is probably far too much to be addressed all at once. The trainee might best approach the rule 'I must be liked immediately' in two somewhat separate mini-presentations and, possibly, sessions, the first focusing on disputing the rule and the second on reformulating it.

The trainee and client also need to have a realistic time limit for the client learning the skill properly. Many aspiring life coaches try to do too much too quickly and end up by doing nothing well. The trainee also needs to be sensitive to the client – clients differ in how quickly they can really understand skills as contrasted with just saying that they do.

## *Developing a Systematic Outline*

Though there can be much interaction as part of the learning process, it is important for coaching trainees to have a clear structure when presenting a skill. Coaching is often better when systematic rather than piecemeal. A clear structure introduces the skill in a logical and easily comprehensible sequence, preventing both trainee and client confusion. For example, a trainee who is helping a client to develop the skill of using coping self-talk to manage anger might develop the following outline:

Introductory definition of self-talk.
STC framework.
What you say to yourself at T.
Negative self-talk and anger.
What is negative self-talk?
Using the STC framework to illustrate the effects of negative self-talk.
Coping self-talk and anger.
Changing what you say to yourself at T.
Dimensions of coping self-talk:
    calming self-talk,
    coping self-talk.
Demonstrating using coping self-talk at T in anger situations:
    before, during and after.
Coaching, rehearsal and practise of the skill of coping self-talk using the STC framework.
Negotiating homework.
Summary – possibly first given by client.

The purpose of the outline is to ensure that the coaching trainee knows the skill thoroughly and to help them to present it well. However, even with a clear structure, trainees should always go at a pace congenial to the client and allow the client to interact as they go along. As a trainee you are not giving a talk but presenting material in a way that shows you are clearly working with the client. With skills that you are presenting for the first time, it can be important that you write out your outline for the sake of both clarity and safety.

Coaching trainees should aim to present skills sufficiently clearly so that clients understand them well enough to instruct themselves when on their own. Methods of presenting skills in a practical 'how to' way include breaking down skills step by step; relating content to clients' own experiences; giving clear demonstrations; and indicating the self-talk that clients might use when confronted with the need to use the skill in their daily lives.

## *Using Language Effectively*

When presenting lifeskills effectively, coaches should make it easy for clients to receive them 'loud and clear'. Coaching trainees may not have good skills at sending clear messages, nor may they adjust their messages to the different kinds of clients they see. The following are some considerations in using language effectively:

*Take the Intelligence Level and Background of Your Client into Account* Just as good writers always write with specific audiences in mind, so skilled coaches prepare what they are going to say with the client in mind. Lifeskills coaching is not just for the college-educated. Clients can differ enormously in educational level, economic status, culture and intelligence, to mention a few factors.

*Use Straightforward and Unambiguous Language* In general where a simple word will suffice, avoid using a more complex one. Even words like empathy may not communicate clearly to some clients. Instead of empathy, you may use terms like active listening or listening and showing understanding.

*Use Words Economically* Shakespeare wrote in *Hamlet* 'Brevity is the soul of wit.' Using too many words can block clear communication of meaning. Furthermore, being long-winded wastes valuable time.

*Avoid Long Sentences* The language of speech differs from written language, with sentence length being one of the main differences. An important reason for using short sentences is that they are likely to add to client comprehension. Remember, 50 per cent of the population is below the average intelligence level!

## *Using Audio-Visual Aids*

Audio-visual aids can be used at many stages of the life coaching process. At the beginning, they can be used when introducing a skill. During and after coaching, they can be used to reinforce and remind clients of important points. When presenting material, accessing clients through their eyes as well as their ears can greatly assist in holding their attention and interest. Furthermore, clients can use audio-visual aids to help them to practise skills. The following are some audio-visual methods for illustrating presentations and practising skills.

## The Whiteboard

A whiteboard is an essential aid to coaching. Just putting up the component parts of a skill on a whiteboard can make it easier for clients to grasp it. In addition, you can work together with clients as you put material onto a whiteboard. Furthermore, at an appropriate time, clients can write down some of the material that has gone on a whiteboard for their records. Whiteboards are much preferable to blackboards since clients see cleaner images and those coaching do not get chalky hands.

## Videotapes and CDs

Videotapes and CDs can be useful for demonstrating skills, especially body messages. Coaching trainees or clients can push the start, stop or pause buttons as necessary. If you make your own visual material for demonstration, strive for as professional a result as possible. Some institutions, such as colleges and universities, have audio-visual centres where you can get advice and help for visual recording. Coaches with large budgets can hire an outside firm to produce visual training material. Video equipment can also be used during and after sessions as clients practise skills.

## Audio Cassettes

Audio cassettes can also be useful for demonstrating skills. In instances where the emphasis is on demonstrating vocal skills, audio may be preferable to video demonstration. Audio cassettes are also useful when demonstrating mind skills since there are no distracting visual images. When making up audio and visual recordings, make sure to use a high quality recording system so that the playback is at or close to a professional standard. Poor quality recordings introduce static into the communication of your messages. Audio aids are possibly most useful when short and informative. Audio cassettes are also easy to use and helpful for practising some skills, for instance practically any skill emphasizing verbal and vocal content.

## Training Manuals and Handouts

Coaching and trainees can help clients to acquire and maintain skills either by using training manuals or by providing them with handouts. Such material needs to convey the messages that the coach is trying to communicate.

Training manuals and handouts can both reinforce these messages for clients and provide them with a basis for practising outside of sessions. Those coaching should always provide written instructions for any homework assignments.

## *Other Audio-Visual Aids*

Overhead projectors, flipcharts, slides and films are four other audio-visual aids, though less commonly used in individual than in group work. Coaching trainees require some basic skill in making up transparencies and using overhead projectors. Skills for making up transparencies include not putting too much information on a single transparency and making transparencies more interesting by using different colours. Skills for using an overhead projector include getting it in focus and placing transparencies on it in the right position and with the right side up.

With flipcharts, many prepared sheets about a skill can be shown in succession. Sheets can be thrown back over the easel as the presentation progresses. Slides are also a possibility, though they need to be prepared beforehand and must be relevant to the client. A disadvantage is that rooms need to be darkened somewhat. Films can be used as part of life coaching presentations, though their use is more appropriate for group rather than for individual coaching.

## *Activity 6.1  Preparing a Systematic Presentation*

Think of a lifeskill in which you may have to coach a client either now or in future.

1.  Set yourself manageable goals for presenting the skill.
2.  Write out a systematic outline for presenting the material using the example in the text as a guide.
3.  Consider whether you will need audio-visual aids and, if so, integrate them into your presentation.
4.  Remember, that you will need to work with and interact with your client in real coaching.

## *Developing Delivery Skills*

This section builds on the section in Chapter 2 where I outlined some verbal, vocal and bodily communication skills. Often coaching trainees are better at receiving information than sending it. Here I focus mainly on delivery skills for sending information.

## Verbal Communication Skills

Good coaching involves clear and precise sending of relevant information geared to the needs and intelligence level of each client. When coaching individuals it is very important that coaching trainees do not overwhelm clients by talking too much. Clients should be encouraged to contribute to the discussion and, when appropriate, be listened to empathically. When as a coaching trainee you present a skill, you need make it easy to understand. Prior preparation is only part of the battle. You may still not have good speaking skills: for instance, using difficult to understand words, unclear sentences or going on for too long. You may also fail to use 'I' messages, as contrasted with 'You' messages, some of the time. Prior to working with clients you can practise delivering content with either other trainees or on your own.

## Vocal Communication Skills

As a coaching trainee you need to be mindful that when presenting information you are responsible for your vocal communication and you cannot rely on matching the way the client communicates. Regarding volume, you need to present information confidently. This entails speaking moderately loudly so that you may be easily heard. Good articulation is also important since unclear speech is difficult to listen to and off-putting. You need to be conscious of the pitch of your voice when presenting information. If you have a problem with being too high pitched or low pitched, you should work on this so as to make it easier for clients to listen to you.

When presenting skills, you need to use an appropriate amount of emphasis. Possibly there is more of a risk of using too little emphasis when you first present a skill since you are focusing on getting the content right rather more than its delivery. You should also pay attention to your speech rate. You may speak too quickly because you are anxious. Alternatively, you may be concentrating so much on what you are saying that you speak too slowly. A final point is that you should not assume that your vocal communication cannot be improved. You and your coaching trainer should always check this out, especially if you plan to do most of your coaching by phone. It may seem obvious but it is too important and easy to ignore.

## *Bodily Communication Skills*

Coaching trainees often need to improve their body messages. Your face may be insufficiently expressive or alternatively too expressive. Some people are better at mirroring other people's facial expressions when listening than sending appropriate facial messages when they speak. When presenting skills, try to make sure that your face shows adequately the emotional content of what you are trying to convey.

The importance in establishing relationships and keeping in touch with clients by using good eye contact cannot be overemphasized. Whether through nervousness, lack of experience, or for other reasons, some coaching trainees make poor contact with clients because they look at them insufficiently. Good eye contact helps clients feel that you are interested in and communicating directly with them. It also enables you to assess their reactions to what you say.

Gestures are movements of parts of the body with the purpose of aiding in the expression of ideas and feelings. Trainees should make sure that their gestures have a purpose, are appropriate to the accompanying words, are made clearly and with moderation, and are sensitive to cultural and regional differences.

Good coaching trainees show confidence, interest and competence by their posture. For instance, you can sit in a relaxed and comfortable way with your body turned towards the client and with a slight forward lean. You need to beware that your posture does not communicate, albeit unintentionally, insufficient interest or sloppiness.

Though not a problem for most coaching trainees, physical distance from the client may be an issue for some. In coaching sessions conducted in Western cultures, it is a good idea to be seated about four feet apart.

## *Activity 6.2   Assessing My Delivery Skills*

1.   Assess your ability to present lifeskills to clients in each of the following categories:

   - your verbal communication;
   - your vocal communication;
   - your bodily communication; and
   - your ability to be facilitative as well as didactic.

2.   Work to improve those areas you have identified as requiring strengthening.

# Managing Presenting Material Anxiety

So far in this chapter I have mainly focused on the overt skills of presenting material. Now I focus on the mind skills or covert skills of managing anxiety. All coaching trainees are likely to be anxious about presenting material and for some the balance of their anxiety may be more debilitating than facilitating. Williams and Thomas (2005) emphasize the power of your thinking habits or mind skills when coaching and state that everyone has the ability to develop creative thinking or mind skills. I here focus on the mind skills of creating rules, perceptions and self-talk.

## Creating Rules Skills

As mentioned in Chapter 2, rules are the 'dos' and 'don'ts' by which people lead their lives. Coaching trainee Leo gets anxious partly because he has the rule that he must present material well immediately. However, the first time he works with a client presenting a new skill it does not go particularly well, which activates his first dose of self-disparagement. His second dose of self-disparagement is because he then becomes anxious and depressed about this overall coaching ability. A third dose of self-disparagement may come if he starts disparaging his worth as a person as well.

Using the Situation–Thoughts–Consequences or STC format, when coaching at S inappropriate feelings and communication at C may be signals that you have created one or more demanding rules at T. Examples of inappropriately demanding rules at T include 'I must present material perfectly well every time', 'I must have my client's total attention and approval' and 'I must be in control at all times'.

Once you have become aware that you possess one or more demanding rules about coaching, what can you do about it? Disputing and restating these demanding rules are two skills that can help you move towards realistic or preferential rules. Ellis (2003, 2005) considers the technique of disputing to be the most typical and often-used method of his rational emotive behaviour therapy. Disputing involves logically challenging the false assumptions that you may hold about yourself, others and the world.

Reverting to Leo who has created the rule 'I must present material well immediately', questions that he might ask himself to dispute this rule include the following:

What evidence exists for the truth of my rule?
What is the worst that might happen if I present material less well than perfectly?
Do I demand the same standards of other people who present material as I demand of myself?
In what ways does presenting material less than perfectly make me worth-less as a person?

You may need to dispute the same rule again and again. This is because such rules have become well-established habits. Ellis strongly emphasizes that people need to work hard to change and regards most of his clients as 'natural resisters who find it exceptionally easy to block themselves from changing and find it unusually hard to resist their resistances' (Ellis, 1987: 370–1).

Restating involves substituting realistic and preferential for demanding characteristics in specific rules. Some of the main characteristics of preferential rules include the following:

*Expressing Preferences Rather than Demands*   Though you would prefer to present material competently, it is not absolutely necessary for your survival.

*A Coping Emphasis*   You focus on managing or coping with your anxiety about presenting material rather than being perfectionist about mastering it altogether.

*Absence of Self-Rating*   Your rules lead to a functional rating of your specific presentation skills for whether they help you attain realistic objectives. Your rules do not lead to rating your whole personhood.

Below is a possible preferential restatement, which will help Leo from the earlier example to manage his presentation anxiety:

*Demanding rule*: 'I must present material well immediately'.
*Preferential rule*: 'Though I would prefer to present material well immediately, this may not be realistic. I have to work and practise at developing my presenting material skills and setbacks are part of the learning process.'

## Creating Perceptions Skills

As coaching trainees you may contribute to getting anxious by misperceiving your ability to present information both by negative self-labelling and by misperceiving clients' reactions to your efforts. Here the STC framework requires alteration to become:

**S** = the situation,
**T** = your perceptions,
**C** = the emotional and behavioural consequences.

The consequences for you of S are influenced by your perceptions of S at T. These consequences do not automatically follow from S. You have a choice about how you perceive at T.

## Perceive Yourself Accurately

Negative self-labels are unrealistically negative perceptions either about yourself or about your specific abilities, in this case your presentation skills. You may perceive yourself as a presenter to be incompetent, boring and inadequate. At best such labels are overgeneralizations, since presentation skills involve many sub-skills, in each of which you may have strengths and weaknesses. Why keep focusing on your negatives? Instead you can engage in what the Iveys call 'positive asset search' to identify your strengths (Ivey and Ivey, 2003). When assessing both negative and positive characteristics, try to make your inferences reflect the facts as closely as possible. In this way, you are likely to arrive at a more balanced set of perceptions concerning your presentation abilities.

## Perceive Others Accurately

If you get anxious when presenting material to clients, the way you perceive situations may sustain your discomfort. Often coaching trainees and clients are unaware that they jump to conclusions rather than saying to themselves 'STOP … THINK … what are my choices in how I perceive this?' Beck observes that frequently people have automatic thoughts and perceptions that influence their emotions (Beck, 1988; Beck and Weishaar, 2005). Either they are not fully conscious of these thoughts and images or it does not occur to them that they warrant special attention. Beck collaborates with his clients in the scientific or detective work of identifying oppressive automatic thoughts.

Here is an example in the STC framework for a coaching trainee, Annette, who gets anxious when presenting a lifeskill to Tariq.

**S** = Tariq seems slow to understand a point she presents.
**T** = Annette perceives: 'Tariq is bored with my coaching him.'
**C** = Annette gets anxious and conducts the session in a tense way.

There are other perceptions that Annette might have had at T. These alternative perceptions include:

'Perhaps I am presenting the skill insufficiently clearly.'
'I am expecting too much of Tariq too soon.'
'Tariq is trying his best to cooperate.'
'Tariq is not fully fluent in English so I must use simpler English and check that he understands.'

If, like Annette, you are prone to having negative automatic thoughts when presenting a lifeskill, how can you combat this? First, become aware of your tendency. Second, monitor your thinking in presenting lifeskills situations and practise making the connections between automatic perceptions and upsetting feelings. Third, question your perceptions by logically analysing them. This process involves engaging in the following kinds of self-talk:

STOP … THINK … what are my choices in how I perceive this situation?
Are my perceptions based on fact or inference?
If my perceptions are based on inference, are there other ways of perceiving the situation more closely related to the facts?
If necessary, what further information do I need to collect?
What is the most accurate perception in relation to the factual evidence?

Let's assume that Annette reviews with her coaching supervisor the accuracy of her perception that Tariq is bored with her coaching him. On doing this she discovered that there were no facts to support this conclusion and that it was an inference on her part. Annette then generated the alternative perceptions just listed. She decided that 'Tariq is not fully fluent in English and I must use simpler English and check that he understands' was the best fitting perception. This perception gave Annette a way of improving her performance and did not involve her in putting herself down unnecessarily.

## Creating Self-Talk Skills

Creating coping self-talk is another mind skill that coaching trainees can use when getting anxious about presenting a lifeskill (Meichenbaum, 1985;

Meichenbaum and Deffenbacher, 1988). The idea is to replace anxious and task-irrelevant self-talk with more constructive statements. In coping self-talk, calming and coaching statements tend to be interspersed.

## Calming Self-Talk

Two important areas of calming self-talk for coaching trainees are as follows. First, tell yourself to stay calm. Sample self-statements include 'Relax', 'Keep calm', 'Take it easy' and 'Breathe slowly and regularly'. Second, you can tell yourself that you can cope. Sample self-statements include 'I can handle this' and 'My anxiety is a signal for me to use my coping skills.'

## Coaching Self-Talk

With coaching self-talk, you require clarity as to the task you are attempting to do. Concentrate on the task at hand. Then instruct yourself in skilled execution of the task like pilots talking themselves through difficult landings.

## Creating Self-Talk for Before, During and After

Coaching trainees can create coping self-talk statements for before, during and after anxiety-evoking lifeskills presentation situations. Possible coping self-talk statements before presenting a lifeskill include the following:

I know I will feel less anxious if I am properly prepared.
Calm down. What is it I have to do?

Possible coping self-talk statements during an anxiety-evoking presentation include:

Stay cool. Take my time. Just aim for a steady performance.
Relax. The client is not expecting perfection and it is unrealistic for me to expect it too.

Possible coping self-talk statements after an anxiety-evoking presentation include:

My fear was not justified by how I felt once I got started.
Each time I cope it seems to get easier.

Creating and using coping self-talk requires work and practise. If you are a coaching trainee who gets anxious about lifeskills presentations, you need to identify the coping self-talk statements that work best for you. Then you need to practise these statements both in imagination and in real-life situations. Imaginal rehearsal, in which you talk yourself through presenting lifeskills situations as you visualize them, has many advantages. You are not restricted to requiring anyone else, you can anticipate and work through difficulties, and you can choose your rehearsal times and rehearse regularly.

### Activity 6.3  Using Mind Skills to Manage Presenting Material Anxiety

## Part A:   Creating Rules

1.  Select a past or future coaching situation in which you wish to work on managing your anxiety as you present material to a client.

    **S** (the situation): Describe the situation that contributed to or may contribute to your anxiety.
    **T** (your rules): Looking out for musts, oughts and shoulds, list any demands you made or might make on yourself, others or the situation.
    **C** (the consequences): Describe how you felt and communicated or might feel and communicate. Indicate any feelings and communications you consider to be inappropriate.

2.  Dispute each of the demands you made or might make in the situation.
3.  Restate one or more of your unrealistic rules in the situation into realistic or self-supporting rules.

## Part B:   Creating Perceptions

1.  Choose a coaching situation in which you have experienced anxiety associated with making a presentation.
2.  Make up a worksheet with the following format:

| Situation | Upsetting perceptions | Different perceptions |
| --- | --- | --- |

3.  Write down the situation and, in the 'Upsetting perceptions' column, any perceptions associated with being anxious about presenting material in that situation. Assess the realism of your upsetting perceptions by logical analysis.

4. In the 'Different perceptions' column, write down as many different perceptions of the situation that you can create. Then evaluate your new perceptions and put a star alongside the one that best explains the situation.
5. Assess the ways in which the emotional and behavioural consequences of your most realistic perception would have been different from your original perception.

## Part C:   Creating Self-Talk

1. Identify and list any negative and anxiety-evoking self-talk statements that contribute to your anxiety about presenting material in coaching.
2. Identify a specific presenting-material-in-coaching situation in which you think that you would feel unreasonably anxious. Write out at least two coping self-talk statements for each of (a) before, (b) during, and (c) after the situation.
3. Rehearse and practise your coping self-talk to help you manage your presenting material anxiety.

# 7
# *Demonstration Skills*

The last chapter focused on presentation skills or the *telling* mode. Along the lines of the old saying 'A picture is worth a thousand words' this chapter focuses on demonstration skills, or the *showing* mode. Sometimes clients will have a correct behaviour in their repertoires and coaches can release the behaviour without needing to model it. On other occasions, it may not be possible to model a behaviour in which the client is being coached (for instance, not eating between meals for a client being coached in weight control). However, on many occasions, coaches and coaching trainees can either model themselves or provide other models of the skills that the client is trying to improve. One of the main ways that people learn is observational learning or learning from models. Mental as well as overt behaviour can be learned this way and so modelling can be auditory as well as visual. Clients can then attempt to reproduce the behaviour. Alternatively, they can use the modelling to improve their own interpersonal style in ways that are realistic for them (Neenan and Dryden, 2002). As a coaching trainee you can consciously promote observational learning of desired skills and sub-skills. Here the more everyday term 'demonstration' is used instead of modelling.

Though demonstration can mainly be done in face-to-face coaching, this is not exclusively the case. For instance, coaches can demonstrate mind skills over the phone and clients can have access to pre-recorded audio and visual demonstrations.

## *Goals of Demonstration*

Demonstrating may be used to initiate new skills strengths, develop existing skills strengths, disinhibit existing skills strengths, and inhibit and lessen existing skills weaknesses. Goals for demonstration and of observational learning can be viewed in the following categories.

## Communication/Action Skills

Communication and action skills demonstrations focus on observable behaviours. When demonstrating communication, coaching trainees should be mindful of sending vocal and body as well as verbal messages.

> Joseph, an executive coach, works with Ellie on her skills for giving instructions to those whom she manages. The communication skills they decide on as goals are: (a) telling her staff what she wants in a clear and orderly way; (b) speaking at a comfortable rather than a rapid rate; (c) being easy to hear rather than too quiet; and (d) making good gaze and eye contact with them. Joseph demonstrates one skill at a time and then coaches and rehearses Ellie in it before moving on to the next skill. Ultimately Joseph demonstrates and coches Ellie in all four skills together. He also encourages Ellie to audio record or, if possible, video record her own competent performance of the skills so she can use herself as a model in future.

## Mind Skills

Mind skills include creating rules, perceptions and self-talk.

> Ellie has reported that she tenses up sometimes when giving instructions to her staff. As part of their goals, Ellie and Joseph agree to target the mind skill of creating realistic rather than perfectionist rules about giving instructions. They identify two sub-goals to work on, namely (a) Ellie's inner demand about communicating her instructions perfectly and (b) her inner demand that others should think her perfectly competent when giving instructions.

## Communication/Action Skills with Accompanying Self-Talk

Here the demonstrator focuses on the goals of communication/action skills and on accompanying self-talk.

> To give instructions effectively as a manager, Ellie needs to combine mind and communication skills. Joseph demonstrates to Ellie how she can use calming and coaching self-talk when practising and giving instructions. Joseph's demonstration intersperses 'think aloud' self-talk with demonstrating communication skills.

## *Considerations in Demonstrating Lifeskills*

Considerations in demonstrating lifeskills include the issue of who demonstrates, methods of demonstration and ways to enhance client attention. I examine each of these considerations in turn.

### *Who Demonstrates?*

Options for who demonstrates include the following. These demonstrator options can be used singly or in combination. Coaches and coaching trainees are likely to be the main source of demonstrations both when initially presenting skills and during the consolidation of the learning period. However, clients can also take part in live and pre-recorded demonstrations of desired skills. Coaching trainees can ask clients to show them what might be desirable ways of thinking and acting. In addition, clients can be asked to demonstrate skills for themselves in their imaginations and use 'self-as-model' edited videotapes of their own performances.

In symbolic demonstration, the demonstration is presented through written materials, cassettes or videotapes, often using third parties as models (Cormier and Nurius, 2002). Coaching trainees can develop symbolic demonstrations for individual clients or for groups of clients. If you are seeing many clients with the same issue, it may be worth developing a standardized demonstration; for instance making a cassette or videotape on dealing with gender-stereotyped behaviour. Cartoon characters can also be used as symbolic demonstrators, for example in teaching decision-making skills to children.

The characteristics of third-party demonstrators can influence how much clients attend, retain and are motivated. In general, the greater the similarity between demonstrators and clients, the greater the effect on clients' subsequent behaviour. How competent should demonstrators be? Kazdin suggests the advantage of demonstrators showing similar behaviours to those of observers but then overcoming problems (Kazdin, 1976). Warmth and personal attractiveness are further considerations. Models without engaging characteristics are likely to be either ignored or rejected.

### *Methods of Demonstration*

Coaches and coaching trainees have many options for how to present demonstrations. These options are not mutually exclusive. As well as live demonstrations, they can be written, pre-recorded or visualized.

## Live

Live demonstrations have the advantage of here-and-now communication. Clients can receive verbal, vocal, body and taking action communication messages as they actually happen. Live demonstrations also allow for the possibility of spontaneity and feedback. Coaching trainees can work with clients to build the specific skills they currently require. In addition, they can interact with clients and, if appropriate, show different or simpler ways to enact skills. However, live demonstrations can have problems, especially if coaching trainees have not mastered the skills that they demonstrate.

## Written

For clients who are not seen face-to-face, much demonstration can take place via the printed page. Mind skills especially lend themselves to written demonstration. Written demonstration can also be used for verbal message skills. Body message skills can also be depicted on the printed page, though there are distinct limitations to depicting vocal messages. Written demonstrations can be supplemented by visual images, such as cartoons. Another advantage is that written demonstrations can be introductory examples for subsequent written or live skills development exercises.

## Pre-recorded

Pre-recorded demonstrations can include audio cassettes, videotapes and sometimes films. Demonstrators can be coaches or coaching trainees, clients or third parties. Pre-recorded demonstrations have some advantages. If you make the material yourself, you can carefully control input and edit out mistakes. The process of making pre-recorded demonstrations allows for successive attempts to rewrite scripts and improve role plays. Once made, clients can view or listen to pre-recorded demonstrations either during their coaching sessions or when rehearsing outside of them. During sessions, coaching trainees and clients can pause or rewind to emphasize points. Successful demonstration tapes and cassettes can also be stored for future use by other clients.

Coaching trainees also have to consider the disadvantages of pre-recorded demonstrations. The demonstrations may not be tailored to the specific needs of individual clients. Considerable time and expense may be required for developing and recording material. In addition, good quality equipment may not be readily available.

*Visualized*

In visualized demonstration, coaches and coaching trainees request that clients visualize the scenes that they describe. Depending on the instructions, clients visualize themselves or, possibly, third parties enacting the skills. Visualized demonstration has the advantage of flexibility. Different scenes can be readily presented to clients' imaginations depending on their needs and rates of learning.

Visual rehearsal can be used after live, pre-recorded and visualized demonstrations. In such instances, visual rehearsal should take place immediately after the demonstration to help with memorizing skills and as a homework assignment too.

Visualized demonstration has disadvantages. It is only appropriate for clients who have the capacity to visualize scenes adequately. Since scenes are never actually demonstrated, even for good visualizers there may be important slippages between what coaching trainees describe and what clients visualize. For example, a client who is asked to visualize being a rewarding listener may misinterpret important body messages, even if these are described.

## Ways to Enhance Client Attention

Bandura (1977: 24) writes 'People cannot learn much by observation unless they attend to and perceive accurately, the significant factors of the modeled behaviour.' How can those coaching enhance the extent to which clients attend? At risk of repetition, the following are some suggestions.

*Orient Clients*   Let clients know how, by watching demonstrations, they can help themselves to achieve their goals. Without engaging in phony selling, convey enthusiasm for observational learning. Make sure that clients know what to look out for in demonstrations and that next it will be their turn to use the demonstrated skill.

*Match Demonstrations to Clients' States of Readiness*   Take into account the intellectual levels and attention spans of clients. Avoid giving boring and lengthy introductions to demonstrations. Be prepared to use demonstrations graduated in difficulty for skills that are complex.

*Reduce Debilitating Anxiety*   Anxiety can interfere with clients' ability to attend and observe. Relaxation may prove helpful for unusually anxious observers. Other ways that coaching trainees can reduce clients' anxiety are by developing rapport with them and informing them that, in subsequent enactments of demonstrated skills, mistakes are okay.

*Reduce Extraneous Distractions* Clients' attention can be badly disrupted by extraneous distractions, such as corridor noise. If necessary, placing a sign on the outside of the door that says that coaching is in progress and requests quiet may be better than doing nothing.

# Demonstrating Communication/Action Skills

Communication and action skills differ from mind skills in that they are 'outer game' skills that act on the environment rather than 'inner game' skills involving thought processes. Communication and action skills involve sending observable verbal, vocal, body and taking action messages. This section focuses in particular on communication. Methods of demonstrating communication skills include live demonstration, using audiotapes and videotapes, and using visualization.

## Live Demonstration

Coaching trainees are likely to use live demonstration more than other ways of demonstrating communication skills. In using live demonstration, you should focus on vocal and body as well as verbal messages. Trainees need to make sure they are offering good and appropriate models. Clients can help you by setting the scene for the skills you are demonstrating and letting you know if you are saying or doing anything that may not be right when they use the demonstrated skills in real life. Live demonstrations lead to clients practising the skills first with trainees, then on their own. Live demonstration can also be used for giving feedback during the process of building skills – both for how the client used the skills and any modifications that the trainee considers would improve the client's performance. Furthermore, the trainee can demonstrate how the client might handle various reactions by other people.

Live demonstration can employ Bandura's participant modelling approach. This approach has been used to train those suffering from phobias (Bandura, 1986). For example, clients can watch those coaching them perform progressively more threatening tasks in relation to feared objects, such as snakes. After each demonstration, clients are given both guidance and ample opportunity to perform the demonstrated behaviour under favourable conditions. Examples of favourable conditions include joint performance of sub-tasks with coaches and clients performing sub-tasks under protective conditions – for instance wearing gloves when touching snakes.

## *Audio Cassette Demonstration*

Audio cassette demonstration is not recommended for coaching trainees who want to include a focus on body messages in skills demonstrations. However, if the main focus is on showing verbal and vocal messages, audio cassette demonstration of communication skills may be appropriate. For example, with a trainee who was coaching a client who gave poor verbal and vocal messages when introducing a talk, making an audio cassette with the trainee demonstrating how to perform better might help the client both now and in homework.

The following is an example of a brief audio cassette demonstration made by a coaching trainee, Kusum, with a salesperson client who has been told that she will not get promoted until she improves her skills of handling clients. In this demonstration the salesperson is dealing with a customer, Angela, who is returning a defective compact disc to the shop and requesting that it be replaced. Within the overall goal of helping the salesperson to become more effective, Kusum wishes to demonstrate the verbal message sub-goals of using 'I' statements, reflecting what the client says and, if the client is right, giving way gracefully; and the vocal message sub-skills of speaking with good volume and at a moderate rate. The salesperson client plays Angela this time round.

| | |
|---|---|
| *Angela*: | Hello. |
| *Coaching trainee*: | Hello. What can I do for you? |
| *Angela*: | Yesterday I bought this compact disc. Here is the receipt. When I got home I found that the disc was scratched. I request that the store replace it. |
| *Coaching trainee*: | You've got a scratched compact disc from us that you want changed. Please show me the scratch since it is very unusual. |
| *Angela*: | There it is. |
| *Coaching trainee*: | Okay, I see it. I'm sorry and I'll change the CD. I know that we still have others in stock. |
| *Angela*: | That's great. Thanks a lot. |

Though only verbal messages have been provided in the above example, it is essential that Kusum, the demonstrator, also models appropriate vocal messages. An assertive verbal message can be countermanded if given with either unassertive or aggressive vocal messages (Alberti and Emmons, 2001). Sometimes coaching trainees giving communication skills demonstrations have to improve their initial efforts. Then they almost always need to work with clients to polish their targeted skills too.

## Videotape Demonstration

Both videotape and film demonstrations of communication skills have the great advantage over audio cassette demonstrations that clients can observe body messages. Since the making of demonstration films necessitates more resources than most coaches have readily available, here the focus is on making videotapes. When making videotapes, coaches have to specify body message sub-goals as well as verbal and voice sub-goals. For instance, in the previous example of the salesperson dealing with Angela returning a compact disc to a store, if the coaching trainee were to make a videotape she or he might also get the salesperson to demonstrate the body messages of adequate eye contact, erect posture and good use of gesture.

In making coaching videos you have the choice of whether or not to do it on your own. If you decide to bring in outside resources, these may range from a professional videotape-making company, to a central audio-visual unit in your institution or organization, to a technician in your department. As with audio cassette recording, use the best available videotape recording equipment and be prepared to retake scenes. If you make the videotape on your own, you may be restricted to one camera angle and not have the facility for editing. Furthermore, your energies may be diverted into working the equipment rather than concentrating on the quality of demonstration. With more resources, both human and technical, you can do a better job. However, the trade-off for a higher quality product may be unjustified time and expense.

In making coaching videotapes, coaches and coaching trainees act as 'movie' directors and, as such, require many of their skills. Once content has been developed, coaches need to train demonstrators in how to deliver it. During the rehearsal process and shooting of scenes, you may decide to revise parts of the demonstration and to emphasize targeted skills differently. Much trial and error goes into making polished demonstration videotapes.

## Visualized Demonstration

Visualized demonstration or 'covert modelling' is not used to demonstrate communication skills when coaching lifeskills nearly as frequently as live demonstrations. Nevertheless, visualized demonstration is a useful coaching skill. Scenes in visualized demonstrations can be standard as well as individual (Cormier and Nurius, 2002). Visualized demonstrations are good precursors to visualized rehearsal and practise outside of coaching sessions.

In general, people visualize best when relaxed (Kazdin, 1976). Coaching trainees can get clients to visualize neutral scenes as a way of checking out that they understand how to visualize. For example, clients may be asked to visualize someone eating dinner with them at home.

Three guidelines for developing visualized demonstrations are as follows:

*Set the Scene*   Describe the situation in which a targeted lifeskill is to be enacted, in sufficient detail so that it is easy for the client to visualize it.

*Describe the Communication Skill(s)*   Describe how the person enacts the targeted behaviours in the situation. The person visualized may be either a third party or the client themselves. Remember to describe clearly verbal, vocal and body as well as any taking action messages. In brief, give full descriptions of any communication skills you demonstrate.

*Depict favourable Consequences for Using the Communication Skill(s)*
Get clients to visualize the demonstrator's behaviour being rewarded (Kazdin, 1976).

Below is an example of a visualized demonstration used for parent effectiveness coaching. The targeted behaviours are active listening, sending an 'I' message and requesting a behaviour change.

**Set the scene:** Picture a family consisting of a father, mother and two 9-year-old twin girls sitting at their dining room table. The meal has just started. Mum asks Dad about how his day has gone and Dad starts to reply. Before he has had a chance to finish, one of the girls, Betty, interrupts and asks if he will take her to her dancing lesson tomorrow. Dad, who has had a hard day at work, feels himself tense up at the interruption.

**Describe the communication skill(s):** After the interruption, Dad turns to Betty, catches her eye and says in a warm but firm voice, 'Honey, I know that it is important for you to get to your dancing lesson. However, I haven't finished answering Mum's question yet. Please let me finish and then we can talk about your concern.' At no stage does Dad raise his voice or give his daughter an angry look. Rather, he calmly asserts his right for respect when he talks.

**Depict favourable consequences for using the communication skill(s):**
Betty says in a relaxed voice and without sulking, 'I'm sorry Dad. I'll wait.' Betty does not feel put down by Dad's response. Dad feels good that he has set a limit on her interrupting. In instances where favourable consequences cannot be guaranteed, it may be better to depict dealing with realistic consequences.

Coaching trainees can develop different visualized demonstrations around targeted skills. These visualizations may be graduated by threat or difficulty. Clients visualize themselves enacting appropriate behaviours in problematic scenes taken from their own lives.

## *Activity 7.1    Demonstrating a Communication Skill*

Do Part A and any other part that you find useful.

## Part A    Live Demonstration

Work with a partner who acts as a client who wants to work on a specific communication skill. The client describes the situation in which the skill is required and plays the other person in the scene. As part of presenting the skill, include a demonstration in which you focus on clearly showing her or him the desired verbal, vocal and body messages. Then swap roles, getting your client to enact the skill and give feedback as necessary.
    Afterwards, reverse roles.

## Part B    Audio Cassette Demonstration

Either with the client and situation you worked on in Part A or for another client and situation, make up an audio cassette focused on coaching and demonstrating the verbal and vocal dimensions of a targeted communication skill.

## Part C    Videotape Demonstration

Either with the client and situation you worked on in Part A or for another client and situation, make up a videotape focused on coaching and demonstrating the verbal, vocal and body dimensions of a targeted communication skill.

## Part D    Visualized Demonstration

Either with the client and situation you worked on in Part A or for another client and situation, used visualized demonstration as part of coaching and demonstrating the verbal, vocal and body dimensions of a targeted communication skill.

# Demonstrating Mind Skills

Coaches and coaching trainees subscribing to the cognitive-behavioral theoretical position are faced with the need to demonstrate not only communication/action skills, or overt behaviours, but also mind skills, or covert behaviours. Mind skills are both lifeskills in themselves and also are relevant to all specific lifeskill areas such as relationships, leisure, work and health. For example, the capacity to identify, dispute and reformulate irrational beliefs or unrealistic rules is both a mind skill in its own right and also a skill that can be applied to all areas in which such beliefs or rules occur (Ellis, 2005).

Mind skills can be demonstrated live. Live demonstrations can be either when skills are initially presented or later as you endeavour to change clients' thinking. Thinking is an inner process mostly involving self-talk. Therefore mind skills lend themselves more readily to written and audio cassette demonstrations than communication skills. The visual images provided by videotapes or films are not required for mind skills. Furthermore, visual images may interfere with demonstrating the thought processes.

## Live Demonstration

In live demonstrations of mind skills, the demonstrators may be either coaches or possibly clients. Many coaching trainees have to work hard at preparing and delivering competent live demonstrations. However, if those coaching are experienced in teaching about and demonstrating specific mind skills, they may dispense with scripts and either make up demonstrations on the spot or demonstrate material used before. Competent impromptu demonstrations may come over as more real than those memorized from prepared scripts.

Coaching trainees should make sure that they understand the mind skills that they are presenting and demonstrating to clients. Many trainees do not demonstrate mind skills well because of inadequate preparation. You need to be able to verbalize clearly the thoughts involved in the skill. You also need to focus on your vocal and bodily delivery. For instance, it is important to be easily audible and to speak clearly. Relevant body messages include keeping good eye contact with clients. You are much more likely to remain focused on your clients if you have mastered the material that you are presenting and demonstrating.

## Written Demonstration

Written demonstration can accompany live demonstration. Coaching trainees and clients can work with a whiteboard to sharpen up verbal demonstrations of mind skills. Take coaching a client in the mind skill of creating rules (Ellis 1999, 2005). The trainee can first elicit and put on the whiteboard statements containing the client's 'musts', 'oughts' and 'shoulds' in a situation. Then trainee and client can select a main unrealistic rule. The trainee can ask the client some of the key questions that can dispute the rule and then write good answers on the whiteboard. Trainee and client can then work together to restate the rule into a more realistic one and this revised rule can be put on the whiteboard. Clients can record the content of all of the above steps to help them to learn the skill of creating realistic rules.

Written demonstrations often form part of instructional manuals or handouts. Coaches and coaching trainees require clear goals for what they need to achieve in each learning unit. Furthermore, if making up a handout, you need to explain clearly the skill or sub-skill being demonstrated so that clients need to know what to look for, both when introduced to the skill and later when rehearsing and practising it. Box 7.1 contains a coaching handout focused on creating realistic rules.

---

### Box 7.1   Handout on How to Create Realistic Rules

One of the main mind skill weaknesses that people have is that, often unawares, they create unrealistic and demanding rules about how they, others and the world should be. Creating demanding rules can lead to negative feelings and inappropriate communication. The purpose of this handout is to make you more aware of how you may be creating unrealistic and demanding rules, to help you to dispute such rules, and then show you how to restate your unrealistic and demanding rules into realistic or preferential ones. The handout is based on a case example of Scott, a 33-year-old insurance salesman.

## Creating a Demanding Rule

### Situation
Scott has just moved to a new insurance firm to join their sales department.

### Thoughts (demanding rule)
'I must be the best salesperson in the department.'

---

## Box 7.1    *(Continued)*

*Consequences*

Feelings and physical reactions: Excessive stress, depression, unable to sleep properly.

Communication/actions: Rushes around without focusing his efforts.

## Disputing

### *Questions that can be used to dispute unrealistic and demanding rules*

1.  Realistic disputing: 'Where is the evidence that I *absolutely must* be the best salesperson in the department?'
    Nowhere – except in my head. I prefer being the best salesperson in the department but I clearly do not have to be.

2.  Logical disputing: 'I very much want to be the best salesperson but how does it follow that I *absolutely must* be? How does not being the best salesperson *prove* that I am a *worthless person*?'
    It doesn't. I can't logically jump from 'I am not the best salesperson' to 'I *am* a poor, lowly *person*.'

3.  Pragmatic disputing: 'If I keep believing, "I absolutely must be the best salesperson", "I am a worthless person if I am not the best," "This lack of success is awful," and "I can't stand it", where will these unrealistic rules get me?'
    Nowhere. I'll make myself very stressed and depressed. I will continue not to sleep well. I will keep rushing around.

## Create a Realistic or Preferential Rule

*Situation:*

Scott has just moved to a new insurance firm to join their sales department.

*Thoughts (realistic rule):*

'I'd prefer to do very well. I need to think carefully about what the job requires and be prepared to learn from others.'

*Consequences:*

Feelings and physical reactions: Much less stress, optimistic, sleeps properly.

*(Continued)*

---

### Box 7.1    (Continued)

Communication/actions: Becomes a much more effective salesperson by targeting his efforts to best effect.

Scott needs to keep vigorously and persistently disputing his unrealistic and demanding rule and changing it to a realistic one. He needs to practise, practise, and practise.

---

A few comments about using demonstration handouts. Written demonstrations can be used in conjunction with live or audio cassette demonstration and should rarely be use alone. They can also be used by those coaching over the phone to build clients' skills. Using demonstration handouts, such as the one shown above, lends itself to being followed by practise and homework to consolidate the targeted skills. Demonstration handouts can also easily be stored and retrieved for revision and reuse.

### Audio Cassette Demonstration

For both individual and group use, audio cassette demonstrations of mind skills have the advantage over written demonstrations since clients can hear how demonstrators think. People talk to themselves when they think. Audio cassette demonstrations much more closely replicate this self-verbalizing process than written demonstrations. Since audio cassette demonstrations are relatively inexpensive to reproduce, clients can receive copies for homework and revision purposes. Clients are likely to require much work and practise to change established patterns of thinking (Ellis, 1987, 2005). Consequently, a demonstration lending itself to repeated listening has much to recommend it.

The initial audio-recorded demonstration of a mind skill to be used is best created either by those coaching or by knowledgeable third parties. It is unreasonable to expect clients to demonstrate skills that they may not understand. However, coaching trainees can encourage clients later in the learning process to make up their own demonstration cassettes. At the conclusion of lifeskills coaching, clients have to listen to their own self-talk without coaches. If clients are encouraged to use themselves as demonstrators of targeted mind skills during coaching, they may be more likely to maintain these skills afterwards. Clients probably require repeated listening to their demonstrations for the mind skills to become part of their everyday repertoires.

Here the focus is on you as a coaching trainee to build the skills of developing your own demonstration audio cassettes rather than encouraging you to use commercial ones. You may still decide to use other people's voices rather than your own. Audio cassettes provide the opportunity to pick up feelings from voice inflections. Consequently, audio cassettes may bring interaction much more to life than the printed page.

Box 7.2 contains the script for an audio-recorded demonstration focusing on Marge, a highly successful accountant, challenging her demanding rule that life must be all work and no play. The instructions, left out in this example, can be given either live, put on the cassette, provided as a handout, or a mixture of these. For instance, those coaching may stop their demonstration cassettes to highlight points and make comments. You may also rewind and play again key sections of demonstrations.

---

### Box 7.2    Script for Audio Cassette Demonstration of Marge's Disputing and Restating a Demanding Rule into a Realistic One

Recently I have not been eating or sleeping properly. I'm feeling depressed and tense. I have to force myself to get through the day. Why do I keep pushing myself so hard? I seem to have created this rule that my life *must* be all work and no play. Let's try disputing this rule. Do I expect other people to sacrifice everything for their careers? Definitely not. I seem to have a double standard in which I'm harder on myself than other people. Do I need the extra money and status that comes from working this hard? I want a good standard of living and for people to recognize my competence. However, I would still earn enough money even if I were to ease off a bit. What I think of myself is more important than needing recognition from others all the time. I know I'm competent. Is the rule about all work and no play helping or harming me? The rule helped me when I was studying for my accountancy exams and getting started. I have just kept going at the same frantic pace ever since. My body and low feelings are telling me to watch my stress level. I'm concerned that, in my early thirties and single, I'm having virtually no social life. There are also a lot of recreational activities I would like, for instance I used to be a good tennis player. It would be fun to play again.

*(Continued)*

---

---

### Box 7.2   (Continued)

Let's try changing the rule about all work and no play into a rule that might be better at this stage of my life. Here's a try: 'I want to earn good money and be respected for my competence as an accountant. However, I am likely to be a more successful person – and not necessarily a less successful accountant – if I lead a more balanced life and treat my social and recreational activities as though they are as important as my work.' This new rule represents a drastic change from my current way of thinking. I will need to work hard to keep it in mind and also to change my behaviour in line with it.

---

If possible, use highly sensitive recording equipment when you make up your audio cassettes. Aim for a professional standard of recording. Most home audio cassette recorders will not achieve the required level of clarity. Audio cassette recorders that eliminate virtually all motor noise and background hiss are on the market. You greatly lessen the effectiveness of audio cassette demonstrations if clients have to struggle with poor quality recordings. Be prepared to rehearse and retake your efforts if inadequate. Notable stage and screen performers go to these lengths when recording, so perhaps you might too.

## Activity 7.2   Demonstrating a Mind Skill

Do Part A and any other part that you find useful.

## Part A   Live Demonstration

Work with a partner who acts as a client who wants to work on a specific mind skill. The client describes the situation for which the mind skill is required. As part of presenting the skill, include a demonstration in which you clearly show the thinking steps involved in the mind skill. Then swap roles, get your client to enact using the mind skill and give feedback as necessary.

Afterwards, reverse roles.

## Part B    Written Demonstration

For the kind of clients you coach or are likely to coach, write out a handout (including a demonstration) of a specific mind skill. Cover the following points:

- your goals;
- clear instructions that identify for the client the key points of the skill you are coaching;
- one or more demonstrations of the targeted mind skill; and
- some questions that the client can do as homework.

## Part C    Audio Cassette Demonstration

For the kind of client you coach or are likely to coach, either for the mind skill you worked on in Part B or for another mind skill, make a demonstration audio cassette.

Think through how you might incorporate the audio cassette demonstration into the overall presentation of your chosen mind skill.

# Demonstrating Communication/Action Skills with Accompanying Self-Talk

Coaches and coaching trainees often need to demonstrate communication/action skills with the self-talk that accompanies them. This is because in real life clients have to instruct themselves through communication and action skills sequences on their own. The following is an example of a communication/action skills plus accompanying self-talk demonstration for a student with examination anxiety. The demonstrator, Brittany, tries to cope with anxiety and stay focused on the task at hand when looking at an examination paper for the first time. The creating self-talk skills goals for the demonstration are to use calming statements ('Calm down') and coaching statements ('Think what it is that I have to do' and 'I need to read the exam paper instructions carefully'). The communication/action skills goals include the use both of anxiety reduction skills (for example, breathing slowly and regularly) and exam taking skills (for example, reading the instructions on the exam carefully). The communication/action skills plus self-talk demonstration in Box 7.3 is based on the work of Meichenbaum (Meichenbaum, 1985; Meichenbaum and Deffenbacher, 1988).

---

### Box 7.3 Example of Demonstrating a Communication/Action Skill with Accompanying Self-Talk

Okay, I'm feeling pretty tense. My anxiety is a signal for me to use my coping skills. Calm down. Breathe slowly and regularly [*Brittany breathes slowly and regularly*]. Think: what is it I have to do? I need to read the exam paper's instructions carefully and look out for how the marks are distributed and how many questions I have to answer [*Brittany reads the instructions carefully*]. Then I must survey all the questions [*Brittany surveys the questions*]. I'm coping well so far. Next I must plan how to spend my time – in what order to do the questions and how much time to allocate to each question. Let's pick an easy question first. Remember to leave time for checking my answers at the end of the exam. [*Brittany outlines her order of answering questions and the time she intends spending on each*]. I don't have to answer the questions perfectly, just do my best. Now let's see what I really wanted in the first question I've chosen to answer. [*Brittany starts working on the first question*].

---

Coaching trainees need to remember when demonstrating skills that clients have to instruct themselves in sequences outside of sessions. For example, when teaching muscular relaxation skills, coaching trainees can demonstrate the talk that accompanies relaxation in either coach-centred or client-centred ways. With coach-centred talk, trainees give instructions from the outside – for example, 'Now close your eyes and get yourself comfortable.' With client-centred talk, trainees demonstrate the instructions as though clients are instructing themselves – for example, 'Now I close my eyes and get myself comfortable.' Demonstrating client-centred rather than coach-centred talk is an important difference when the goal is to coach clients in how to use progressive muscular relaxation skills on their own.

### Activity 7.3 Demonstrating a Communication/Action Skill with Accompanying Self-Talk

Work with a partner and together select a skill on which to present and then demonstrate a communication/action skill with accompanying self-talk to them.

1. Within the context of your overall goal, set clear communication/action skill and self-talk goals for your demonstration.
2. Develop a communication/action skill plus self-talk demonstration along the lines of the example in Box 7.3.
3. Enact the demonstration and keep working on it until you are satisfied with it.

   If appropriate, reverse roles.

# 8
# Consolidation Skills

The Chinese proverb says 'I hear, I forget. I see, I remember. I do, I understand.' Learning by doing is essential to successful coaching. Knowledge gained by exploring oneself, hearing and observing gets clarified and consolidated when clients learn by doing. You do not learn to drive a car without driving. Likewise clients acquiring and strengthening particular lifeskills need relevant activities that help them to improve the skills and to integrate them into their daily lives. The following are some examples of learning by doing. Note that in some of the examples, learning by doing focuses on mind skills as well as on communication/action skills.

> Joshua, 27, who has difficulties at job interviews role-plays with his coach using the communication skills of answering questions briefly and to the point, being easy to hear and keeping good eye contact.

> Charlotte, 34, reports that she sometimes gets sexually harassed where she works. To date, she has put up with what has gone on. After discussing with Charlotte what might be appropriate, Ursula her coach demonstrates some communication skills for dealing with sexual harassment assertively. She then gets Charlotte practising using the skills in the session through role-playing and encourages her to try using them at work.

> Anita, 56, is a patient with chronic lower back pain. Robin, her coach, demonstrates and gets her practising progressive muscular relaxation and also identifying maladaptive thoughts linked with negative emotions connected with pain, and replacing them with more adaptive thoughts.

> Don, 46, is an executive being sent by his company to an Arab country. To help him develop his cross-cultural awareness and skills, Pervez his coach gets him participating in role-plays of situations where he is dealing with employees from that country.

These are just a few examples of the use of learning by doing in coaching. Like demonstrating, learning by doing can focus on communication/action skills, mind skills, or communication/action skills and self-talk. Often structured activities are integrated with the learning sequence containing the initial demonstration. For example, rehearsal and feedback takes place immediately after a demonstration. Later on, as clients work with the skills, learning by doing takes place both inside and outside of coaching sessions.

## Facilitating Learning by Doing

Coaching trainees require skills to facilitate learning by doing. Even at the best of times, clients come to coaching with various levels of commitment. Trainees cannot assume that clients will automatically participate in learning by doing. They may resist such activities for many reasons including lack of a trusting atmosphere, not seeing the point of particular activities and shyness.

How can coaching trainees enhance clients' motivation and commitment to learning by doing? Here are some suggestions. First, trainees can create a safe and trusting emotional climate in which clients are prepared to take risks. Such risks include disclosing problems, admitting mistakes and not performing as competently as they would like at first. Second, trainees can allow clients to share and explore their fears about performing. Trainees can show sensitivity to clients having to try different behaviours. They can make comments like 'It's okay to feel uneasy about trying to act differently' and 'It's okay to make mistakes when learning any new skill.' If necessary, trainees can reassure clients that they will not be coerced into divulging material or doing any activity about which they feel uncomfortable.

Third, trainees can ensure that the reasons for doing each activity are clear. It can be a good idea to check out with clients whether an activity is likely to work for them. Be sensitive to any reservations clients may have. Fourth, trainees can enhance clients' motivation by helping them process their experiences of learning by doing. Often doing activities provides valuable cognitive and emotional insights; trainees can help clients to share and work through these insights. Fifth, trainees can encourage involvement in learning by doing by facilitating feedback on the process from clients. Trainees can create a norm that, 'It's okay to give and receive constructive feedback.' The issue of feedback is explored further later in the chapter.

# Plan Sub-Goals and Sequence-Graded Tasks

When coaches and coaching trainees attempt to develop clients' communication and action skills, planning sub-goals and sequencing graded tasks overlap. Coaching trainees may plan sub-goals in two main ways.

## Sequence Sub-Skills

When assisting clients to learn complex skills, coaching trainees can break the skills down into their component parts. Then they can decide in what order they wish to train each component. For example, Andy and his trainee, Pam, have the overall goal of enabling Andy to make assertive requests to his boss, Jeff. Andy and Pam decide during their sessions to focus first on verbal messages, second on voice messages, third on body messages and finally on putting all three messages together.

## Sequence-Graded Tasks

Sequencing graded tasks is sometimes called graded task assignment (Beck and Weishaar, 2005) or setting proximal sub-goals (Bandura, 1986). A useful distinction is that between setting distant and proximal or nearer goals. The research evidence is equivocal regarding the effectiveness of setting distant goals. More certain appears the desirability of setting proximal goals or sub-goals (Bandura, 1986). Bandura observes that 'Subgoals provide present guides and inducements for action, while subgoal attainments produce efficacy information and self-satisfactions that sustain one's efforts along the way.' (Bandura, 1986: 475).

The following is an example of sequencing graded tasks to develop communication skills:

Becky, 27, is a new employee at an insurance company, where she works in a room with eight colleagues. At her last job Becky felt isolated from her co-workers and she does not want this to happen again. Together Becky and her coach draw up a sequence of graded tasks that Becky thinks she can complete before their next session.

1. Say 'hello' to all my colleagues when I get in to the office.
2. Ask at least two colleagues how they are getting on.
3. Have a brief conversation with a colleague in which I reveal something about my work.
4. Have a slightly longer conversation with a friendly colleague in which I reveal something about my private life, for instance where I live.

Near the start of the next session, Becky and her coach review progress in attaining each task. The coach encourages Becky to share her thoughts and feelings about progress. The coach emphasizes the explanation that Becky achieves her sub-goals as a result of her willingness to take risks, her effort and her skill. As a result of the feedback Becky gets both from others and herself about her growing skills, the coach and she develop further graded tasks for the next period between sessions. At progress reviews the coach rewards Becky for working to develop her skills whether or not she is successful. For instance, when Becky goes on to ask a colleague out for a coffee, the coach will reward her, even if her offer was refused. The coach encourages Becky to view as learning experiences all attempts to attain graded tasks.

### Skills for Sequencing and Reviewing Graded Tasks

The following are some coach and trainee skills for sequencing and reviewing graded tasks. Always make links between tasks and skills; the purpose of graded tasks is not only to assist clients to attain specific goals but also to help them develop specific skills. Encourage clients to view graded tasks as ways of developing skills for handling not just immediate but future situations.

Work with clients to assess whether they feel willing and able to work on graded tasks. Discuss with them the tasks that are important for them. When sequencing tasks, go at a comfortable pace. Start with small steps that clients think they can achieve (Luciani, 2004). Be prepared to build in intermediate steps if clients think the progression of tasks is too steep. Graded tasks should be stepping stones for clients to develop skills and confidence.

Before they attempt graded tasks, encourage clients to assess what skills they need to attain them. When reviewing progress, assist clients to evaluate their use of targeted skills. To avoid connotations of failure, encourage clients to view attempting each graded task as an experiment in which they gain valuable information about themselves. Even if they are unsuccessful, attempting tasks provides clients with useful learning experiences about how they think, feel and communicate.

Help clients to share their feelings and thoughts about attempting graded tasks. Where necessary, work with clients' poor mind skills. Encourage clients not only to acknowledge their successes but also help them to realize that success results from willingness to take risks, expending effort and using targeted skills. In collaboration with clients, sequence either easier or more difficult tasks as necessary. Though some graded tasks are performed within coaching sessions, most are performed outside of such sessions. Where feasible, encourage clients to rehearse and practise graded tasks before trying them. Repeated success experiences with specific tasks consolidate clients' skills and confidence.

## Activity 8.1    Arranging a Graded Task Plan with a Client

Conduct a coaching session with a partner as 'client', with the goal of developing a specific communication/action skills strength. Together you decide that the best way to help your client is for her/him to work through a sequence of graded tasks between sessions. Sequence progressively difficult graded tasks using the following skills:

- encouraging realistic assessment of existing skills;
- generating tasks involving using the targeted skill(s);
- sequencing graded tasks in cooperation with the client;
- paying attention to feelings and thoughts; and
- encouraging homework and practise.

Afterwards discuss your coaching session with your 'client', including your skills in assisting the sequencing of graded tasks. Then reverse roles.

# Rehearse and Role-Play

Learning any skill generally requires repeated performances of targeted behaviours. Rehearsals may take place immediately after initial demonstrations of skills, later in coaching and before, when and after clients apply targeted skills in their daily lives. In role plays, clients rehearse communication and action skills and sometimes mind skills in simulated or pretend situations involving one or more others. Most often coaching trainees play the part of the other person but sometimes trainees and clients switch roles.

## Skills for Assisting Rehearsal

The following are some skills for role play rehearsals in coaching. Some clients find the idea of role-playing off-putting. For example, they may be self-conscious about their acting skills. Trainees can explain the reasons for using role plays to ease clients' anxieties and help motivate them. Here is a rationale used by coach, Jen, for role play rehearsal with a client, Bob, who inwardly gets angry when his secretary, Jane, comes in late but outwardly does nothing about it:

Bob, I think it would be helpful if, after my demonstrating the skills we agreed on to cope better with Jane next time she comes in late, we change roles.

I realize that it may seem artificial acting the scene here. However, role-playing gives you the chance to rehearse different ways you might behave – your words, voice messages and body messages – so that you are better prepared for the real event. It is safer to make mistakes here where it doesn't count for real. There is no substitute for learning by doing. What do you think about this approach?

Already if you have given a demonstration, you have elicited information about the physical setting of proposed scenes, what other characters are involved and how they behave. If you are then to role-play someone, for instance Jane, when the client rehearses you should make sure to have sufficient information about Jane's verbal, voice and body messages so that you can get into the role. Depending on what sort of office trainees have, you may be able to move the furniture around to create a 'stage', for instance a family living room.

You can usually spend time well if you conduct assessment role plays in which clients demonstrate how they currently act in problem situations. You can elicit much relevant information about non-verbal communication that may not be apparent if clients only talk about how they communicate and act. Assessment role plays can also reveal how clients think in situations.

Trainees cooperate with clients to formulate new and better ways of communicating that both use targeted lifeskills and yet feel 'comfortable'. As a coach you should facilitate clients' contributions to the discussion prior to making your own suggestions. For instance, you can ask: 'How might you use your new skills to behave differently in the situation?' Together with clients you can generate and review alternative scripts and appropriate voice and body messages. As part of this process you can demonstrate the different verbal, voice and body message components of appropriate communication and action skills. You can also explore with clients how to cope with different responses by others.

After demonstrating, once the client is reasonably clear about their new role and you understand your 'part', trial enactments or rehearsals can take place. Trainees should avoid trying to do too much or anything too difficult too soon. You may allow role plays to run their course. Alternatively, you may intervene at one or more points along the way to allow client self-assessment and provide feedback. Rehearsal role plays are dry runs of how to use communication and mind skills in specific situations. Video feedback may be used as part of coaching both during and after role plays. Trainees may require a number of rehearsals to build clients' skills. Some of these role plays may involve responding in different ways to clients. For example, clients asking for a pay rise may have their requests accepted, postponed or rejected in separate role plays.

Role reversal and mirroring are psychodrama techniques that trainees may use (Blatner, 2005; Moreno, 1959). In role reversal, trainees get clients to play the other person in interactions. Role reversals force clients to get some way into another's internal viewpoint. With mirroring, trainees 'mirror back' clients' verbal, voice and body messages. Clients see themselves as others experience them.

Trainees may rehearse clients' mind skills alongside their communication/action skills. For instance, you can rehearse clients in the calming and coaching dimensions of appropriate self-talk to accompany new communication skills. You can also rehearse clients in other mind skills relevant to targeted communication/action skills.

Processing involves spending time dealing with clients' thoughts and feelings generated by role plays. Together coaching trainees and clients can discuss things learned from role plays and make plans to transfer rehearsed skills to daily life. You can ask clients processing questions like: 'How were you feeling in that role play?', 'How well do you think you used your skills in that rehearsal?', 'What have you learned in that role play that is useful for real life?' and 'What difficulties do you anticipate in implementing your changed behaviour and how can you overcome them?' After processing the previous role play, trainees and clients may move on to the next role play, either with the same or with another situation.

Let's revert to the example of coach Jen talking to Bob about rehearsing dealing with his secretary Jane coming in to work late:

> Let's rehearse the skills, this time with you playing yourself. First, when Jane is late but before she arrives, rehearse the mind skill of creating coping self-talk – its calming and coaching dimensions. Speak your self-talk aloud. *(Bob does this and Jen asks him to evaluate what he just said and together they work to improve it over two more rehearsals).*
>
> Now let's rehearse how you communicate with Jane when she arrives late. You say 'good morning' to her in a friendly way. You give her time to get settled and then your verbal message is 'Jane, I've noticed you've been late a few times now. In future, unless something unavoidable holds you up, I want you always to come to work on time.' Your vocal messages include speaking calmly and clearly. Your body messages are keeping your eye contact and gaze in her direction, having a pleasant facial expression and with your body turned towards her. Now, let's practise that with me playing Jane until you feel comfortable in your role. *(Jen rehearses with Bob a few times until he acts and feels all right.)*

### *Activity 8.2   Developing Role-Playing and Rehearsal Skills*

Conduct a session with a partner as 'client' in which you aim to help her/him use creating coping self-talk and one or more targeted communication skills for a specific situation in her/his personal or working life. Conduct one or more role play rehearsals using the following skills:

- using role-playing to assess current communication;
- formulating changed communication;
- creating relevant coping self-talk;
- demonstrating targeted communication skills and coping self-talk;
- rehearsing the client who uses targeted communication skills and coping self-talk;
- processing each role play rehearsal; and
- encouraging the client to rehearse in her/his imagination (as homework) competent performance of the communication skills accompanied by coping self-talk rehearsed in the coaching session.

Afterwards discuss and get feedback from your 'client' on your use of role play rehearsal skills. Then reverse roles.

# *Assist Clients to Experiment*

A major concern of all coaches and coaching trainees is that of how best to help clients take the risks of changing how they behave. Another major concern is how best to help them transfer trained skills to their worlds outside of the coaching. Communication and action skills experiments provide an excellent way to approach both concerns. Clients, in conjunction with coaching trainees, can hypothesize about the consequences of using the skills they are learning in coaching outside of coaching. Then clients implement the skills and evaluate the consequences of their changed behaviour.

An advantage of viewing changing communication and action skills in experimental terms is that it helps clients to be detached about what they do and its results. When experiments do not work out quite as planned, clients do not have to think they have failed. Rather each experiment is a learning experience that provides information useful for developing communication/action skills.

Often experiments simultaneously focus on changing both mind skills and communication/action skills. For instance, Tom wants to increase his skills of talking about himself to his girlfriend, Olivia. An experiment focused solely on communication skills might target improving Tom's verbal, vocal and bodily communication skills of self-disclosing. An experiment focused solely on mind skills might target Tom's skills of creating more helpful perceptions about his self-disclosing. An experiment focused on both communication skills and mind skills would target improving both how Tom communicates his disclosures and also his perceptions. In this section, for the sake of simplicity, I focus solely on designing and implementing changing communication/action skills experiments.

## Steps in Communication/Action Skills Experiments

Experiments focus on the use of targeted skills in specific situations or relationships. There are six main steps in designing, conducting and evaluating communication/action skills experiments.

*1. Assess*   Coaching trainees collaborate with clients to assess their good and poor communication/action skills in the targeted area.

*2. Formulate Changed Communication/Action Skills*   Trainees and clients work out how to behave differently by using improved communication/action skills. Regarding communication, they pay attention to vocal and body as well as verbal communication.

*3. Make an 'If ... then ... ' Statement*   The 'If' part of the statement relates to clients rehearsing, practising and then using their changed communication/action skills. The 'then ... ' part of the statement indicates the specific consequences that they predict will follow from using their changed skills.

*4. Rehearse and Practise*   Probably with assistance from their coaching trainees, clients need to rehearse and practise changed communication/action skills to have a reasonable chance of implementing them properly outside of coaching.

*5. Try Out Changed Communication and Action Skills*   Clients implement changed communication/action skills in actual situations.

*6. Evaluate*   Initially clients should evaluate their use of changed communication/action skills on their own. This evaluation should focus on questions like 'How well did I use my changed communication/action skills?',

'What were the positive and negative consequences of using the targeted skills for myself and for others?', 'Have my predictions been confirmed or negated?' and 'Do I want to use my changed communication/action skills in future?' Afterwards trainees can assist clients in processing what they learned from their experiments. Some clients may just require encouragement to keep persisting in their changed behaviours, whilst others may require additional rehearsing. Sometimes, trainees and clients may decide to modify the client's use of communication/action skills in light of experience.

---

### Box 8.1 Example of Designing a Communication Skills Experiment

What follows is an illustrative outline for an experiment in which Tom addresses the question: 'What happens when I use improved communication skills to self-disclose more to Olivia?'

## Part A  Assessment

1. For a period of a week, monitor on a worksheet how I self-disclose to Olivia. Focus on strengths and weaknesses in each of the following sub-skills of self-disclosing: verbal, vocal, body, touch and action-taking communication. Use the following column headings on my worksheet:

| Situation | Self-disclosing communication |
|---|---|
| *What? When? Where?* | *Verbal, vocal, bodily, touch, action* |

2. List all the information about myself that I either fail to or inadequately convey in our relationship.

_____

_____

_____

_____

3. Based on the answers to questions 1 and 2 above, assess my good and poor communication skills at self-disclosing to Olivia.

| Self-disclosing to Olivia (my good skills) | Self-disclosing to Olivia (my poor skills) |
|---|---|

*(Continued)*

---

---

### Box 8.1    (Continued)

## Part B    Make an 'If ... then ...' Statement

Make an 'If ... then' statement along the lines of:
'**If** I use the following changed communication skills [*specify*] to self-disclose to Olivia during the next week, **then** these specific consequences are likely to follow' [for instance, (a) I will feel better about myself for being open, and (b) Olivia will feel and act more positively toward me].

**If**_____

_____

**then**

(a) _____

(b) _____

(c) _____

(d) _____

## Part C    Implement and Evaluate Using My Changed Communication Skills

During the coming week, try out using my changed communication skills in self-disclosing to Olivia. What are the positive and negative consequences for Olivia and me? Have my predictions been confirmed or negated? Have I learned anything useful from this experiment? If so, what?

_____

_____

_____

_____

---

## *Provide Feedback*

'How did I do?' and 'How am I doing?' are questions that clients ask of themselves and others. Clients require knowledge of the consequences of their attempts to develop specific lifeskills. Feedback and monitoring can let clients know whether they are on the right track and in what ways they need to alter behaviour.

## *Sources of Feedback*

Effective coaches and trainees are managers of feedback to clients rather than always providing feedback themselves. As well as their own feedback, they are always building clients' skills of self-feedback or of monitoring how well they are using specific skills. Though the distinction is somewhat arbitrary, here I first deal with providing feedback to clients and then with encouraging clients to monitor themselves.

Coaches and clients can use audio-visual feedback both when assessing and when building new skills. Peltier (2001) observes that video provides feedback without much verbal criticism and that successful athletic coaches would not think of coaching without using videotape. Regarding coaching executives, he writes 'Show clients how they look, how they act, and how they speak and sound' (2001: 178). Using videotape and audio cassettes can also be important in relationship coaching, and often in health coaching. For example, audio-visual feedback is useful for rehearsing a client in how best to deliver a difficult message to a partner or in learning to say no to drinking too much alcohol.

Trainees and clients can also get feedback from third parties, for instance partners, parents, teachers, colleagues and bosses. Clients are always getting feedback from such sources anyway and so it is a matter of how much the collection of feedback is formalized as part of the coaching process.

## *Kinds of Feedback*

As managers of feedback, coaches and coaching trainees need to bear a number of feedback dimensions in mind (Egan, 2002).

## *Self or External Feedback*

As a guideline, when they undertake a task inside or outside of coaching, clients should be the first to comment on their learnings and reactions. Then the coaching trainee may provide some feedback but clients should be given the further opportunity to comment on how they perceive it.

## *Behavioural or Emotional Feedback*

A distinction exists between behavioural feedback, 'how you behave', and emotional feedback, 'I feel such and such about you or the way you have behaved'. In lifeskills coaching, behavioural feedback is emphasized. Where possible, emotional feedback should be preceded by behavioural feedback, 'When your behaviour contains the following element(s), I feel such and such'.

## Specific or Non-Specific Feedback

Imagine a behaviour rehearsal on how to ask for a pay rise. Afterwards the coaching trainee says to the client: 'I don't think you did that very well', and leaves it at that. The client has not been provided with specific feedback on how to improve but has instead given negative feedback leading nowhere. Feedback should always be specific and concentrate on targeted behaviours. After a role play in which the client was asking for a pay rise, an example of specific feedback to the working participant, Les, might be: 'Les, when you asked Jan for a pay rise I thought you did not make much eye contact with her and you spoke in a very quiet voice.' If the behaviour rehearsal had been videotaped, the trainee could say to the client: 'During the playback, I want you to notice how well you made eye contact with Jan and how loudly you spoke to her.' Here, the trainee cues the participant what to look for specifically during the video feedback. When giving specific feedback, try not to cover more than two or three points at any one time; recipients suffer from and get confused by feedback overload.

## Confirmatory, Corrective and Motivating Feedback

Feedback can be confirmatory, corrective and motivating. Confirmatory feedback lets participants know which specific behaviours they are developing along the right lines. Corrective feedback lets participants know which specific behaviours require altering and in what ways. Much feedback is both confirmatory and corrective: for example, 'Les, when you asked Jan for a pay rise you made good eye contact [*confirmatory feedback*]. However, I thought you spoke with too quiet a voice [*corrective feedback*].'

Motivating feedback points out the consequences of good and poor use of skills and includes suggestions for improving performance: 'Les, the consequence of your speaking in a quiet voice was that you seemed diffident about wanting a pay rise, if you spoke louder Jan might take more notice [*motivating feedback*].' Start where possible by giving confirmatory feedback to clients.

## *'I' Message or 'You' Message Feedback*

A way of detoxifying feedback is to use 'I' messages rather than 'You' messages. Givers of feedback should always take responsibility and locate its source clearly in themselves. Locating the source of feedback in senders reduces the chance of it being received defensively. For example, the message 'Les, I think your voice should be louder when you ask Jan for a pay rise' is gentler and a more open invitation for discussion than, 'Les, your voice should be louder when you ask Jan for a pay rise.' The trainee acknowledges that feedback reflects her or his perception.

## *Verbal or Demonstrated Feedback*

Feedback may be given largely by means of words. However, often feedback can be communicated even more clearly and received even more accurately if verbal description is accompanied by demonstration: for instance, by videotapes or audio cassettes. Feedback can also be demonstrated without audio-visual aids. For instance, in the previous example the trainee could mirror Les's vocal messages when asking Jan for a pay rise. In addition, she or he could demonstrate more appropriate behaviour.

## *Feedback or Confrontation*

How can feedback be distinguished from confrontation? Much feedback is either in line with or reasonably close to clients' existing perceptions. Such feedback does not provide any major challenge or threat to their self-image. Confrontation is a category of feedback where clients' self-images are challenged. In coaching, confrontations may focus on inconsistencies, for instance between words and actions; on distortions of reality, for instance selecting out inconvenient feedback; or on not owning responsibility for the consequences of one's behaviour. How as well as what trainees confront is important. Given the right trusting atmosphere, constructive confrontations have their place in coaching. However, where possible help clients to confront themselves: for example, by asking them to search for evidence to back their statements. Furthermore, use a minimum amount of 'muscle'. Although sometimes necessary, strong confrontations are generally to be avoided since they can create resistances.

## Feedback or Reward

As well as specific feedback concerning how clients perform behaviours, trainees may also provide social rewards or reinforcers. Praise and encouragement are important sources of reward. Trainees can use reward when participants achieve targeted behaviours either inside or outside of coaching. Rewards can be non-verbal as well as verbal. Applause, head nods, smiles and pats on the back are each examples of non-verbal rewards. In addition, forms of reward like money, soft drinks, candy and exchangeable tokens can be used in lifeskills coaching. Such rewards should be appropriate to the clients in question. Coaching trainees need to beware of clients only performing targeted behaviours under conditions of external reward rather than self-reward.

## Socio-Cultural Feedback Considerations

Feedback needs to take into account the social and cultural milieu of clients. Coaching trainees who come from different backgrounds to some or all of their clients require sensitivity to these differences. Trainees may require awareness of differing rules governing feedback in other cultures and social groupings. Clients can be encouraged to relate how feedback is handled in their own cultures.

## Check that Feedback is Received Clearly

Williams and Thomas (2005) state that one way to do this is to have the client rephrase the feedback according to their understanding of what you have said. If what the client says corresponds to what you meant, then you can be more certain that your feedback has been accurately received. Box 8.2 provides ten guidelines for providing feedback.

---

### Box 8.2   Ten Guidelines for Providing Feedback

1. Encourage the client to comment first, before giving feedback.
2. Give feedback on behaviour rather than on what you feel.
3. Give specific feedback.
4. Where possible, start by giving confirmatory feedback and then give corrective and motivating feedback.

---

---

### Box 8.2    (Continued)

5.   Give 'I' message rather than 'You' message feedback.
6.   Consider demonstrating your feedback.
7.   Where possible, encourage clients to confront themselves, before you confront them.
8.   Alongside specific feedback, consider providing a reward.
9.   Take socio-cultural considerations into account.
10.  Check that your feedback has been received clearly.

---

## *Activity 8.3    Developing skills for providing feedback*

### Part A  Verbal Feedback

Coach a partner in a skill upon which you have previously agreed. As part of rehearsing the skill, go through each of the guidelines in Box 8.2, providing feedback to your partner on her/his performance. Afterwards, discuss and reverse roles.

### Part B  Audio-visual Feedback

For the skill in which you were coaching your partner in Part A, or for another skill, as part of rehearsing the skill provide audio cassette or video feedback to her/him. Let the 'client' comment on the feedback before adding your comments. Afterwards, reverse roles.

# *Encourage Monitoring*

Clients can obtain feedback from monitoring themselves:

Fiona, 26, is seeing a coach, Barrie, to develop her job-seeking skills and help her get re-employed. She is keeping a record of her job-seeking activities: for instance, making phone enquiries and written applications.

Miles, 42, is working on keeping fit after a heart attack. He keeps a chart of his daily exercise, for instance walking or jogging, how far, for how long and so on.

Allen, 33, is striving to develop a more balanced lifestyle. His coach, Arnold, encourages him to set aside time for pleasant events. Allen monitors the time he sets aside and what he does with it.

The following are some ways that coaching trainees can assist clients to monitor themselves and to develop self-monitoring skills.

## Offer Reasons for Monitoring

Clients are not in the habit of systematically recording observations about how they act; trainees need to motivate them to do so. For instance, they can explain: 'Counting how many times you perform a behaviour daily not only indicates how severe your problem is but also gives us a baseline against which to measure your progress in dealing with it' or 'Systematically writing down how you send verbal, vocal and body messages after each time you go for an interview provides us with information to build your skills.'

## Train Clients in Discrimination and Recording

Clients are not naturally accurate self-observers (Thoresen and Mahoney, 1974). Consequently, trainees need to educate them in how to discriminate and record specific behaviours. Clients require clarity not only about what to record but also about how to record it. Clients also require awareness of any tendencies they have to misperceive or selectively perceive their actions: for example, being more inclined to notice weaknesses than strengths.

## Design Simple and Clear Recording Logs

Trainees should always consider supplying the logs themselves and not expect clients to make up their own logs. They may not do so in the first place and, if they do, they may get them wrong. Simple recording systems enhance comprehension and recording accuracy.

## Use Reward Skills

Trainees can reward clients with interest and praise when they fill in logs. This guideline is based on the basic behavioural principle that actions that are rewarding are more likely to be repeated. Furthermore, they can always reward clients for their efforts by debriefing them.

## Encourage Clients to Evaluate Monitoring Information

When clients share monitoring logs with trainees, trainees can help them to use this information for self-exploration and evaluation. Assist clients to understand the meaning of the information they have collected. However, do not do their work for them. When coaching ends, trainees will not be around to assess the implications of their frequency counts and monitoring logs: train clients to do this for themselves.

## Use Other Skills-Building Strategies

Trainees should not expect clients to develop communication/action skills on the basis of self-observation alone. They are likely to require other interventions, for example behaviour rehearsals and self-reward, to develop these skills. Furthermore, they require work and practise to acquire and maintain skills.

# Assist Clients to Deliver Self-Reward

Coaching trainees can assist clients in learning how to deliver positive self-reward. There are two main categories of reward that clients can self-administer: external and internal.

*External reward* includes: (1) self-administration of new rewards that are outside the client's everyday life, such as a new item of clothing or a special event, and (2) initial denial of some pleasant everyday experience and later administration of it contingent upon a desired action. Wherever possible a positive self-reward should be relevant to the targeted goals: for instance, clients achieving weight loss goals can reward themselves by buying slimmer-fitting clothes.

*Internal reward* includes self-talk statements like 'That's great', 'I did it' or 'Well done' that clearly indicate the client's satisfaction at achieving a sub-goal or goal. Clients can also use their imaginations to visualize significant others praising their efforts.

Coaching trainees can collaborate with clients to determine the precise conditions for administering rewards to themselves as they work to improve their mind skills and communication and action skills. In making positive self-reward plans, pertinent considerations can include identifying rewards, sequencing progressive tasks, and making the connections between achievements and rewards very clear. Clients should know that, in general, it is best that they reward themselves either immediately or shortly after performing targeted skills or sub-skills.

Trainees can encourage clients to draw up contracts that specify the relationship between administering positive self-rewards and developing targeted mind skills and communication and action skills. Contracts should establish clear-cut criteria for achievement and specify the means whereby behaviour is observed, measured and recorded. Contracts can be unilateral or bilateral. In unilateral contracts clients obligate themselves to personal change programmes independent of contributions from others. Bilateral contracts, which are commonly used in relationship coaching, stipulate obligations and rewards for each of the parties. For example, partners can contract with one another to increase their exchange of caring behaviours for a specified time period.

Not all clients like self-reward plans or follow them. Some clients consider the use of self-reward too mechanical. Furthermore, trainees may introduce self-reward ideas too soon, before clients are sufficiently motivated to change. Trainees should assess how well clients accept the idea of self-reward and their motivation for change.

## *Negotiate Homework*

After presenting, demonstrating and rehearsing clients in new or different skills, coaches and trainees can negotiate relevant homework assignments. Homework assignments or between-session activities include completing self-monitoring sheets and filling out worksheets for developing mind skills that influence feelings, communications and actions. Other assignments can entail reading self-help books, listening to cassettes, watching videotapes, observing people with good communication skills, and trying out improved communication and action skills in real life (Dryden and Feltham, 1992; Greenberger and Padesdy, 1995).

Many reasons exist for asking clients to perform homework assignments (Cormier and Nurius, 2002; Egan, 2002). These reasons include speeding up the learning process and encouraging clients to monitor, rehearse and practise changed thinking and communications/actions. Furthermore, homework activities can help the transfer of trained mind skills and communication/action skills to real life, which may involve uncovering difficulties in applying them in specific problem situations. In addition, homework assignments can increase clients' sense of self-control and of personal responsibility for developing targeted mind skills and communication/action skills.

## Skills for Negotiating Homework

The following are some central skills for negotiating homework assignments. These skills can increase the chances of clients complying to do agreed-upon activities.

### Offer Reasons for Assignments

Coaching trainees can often enhance clients' motivation for completing homework assignments if they explain their importance. At the start of 'tell, show and do' sequences, they can introduce the idea of practise.

> Now, Helena, first I am going to describe _____ [*specify which*] skills, then I am going to demonstrate it/them for you, then I am going to rehearse you in it/them, and then, if agreeable, we will discuss some ways to practise your _____ [*specify which*] skills in real life. To gain competence in developing any skill requires practise.

### Negotiate Realistic Assignments

I use the word negotiate to highlight the importance of client participation in homework assignment decisions. I assume that clients are more likely to comply with assignments that they have had a say in designing. The following are three key aspects of realistic assignments. First, such assignments either consolidate earlier learning or set the stage for the learning activities of the next session. Do not introduce any new skills and ideas that clients will have had insufficient time to assimilate before the session ends.

Second, the assignments are of appropriate difficulty. The tasks take into account clients' understanding of and readiness to perform targeted skills. Where appropriate, suggest graded steps. Third, the amount of work entailed in the assignments is realistic for the client's circumstances and motivation. It is preferable for clients to make a definite commitment to a small amount of homework than to make a vague commitment to a larger amount. Encourage clients to view homework in terms of learning contracts not just to the coach but, more importantly, to themselves.

## *Give Clear Instructions in Take-Away Form*

How can clients know precisely what to do? What, when, how often, and how it is to be recorded are each pertinent questions. Sometimes clients have already received handouts summarizing the main learning points of a skill. Where possible, give instructions in take-away form. Trainees can design their own homework assignment forms. Either trainee or client should write down clear instructions for homework assignments on these forms. Writing instructions on scraps of paper is generally not good enough. Trainees should always check what clients write to make sure they have taken down the instructions correctly. If trainees want clients to fill out forms such as monitoring logs, they should provide these forms themselves. This practise ensures the transmission of clear instructions and saves clients the extra effort of having to write out forms before filling them in.

## *Aim to Increase Compliance*

One of the central problems in assigning homework activities is getting clients to do them. Often I have observed trainees rush through negotiating homework assignments at the end of sessions in ways that virtually guaranteed client non-compliance. Common mistakes included not leaving enough time, inviting insufficient client participation, giving vague verbal instructions and not checking whether clients clearly understood what they were meant to do. Box 8.3 lists nine guidelines recommended by psychologists Dennis Greenberger and Christine Padesky (1995: 24–7) for increasing the chances of client compliance.

---

### Box 8.3   Guidelines for Increasing Clients' Compliance with Homework Assignments

1. Make assignments small.
2. Assign tasks within the client's skill level.
3. Make assignments relevant and interesting.
4. Collaborate with the client in developing learning assignments.
5. Provide a clear rationale for the assignment and a written summary.
6. Begin the assignment during the session.
7. Identify and problem-solve impediments to the assignment.
8. Emphasize learning, not a desired outcome.
9. Show interest, and follow up in the next appointment.

---

## Anticipate Difficulties and Setbacks

Explore with clients their motivation for completing homework assignments. Where possible, identify and help clients to work through resistances. In addition, identify rewards for completing assignments. If trainees have negotiated realistic amounts of homework, hopefully clients will comply. Sometimes implementing a skill requires asking clients to give up long-established habits. Here it can be especially important not to assign too difficult an assignment too soon. Where possible, trainees and clients should try to build in some early successes to encourage clients to keep working on their skills.

Some clients return to very unsupportive environments. Here trainees may need to prepare clients more thoroughly prior to suggesting they implement targeted skills in real-life settings. Such preparation is likely to include devising strategies for coping with negative feedback.

## Signal a Joint Progress Review

Coaching trainees should signal a joint progress review by letting clients know that at or around the start of the next session, they will ask them how they fared in their homework assignments. Clients who know that their coaches are interested in and supportive of their attempts to complete homework assignments are more likely to be motivated to do so, that is so long as trainees avoid becoming controlling and judgmental.

## *Activity 8.4    Developing Skills for Negotiating Homework*

## Part A    Considering Negotiating Homework Assignments

Imagine that you have just coached a client in a specific skill or sub-skill that you have presented and demonstrated. You are now thinking about setting the client one or more homework assignments. How might you take into account each of the following considerations for negotiating homework assignment?

- Offering reasons for assignments.
- Negotiating realistic assignments.
- Giving clear instructions in take-away form.
- Anticipating difficulties and setbacks.
- Signalling a joint progress review.

## Part B    Rehearsing and Practising Negotiating Homework Assignments

Work with a partner acting as client to improve a specific mind skill and/or communication skill in her/his work or personal relationships. Now rehearse and practise how to negotiate one or more homework assignments so that your client can use the time before the next coaching session to good effect. To increase your client's chances of compliance, observe the guidelines provided in Box 8.3.

Afterwards, hold a sharing-and-discussion session focused on your use of negotiating homework assignments skills. If necessary, practise more until you consider that you have obtained some competence in negotiating homework assignments. Then reverse roles.

# 9
# Group Coaching

Life coaching may be conducted in groups either in addition to individual work or on its own. Williams and Davis (2002) list three areas of group coaching: (1) as added value with existing clients; (2) for specific niche markets; and (3) using a personal development book as the tool for discussion and exploration. Whitworth and her colleagues (1998) also mention areas of group coaching, including couples coaching and coaching work teams. However, to date the main focus of the coaching literature has been on individual rather than group work. Though both the aforementioned works emphasize group coaching by phone teleconferencing, group coaching is frequently performed face-to-face, such as Relate's preparation for marriage courses.

What are some of the reasons for life coaching in groups? Availability is one reason. It may be difficult to coach sufficient people working on an individual basis alone: for instance, coaching college students in relationship skills or patients in health care skills. Related to availability are considerations of cost. For some people, either they get their coaching in group form or they do not get it at all. In addition, some agencies may opt for group coaching as a way of maximizing scarce resources, as can be the case with educational institutions. For these reasons alone, it is likely that there will be an increase in group coaching in years to come to meet the needs of ordinary people, unlike the well-off who can afford individual work.

For some coaches and clients, group coaching may even have some advantages over individual coaching. Yalom's (1995) 12 therapeutic factors can apply to coaching groups as well as to psychotherapy groups. These factors are as follows:

1. Altruism – thinking of and helping others.
2. Group cohesiveness – a sense of belonging to, feeling accepted by and finding the group and its members attractive.
3. Universality – learning that others have the same thoughts and problems too.
4. Interpersonal learning (input) – learning how I come across to others and why.
5. Interpersonal learning (output) – the opportunity to be more trustful and to work on how I relate to others.
6. Guidance – either the group leader or group members making suggestions or giving advice to me.
7. Catharsis – being able to ventilate and to learn how to express my feelings.
8. Identification – finding role models in the behaviour of either the group leader or other group members.
9. Family re-enactment – being in a simulated family that helped me understand the influences on me of my original family.
10. Self-understanding – learning about how, through the influences of my childhood and development, I distort my perceptions of myself and of others.
11. Instillation of hope – seeing other group members improve and solve their problems.
12. Existential factors – learning to acknowledge more fully the existential parameters of death, freedom, responsibility and isolation, and to make the most of my life.

It is important for coaching trainees to learn the skills not just of working with individuals in groups but of helping clients to help one another. A willingness to work on real rather than surface issues may come about through the climate of cohesiveness, safety, trust and acceptance that trainees are able to foster in groups. Trainees should seek to create norms or rules conducive to the group's work: for instance, honesty, openness and willingness to assume personal responsibility for building skills strengths. Much of the learning in life coaching groups takes place between clients. Universality, instillation of hope and identification may come from other clients' disclosures. Interpersonal learning and self-understanding come from sharing and feedback within the group as well as from the advice and suggestions of the other clients. In addition, altruism is is more likely to be experienced if coaches are skilled at releasing the group's healing potential than if not.

# Preparing Coaching Groups

There are many considerations in setting up life coaching groups, only some of which are addressed here.

## Know the Subject Matter

A distinction exists between a coaching trainee's knowledge of subject matter and their delivery skills. Though it may seem obvious, if you are going to run a successful coaching group, it is essential to have a good grasp of your subject matter. There are three main kinds of subject matter knowledge that group coaches require. First, there is theoretical knowledge. Theoretical knowledge involves familiarity with explanations of how people acquire, maintain and can change their lifeskills both in general and in any specific lifeskills area for which a coaching group is envisaged. Second, there is research knowledge. What is the relevant research that has been conducted in the lifeskills area and what is its relevance to designing and leading your group? Third, there is experiential knowledge. For example, an experienced coach running a group for parents and adolescents on managing parent–adolescent conflict may have a fund of case knowledge derived from working with such problems, both with families and in previous groups. In addition, that coach may have received initial training on running coaching groups plus further supervision.

Apart from the obvious point that if you do not know your subject, you are unlikely to be able to coach clients in it well, there are a number of other reasons for possessing a good knowledge base. Knowing your subject releases time and energy for concentrating on how best to put it across. Furthermore, you are more likely to be confident if you know your material. A side effect of this confidence may be that you handle the relationships in the group better. You are also more likely to be a source of influence for clients if they perceive you as having expertise.

## Clarify and State Goals and Sub-Goals

The overall goal is the focus of the group stated in broad terms. The goals of some life coaching groups are only stated broadly: for instance, for a group supporting the work that the coach does on an individual basis. However, with more focused groups, having set out the broad skills focus of the life coaching group, the coaching trainee still needs to break these skills down into operational or working sub-goals. Say the overall goals of an assertion group are to develop clients' skills in setting limits and saying no, and in making assertive requests for behaviour change. Clients still do not know how to work towards these goals. Consequently, the trainee needs to identify what mind skills and communication skills are relevant to attaining them. Basically, when you state sub-goals in working terms, you state the specific steps in helping clients acquire the overall goals. Coaches in business and industry often use the term 'task analysis' for the process of reviewing each task selected for training.

## *Choose the Number of Coaches*

You can conduct life coaching groups on your own or with others. Some of the potential advantages for clients of having more than one coach include the following. Coaches may differ in basic characteristics such as age, gender and race. In lifeskills areas such as managing marital conflict clients may benefit from having female and male coaches. Co-coaching also allows for differences in leader personality, thus increasing the likelihood that clients will feel comfortable with at least one coach. Further reasons for having more than one coach are that it increases the range of available resources, especially where coaches have different strengths, and that individual clients may get more attention.

There are also potential advantages from working together for coaches. Working with another, you may offer lifeskills programmes to larger groups of clients than if coaching on your own. Some coaches prefer working with another coach. Coaches can support each other both emotionally and also in the mechanics of planning, designing and running the group. Coaches may also decide to perform different functions within the group: for instance, one may be more task-oriented while the other is more sensitive to relationship issues and to individual participants' anxieties and difficulties in acquiring skills. Either as co-equals or in the 'apprenticeship' model those coaching may learn from each other. This learning may take place both by observing and also from discussion and feedback between group sessions.

Below are some guidelines for effective co-coaching:

1. Work with coaches who have compatible theoretical positions and values to yourself.
2. Work with coaches whose training skills and experience you respect.
3. Work with coaches with whom you feel you can engage in frank discussion and with whom you can have a collaborative rather than a competitive relationship.
4. Coaches need to share in all aspects of the planning and running of the group, even if you decide on a division of labour.
5. Coaches need to commit time and energy to working with each other both before the group starts and also between sessions.
6. The status and role relationships between coaches require being clearly understood by each. If the coaches wish to perform different functions in the training group, you should agree on this. If one of the coaches is to exercise more power and authority, the other coach should be comfortable about this.

## *Characteristics of Groups*

### *Open or Closed Group*

One decision is whether the group should be open or closed. Life coaching groups are often closed. In many groups, clients receive cumulative instruction in specific skills, say for six to ten weeks. Other clients are not allowed to enter because they have missed out on earlier steps. In instances where groups are used to support long-term coaching, new clients are more likely to be able to join.

### *Group Size*

Though about eight members is a good size for therapy groups, life coaching groups tend to vary more in size. Practical considerations determining group size include whether there are co-leaders, the number of clients available for coaching, the focus of the group and coach confidence and skills. For instance, if life coaching is being done in a school, it is possible that a whole class will be involved. Confident coaches, who know how to run groups creatively including the possibility of using various forms of sub-grouping, can run larger groups well, whereas trainees should start by coaching relatively small groups.

### *Group Composition*

Life coaching groups that include their specific skills focus in their titles by definition can have a high degree of homogeneity. Coaching groups often target specific clienteles: for example, stressed executives or prospective fathers. A further way in which coaching groups can be homogenous is in the level at which they are offered – coaching in public speaking skills can be either basic or more advanced. Entry to the more advanced group might be conditional on successful completion of the less advanced group.

Some coaching groups are more likely to attain their goals if the clients are somewhat heterogeneous. Examples include a dating skills group composed of both females and males; a cross-cultural awareness and communication group composed of clients from different cultures; an inter-racial communication group composed of clients from different races; a coping with death and dying group composed of those dying as well as those living; a hospital group on inter-professional communication composed of clients from different professions, for example doctors and nurses; and a managing conflict group in industry composed of representatives from both unions and management.

## Group Selection

Group selection and composition are interrelated in that you try to select according to your criteria for group composition. There are at least four main ways of selecting participants for life coaching groups, albeit sometimes interrelated. First there is self-selection. A coaching group may be advertised and filled on a 'first come, first served' basis. Clients have decided on their own accord that they need to develop their skills. Sometimes self-selection includes having sufficient finances to pay for the group.

Second, there is coach selection. Coaches have their own criteria for inclusion and exclusion. They may recommend existing clients and/or conduct intake interviews in which they and potential group members can assess their mutual suitability. Third, there is third party selection. An example of selection by a third party is that of salespeople sent on effective communication courses by their sales managers. Third party selection is common in business and industry and may be viewed as either reward or punishment. Fourth, there is compulsory whole group selection. An example of this would be career education skills groups offered to all students as part of a secondary school curriculum.

A number of the above methods of selection contained elements of compulsion. Though it is possible to select people to be physically present in coaching groups, they select themselves to be psychologically present. Many coaches would much prefer not to have unwilling participants in their groups. However, sometime the coaches too are part of systems that restrict choice.

## Setting Up the Group

### Format and Length

Massed life coaching groups are intensive in that all sessions are conducted over a relatively brief period of time. Clients are likely to attend full-time. Examples of massed life coaching groups include a two-day workshop on job seeking skills for unemployed people and a one-week training course on leadership skills for newly appointed supervisors.

Spaced life coaching groups have coaching sessions spaced out; sessions may be held, weekly, biweekly or monthly, for example. Because they are less intensive, spaced groups tend to take place over a longer period of time than massed groups: say, from one month to six months. Examples of spaced life coaching groups include a one-session-a-week group on parenting skills lasting for two months and a twice-weekly career education course for high school students lasting one semester.

In massed–spaced combination, the massed element may come either at the start of or during the coaching group but rarely comes at the end. The massed section gives clients an intensive exposure to skills that then get consolidated and developed in spaced sessions and practise. An example of a massed–spaced combination is a weekend group on relationship skills run by a church minister followed by six sessions one weekday evening each week. In addition, whatever the format and length of the group, those coaching can make provision for follow-up and support.

## Location and Facilities

Where you have a choice, there are questions regarding the location, physical setting and facilities options that you need to consider. Below is a simple 12-point checklist of relevant questions.

1. If necessary, can I obtain permission to use the location?
2. Will I be able to use the same location for the whole of my coaching group?
3. Is the location easily accessible?
4. Are the physical facilities the right size?
5. Does the location offer suitable privacy?
6. Is the location free from undue noise and other unnecessary distractions?
7. Is the heating, cooling, lighting and ventilation adequate?
8. Is the decor pleasant?
9. Can the space be used flexibly?
10. Are the audio-visual facilities good?
11. Is the furniture conducive to the tasks of my group?
13. If necessary, are there adequate refreshment, toilet and parking facilities?

The above checklist is illustrative rather than exhaustive. Many coaches are forced to accept physical facilities that are far from ideal. Hopefully, the quality of your work shines through!

## Design a Coaching Programme

Programme design is major task of preparing focused skills coaching groups. Coaching group leaders have the final responsibility of putting their programmes together and implementing them. Different approaches exist to constructing programmes. For instance, coaching trainees can design programmes around existing coaching manuals/packages. Usually it is worth researching what, if any, coaching manuals and packages already exist in your lifeskills areas of interest. If you can locate suitable coaching material, some of the work of designing programmes will be done for you. However, you still adapt existing material to the specific needs of your groups.

As a group coach you can also design all aspects of your programmes on your own. Allow for flexibility within programmes designed by you in advance. For example, programmes may be altered after feedback and consultation with participants. Furthermore, in most life coaching programmes there is a role for individuals working toward personal goals as well as toward group goals. Hence, some degree of latitude is required to cater for individual needs.

You make trade-offs and compromises all the time as you try to design a programme that coaches clients in the skills in question as systematically as possible. Questions you may ask yourself include 'Given limited time, how can it best be divided between the skills I want to coach?', 'What is a good balance between didactic and facilitative input?', 'What is a good balance between working with either the whole group or breaking down into pairs or sub-groups?', 'How can I best incorporate structured learning activities?' and 'How can I make allowance for individual needs within the context of a group approach?' Rarely are the answers to these questions straightforward. Try not to get discouraged if your programme does not fall neatly into place at your first design attempt.

## Activity 9.1   Preparing a Life Coaching Group

For a life coaching group that you may wish to lead, write out or discuss with another or others the choices you intend to make concerning each of the following preparatory considerations. Refer back to the text if you are in doubt about the meaning of any of the categories.

- goals and sub-goals;
- number of coaches;
- open or closed group;
- group size;
- group composition;
- group selection;
- format and length of group;

- location and facilities;
- programme design; and
- any other considerations.

Summarize what seem to be the main concerns in preparing your life coaching group.

# Leading Coaching Group Sessions

Life coaching sessions are microcosms of overall groups. Though each session has its preparatory, initial, working and ending stages, here I focus on the last three stages. Life coaches and trainees are managers of learning. For any given session, the trainee's function is to design and implement learning experiences to help the group attain targeted skills. The trainee may perform numerous roles: energizer, facilitator, public speaker, demonstrator and role play director, among others. Throughout any session, there will always be tension, as well as sometimes harmony, between your didactic and facilitative roles. There is no such thing as the perfect group session. You are constantly making choices between conflicting demands regarding both content and process.

## The Initial Stage

It is important that sessions get off to a good start. If the opening minutes are a 'downer', this negative atmosphere may be hard to retrieve. There are a number of functions to be performed early in group sessions. Coaches and coaching trainees require the skills to perform these functions adequately.

### Set a Positive Emotional Climate

Below are a few simple guidelines for setting positive emotional climates at the start of sessions. Effective group coaches strive for businesslike, yet friendly, atmospheres.

*Arrive Fresh* You require sufficient energy to interact well with a group of participants over the whole session. If you start the session tired and out of sorts, not only may your own performance suffer, but you risk de-motivating the group.

*Arrive a Few Minutes Early*   If you arrive a few minutes early, you can sort out your materials and compose yourself. If you arrive late, you risk sending negative messages about the importance both of punctuality and the group's work.

*Welcome Participants*   Another advantage of arriving early is that you can welcome participants as they arrive. A pleasant welcome to each participant helps create a positive emotional climate, reinforces punctuality and enhances leader attractiveness.

*Start Punctually*   Starting on time is one of the most effective ways of creating the norm that clients come on time, if not early.

*Show Commitment when Introducing Sessions*   Presumably you consider the work of the session important. Without being overwhelming, let your commitment to the work of the group show by means of positive verbal, vocal and body messages.

## Outline the Session

At the end of the preceding session, you may have discussed with clients the agenda for this session. Nevertheless, it is a good idea at the start of a session to state what the targeted skills are and to outline how time will be spent. Most clients like to know both where they are going and also how the coach intends to help them get there. Outlining sessions may reduce anxieties and help clients see how the different items fit together. In addition to verbal statements, session goals and outlines can be written on whiteboards. When outlining sessions, be prepared to answer questions and clarify the group's understanding of them. In some instances, in light of group feedback, you may decide to renegotiate and alter parts of sessions.

## Review the Previous Session and Homework

Life coaching groups use cumulative learning. Sessions build on what has gone before. Coaching trainees can provide brief reviews of the main learnings of the previous session. Alternatively, they can turn the review into a warm-up activity in which clients pair off and summarize for each other their main learnings from the previous session. Reviewing the previous session is especially useful for those clients who were unable to attend it. Non-attending clients should in addition receive any handouts from missed sessions.

An important task when starting a session is to review between-session homework. Gazda observes: 'Homework is much the content of the session itself; therefore those who do not complete the homework cut down on their potential involvement in the group' (Gazda, 1989: 435). Trainees need be alert to whether or not and how well clients do homework. If homework is not being done satisfactorily, you should explore reasons for this. Often clients will want to discuss specific difficulties they experience with homework tasks and with practising targeted skills.

*Deal with New and
Unfinished Business*

Coaching trainees need to be sensitive to new business that clients bring into groups and to unfinished business from previous sessions. Many things may have happened in clients' lives since the last session. Clients may bring new joys, hurts and momentous events into sessions. In addition, they may be faced with immediate pressing situations involving use of targeted skills. There are no simple answers on how to deal with new business brought into groups. Probably it is best to allow major emotions to be aired. Bottling up strong emotions can act as a block to participation and learning.

Clients themselves may act as gatekeepers for relevance. For example, they may appreciate the chance to get support during a personal crisis but be very sensitive about disrupting the group's skills learning. Furthermore, though not guaranteed, personal crises can be good material for illustrating and working on targeted skills. Sometimes, arising from previous sessions, both clients and trainee may have issues that they wish to bring up. Again, it is probably wise to allow such issues to be aired. Both trainee and group can then decide how much attention these issues merit.

Activity 9.2 is designed to raise your awareness of some issues and coaching skills for the initial stage of sessions.

## Activity 9.2   Starting a Coaching Group Session

Carry out the following activities:

1.  Make up a worksheet by drawing a line down the middle of a page and at the top of the left column writing 'Harmful activities' and at the top of the right column 'Helpful activities'. Think back over any life coaching groups in which you have participated either as client or coach. In the relevant columns, list harmful and helpful activities when starting sessions.

2.  Discuss the role and importance of each of the following skills in the initial stage of training sessions:

    (1)   setting a positive emotional climate;
    (2)   outlining sessions;
    (3)   reviewing the previous session;
    (4)   reviewing homework; and
    (5)   dealing with new and unfinished business.

3.  If possible, work with colleagues and role-play starting a life coaching session in the middle of a group's life. After the role play, discuss the major learnings for when you lead coaching group sessions in future. If possible, give everyone the chance to be a coach in a different role play.

## The Working Stage

There is no clear working stage to life coaching sessions. The work of the group takes place in the initial and ending stages as well. Here the working stage is defined as the middle section of the session – say, after the first ten minutes and up to the last ten minutes. The working stage is the large central heart of the session. During this period new material is introduced and previous material worked over.

### Maintain a Skills Focus

Clients join life coaching groups to acquire and develop specific skills, be they communication skills, mind skills or both. These skills entail learning specific behaviours. Trainees coaching groups, as managers of learning, need to beware of allowing sessions to lose much, if not all, of their skills focus. Sometimes sessions are not planned with sufficient skills emphasis

146

in the preparatory stage. For instance, trainees are insufficiently specific about targeted skills. In addition, trainees may have wrongly planned the balance between discussion and structured skills development.

Three ways in which trainees may dilute the skills focus of a session are by focusing too much on feelings, relationships and problems. In each instance the issue is likely to be one of balance rather than rightness or wrongness. In regard to focusing overly on feelings take the example of a spouse in a managing conflict group who comes to a session extremely agitated after a marital fight. One option is for the leader to focus only on feelings; for example, 'Tell us more about how you felt in the situation?' Another option is to focus only on communication; for example, 'How did you communicate in the situation and how could you have improved on it?' Still another option is to focus on both feelings and communication; 'You are extremely upset, what was good and what was possibly not so good about the way you managed your feelings and communicated?' In the last example, the trainee's response both reflects a feeling and also focuses on feelings in the context of developing skills.

Trainees may focus overly on the relationships within the group. In life coaching, such relationships are important mainly to the extent that they enhance or obstruct the group's learning. If relationship issues within the group can be used to illustrate targeted skills, they may merit attention. Otherwise, trainees should resist turning coaching group sessions into encounter group sessions. In addition, when participants bring problem situations into sessions, trainees need to be careful about focusing too much on the emotions and details of problems rather on the application of targeted skills to problems.

## Use the Group Creatively

Many coaches and trainees either by choice or by necessity work in groups of over eight clients. These coaches are faced with trying to design learning experiences that overcome some of the disadvantages of large group size. One way of mitigating or getting around the problem of large group size is to use co-leaders or coaches' aides. However, bringing in extra coaches is not always possible. Another way is to use good audio-visual presentations. You then use your energy for managing the group. A third way is to be creative in your use of the group. Varying its format is recommended even for small groups of six to eight.

You can vary the tasks, numbers and seating in your groups. Already, in the chapter on consolidating skills, suggestions have been made for varying the tasks in which the group engages. Numerical variations include working with the whole group or breaking it down into small groups, quartets, triads, dyads or even singles. Those coaching may make decisions on the size of working groups either on their own or in consultation with clients. You can also vary the seating pattern of the group from that of a horseshoe. Seating variations include circular, be it the whole group or for sub-groups; the fishbowl, with inner and outer rings; and having a 'stage' for role plays in some part of the room with the audience in a semi-circle – the stage's location may depend on where a video camera is mounted.

## Actively Involve Participants

Getting and keeping participants actively involved is a major skill of effective group coaches. It is all too easy for clients' attention spans and motivation to falter during what may be a long working stage of over an hour or more. Already, some suggestions have been made for getting clients involved at a session's start. Throughout a session, breaking the group down in various ways can encourage involvement. Furthermore, judicious use of structured activities can provide excellent opportunities for participation. Below are some additional suggestions for how coaches and trainees can get and keep clients actively involved.

*Tune In and Check Out*   Coaching trainees as managers of learning should pay close attention to whether items in a session work for clients. You require empathy to how learning experiences are understood and received. For instance, if you sense that participants are getting restless with a presentation you may either try to be more stimulating or move on to something more active. You also require 'checking out' skills. For example, if you perceive that clients show little energy or interest for specific activities you can check out your perception with the group. Tuning in and checking out skills are also applicable to working with individuals. You require sensitivity to individual differences in learning styles and attention spans. However, you can distort the group's work if you pay too much attention to unrepresentative feedback from individuals. Nevertheless, helping individual participants through learning blocks may be good for both individuals and groups.

*Ask 'Drawing In' Questions*   Good group coaches rarely, if ever, allow clients to be passive for long periods of time. Active participation covers thinking as well as doing. Even when giving presentations, try to keep participants' minds active. You can ask questions that have the effect of drawing clients in to sessions. Such questions may be either for anyone in the group to answer, or may entail going round the group with each person answering, or may be addressed to individuals – possibly those who have not participated much to that point. The following are examples of 'drawing in' questions:

Can anyone give me an example of ----------?
Has anyone experienced ------------?
What are your reactions to ----------?
What skills does she/he need to manage the situation better?
Does the demonstration trigger off anything in how any of you might behave differently?
Does anyone have any specific feedback that they would like to give to----------[*mention name*] after observing that role play?

In all the above instances, if you ask questions of the group, your body messages should match your intentions. For example, your eyes should scan the group rather than be fixed on one individual. Any arm movements should show openness to the group, for instance a sweeping gesture, rather than closing off options (for instance, by pointing at someone).

*Reward Helpful Involvement*    Coaches and trainees can literally encourage – give courage to – clients who share experiences, answer questions and take part in activities. You can give both verbal and non-verbal rewards. Examples of verbal rewards for active involvement include 'Thanks for volunteering for the role play', 'That's a good example' and 'I appreciate your sharing that with the group'. Sometimes you may choose to reflect clients' answers to show and check out that you have heard them correctly. In addition, you can support clients as they take part in activities and exercises, for instance by showing consideration for their thoughts and feelings. Examples of non-verbal rewards for getting actively involved include head nods, smiles, pats on the back and so on.

*Curtail Harmful Involvement*    Clients singly or as a group can disrupt the coach and each other by interrupting, showing off, making a joke of the proceedings, talking loudly to each other, and throwing paper darts, among other behaviours. Sometimes destructive behaviours are best ignored. Either the behaviours will drop off of their own accord or other clients will deal with perpetrators.

If the disruptive behaviours persist in interfering with the learning of the remainder of the group, you must consider how best to intervene, and make your interventions appropriate to the behaviours you want to curtail.

For instance, if clients ramble on vaguely, they can be asked to talk about specific behaviours. If clients present discipline problems, there are a number of options. Part of the skill of the group leader is to get potentially disruptive elements in the group 'on side' rather than 'off side'. Consequently, use the minimum 'muscle' necessary to achieve the desired results. Sometimes humour can defuse situations of potential conflict. Giving disruptive clients 'the teacher's eye' may be sufficient to curtail their behaviour. You can also help disruptive clients explore their resistances. Moving further up the hierarchy of 'muscle', you can make behaviour change requests in a firmer voice and, if necessary, repeat them. In addition, you and the other clients can point out the consequences of the disruptive behaviour on the learning environment.

*Use Mini-Breaks*    'Take five'. Sometimes the use of mini-breaks can help keep clients actively involved. Both having brief breaks or time out periods and also providing coffee, tea and soft drinks may be conducive to involvement. In addition, the opportunity for fresh air and physical movement may help.

## Make Balancing Choices

During a session, coaching group leaders are faced with numerous choices concening what is a good balance between conflicting considerations. Some of the considerations you have to balance include: being didactic or facilitative; making decisions alone or sharing decisions with the group; presenting and demonstrating versus doing activities; how much to work with individuals; whether to work with the whole group or break it down; how much to focus on communication skills or mind skills; whether to adhere to or deviate from session plans; whether to allow discussion or cut it off; and whether to be serious or humorous.

Constant tensions between conflicting considerations exist in all coaching groups. Coaching trainees can make some of the above choices in advance. However, what actually happens depends on the choices you make during sessions. Trainees who decide in advance what their main session goals are, how they want the emotional climate in sessions to be, and what their own role is are in stronger positions to make balancing decisions than those who are unclear about these issues. If you think that you have got the balance between some of these considerations wrong, you can often retrieve situations either later in the same session or in subsequent sessions.

### *Keep the Session Moving*

Group coaches need to keep sessions moving. Keeping a session moving does not mean pressurizing participants all the time. Rather, assuming the time distribution has been well planned, you can keep the group moving at a comfortable pace to complete the session's various tasks. Giving an outline at the session's start can help keep it moving. As a result clients should be clear about the ground to be covered. The outline also provides a positive context for your transition statements. Here are some possible transition statements:

> Well, that's the end of my initial presentation of how to generate and evaluate different perceptions in situations you find difficult. If there are no further questions, I would now like to coach one of you through the steps of this skill in relation to a specific situation.
>
> Does anyone have anything pressing they would like to add before we move on to?
>
> Does Wayne have anything to add or does anyone else have anything that they would like to feed back to Wayne before we move on to the next role play?
>
> Though this is an interesting discussion, we seem to be getting away from the skills building purpose of this session. I suggest we curtail the discussion and move on.

## *The Ending Stage*

Effective group coaches pay close attention to how they end sessions. Much of the work of lifeskills coaching groups goes on between sessions. Therefore, coaches and trainees have the added reason of taking full advantage of between-session time for ending sessions well.

### *Ending Stage Tasks*

Quite apart from calling a halt to the proceedings, a number of tasks may be performed in the ending stage of a session. These tasks include the following:

*Summarize*   The main points of the session can be summarized either by the coach or by clients. You can check that clients not only know what to do but also how to instruct themselves when using targeted skills.

*Correct Misunderstandings*   If clients misunderstand some of the session's learnings, you may be able to put them right before the session ends. However, you must defer major corrective instruction and coaching to the next session.

*Set and Formulate Homework*   Sometimes trainees will ask clients to complete prepared homework tasks. On other occasions, you may work with clients to design individual behaviour change experiments and other activities. You need to ensure that clients are clear about what is wanted in homework tasks. You can also help clients to identify and work through blocks to doing homework.

*Obtain Feedback*   Trainees can check out with clients their reactions to the session – what seemed to work for them and what did not.

*Consult*   Trainees can share with participants their ideas for the agenda and activities for the next session. Clients can be asked for their reactions and suggestions.

*Deal with Unfinished Business*   With their emphasis on behaviours rather than emotions, coaching group sessions tend to end with less unfinished business than counselling group sessions. Nevertheless, if there are feelings and hidden agendas that may interfere with the group's work, it is probably best for these to be aired. You can then decide whether these emotions and agendas merit more attention either now or in future.

*Arrange for Mutual Support*   Trainees can raise the issue of clients supporting each other, perhaps in a 'buddy' system, between sessions. For example, clients might phone their buddy at least once to discuss progress.

*Indicate Between-Session Contact*   Trainees may indicate what, if any, between-session contact you are prepared to have with clients. Many coaches discourage clients asking routine questions, for instance concerning homework, between sessions. They expect clients to stay alert and ask such questions during sessions.

## Ending Stage Skills

During the ending stage of sessions coaches use numerous skills: facilitating, checking out, summarizing and setting homework, among others. Here a few further skills are discussed specific to the ending stage:

*End on Time*   It is a good discipline for both coaches and the group that sessions start and end on time. Ending on time has the following advantages for you: providing a firm limit on session content, letting you get away gracefully and cuing clients to raise important issues during the session. Clients appreciate it if the contract on session length is kept and they can make arrangements accordingly.

*Allow Time for Ending*   When designing and managing sessions, trainees need to allow sufficient time to end the session well. Allowing sufficient time for ending means paying attention to timekeeping throughout the session so that there is not a build up of work by the end. Depending on the length of the whole session and on your aim to achieve at the ending stage, perhaps 5 to 20 minutes may be set aside for it.

*Make a Transition Statement*   When outlining the life coaching programme at the first session, trainees may make it clear to clients that in each session there will be an initial, a working and an ending stage. Nevertheless, when the time comes for the ending stage in each session, you still need to make transition statements. Such transition statements shift the focus of the group to the work of the ending stage. The following are examples of transition statements:

> I realize that this is an important issue for you and perhaps we can come back to it. However, we have about ten minutes left now. I would like to spend this time to get the group to summarize its main learnings from the session and to clarify homework.

> We are coming to the end of the session now. The time has come to consolidate learnings, sort out homework and look ahead to the next session.

*Actively Involve Participants*   During the ending stage of sessions, as in earlier stages, trainees can actively involve participants. For example, when summarizing one format is for the coach to summarize, another format is for one or more clients to summarize. The listening clients can then be asked to either verify or correct the summaries. You can also ask questions to be answered by anyone in the group, for example, 'Does anyone have any feedback they want to give about the session?' or do rounds in which each client gets the opportunity to speak, for example, 'I'm now going to give each of you the opportunity to comment on what, if anything, you've learned from today's session.

*Strengthen Commitment to Between-Session Work*   Trainees can encourage clients to use the time between sessions fruitfully. Homework tasks and using targeted skills outside the group should be presented in a positive light. The time between sessions is really an extension of the session in which clients get the opportunity to practise, develop and consolidate skills. When devising homework tasks, you can check that they have relevance for clients' personal goals. Sometimes you may need to help clients state homework goals specifically, realistically and with a time frame. You may also explore with clients the pay-offs for doing between-session homework and changing their behaviour.

## Activity 9.3    Leading a Coaching Group Session

1.  In regard to either your life coaching group from Activity 9.1 or for another life coaching group, discuss how you might use each of the following coaching skills for the working stage of your session:

    (a)   maintaining a skills focus;
    (b)   using the group creatively;
    (c)   actively involving clients;
    (d)   making balancing choices; and
    (e)   keeping the session moving.

2.  In regard to the same group, discuss how you might use each of the following coaching skills for the ending stage of your session:

    (a)   ending on time;
    (b)   allowing time for ending;
    (c)   making a transition statement;
    (d)   actively involving clients; and
    (e)   strengthening commitment to homework.

3.  If possible, work with colleagues and role-play leading the whole of a coaching group session. After the role play discuss major learnings for when you lead coaching group sessions in future. If possible, give everyone the chance to be the coach in a different role play – to save time, sessions may have to be co-coached.

# 10
# Relationship Skills Coaching

This and the next two chapters focus on specific areas of life coaching: namely relationship skills, work and occupation skills, and health skills. People learn how to relate, for good or ill, mainly from the demonstrations and rewards provided by parents, peers, teachers and others. Few people are brought up to view how they relate in skills terms. For instance, the concept of mind skills is not widespread. Nor, despite their central importance throughout life, are many people systematically coached in relationship skills; overt communication skills are rarely broken down into their verbal, vocal and bodily elements. These reasons contribute to the vast number of relationship problems that people experience. In addition, few people currently attain and maintain really outstanding relationships.

There are a number of ways of viewing relationship skills coaching. Its goals can range from helping young people acquire basic skills to dealing with problems, handling transitions from one life stage to the next, and helping people gain greater happiness and fulfillment. Further goals include coaching people in skills for finding relationships, starting relationships, improving relationships, building partnerships, managing problems, rejuvenating relationships and, where necessary, ending relationships. Relationships in which people require skills can be intimate relationships, relating to both younger and older family members, friendships, getting along with neighbours, relating to school and work colleagues and relating to those in authority, among others.

Though this chapter focuses on individual coaching, relationship coaching is frequently done with couples and families. In addition, group relationship coaching is quite common, for instance for students, couples and work colleagues. Here are some examples of relationship skills coaching:

> Ellie, 28, coaches Emily, 17, in the mind skills and communication skills of having genuine friendships with males that have the opportunity of growing into an intimate relationship. Ellie is careful not to impose any deadlines or pressures to perform on Emily. Rather Emily is coached to explore and learn what she likes, as well as specific skills for relating to others.

> Robin, 38, coaches Bruce, 32, in the mind skills and communication skills of being more forthcoming and assertive in both his personal and work relationships. Up until now, Bruce has been too ready to agree and go along with what other people want rather than risk not being liked for seeking what he really wants.

> Megan, 47, coaches Ray, 44, in the skills of being a good parent to his children Bettina, 12, and Richard, 10. Ray came from a broken family where the children's needs were not adequately attended to and he wants to make sure not to repeat this with his children.

> Tom, 62, seeks out a coach, Brian, 57, because he has recently retired and now wants to build his skills of finding and making friends both with and independently of his wife, Sarah, 60. Prior to retiring Tom had a job that he felt left him with little time and energy for his personal life apart from his immediate family.

> Charlize, 52, coaches Shirley, 35, in the skills of managing conflict better with her husband Jeff, 37. Shirley wants to save the relationship before matters get really bad and realizes that she has to examine her own behaviour closely and not just complain about how Jeff treats her.

## What are Relationship Skills?

Already I have indicated that lifeskills are areas of choice that may be well or poorly made and this holds true for relationship skills. Relationship skills entail people in using mind skills and communication skills. Furthermore, communication skills can be thought of as having verbal, vocal, bodily, touch and taking action elements. Box 10.1 lists some relationship skills.

---

### Box 10.1   Some Relationship Skills

- Skills for listening and showing understanding.
- Skills for choosing and starting relationships.
- Skills for managing shyness.
- Skills for developing intimacy.
- Skills for sexual relationship.
- Assertiveness skills.
- Skills for anger management.
- Skills for managing relationship problems.

---

For various relationships people require a *repertoire* of relationship skills. Sometimes they may not have a particular skill in their repertoire: for instance, the ability to say no to an unreasonable request. Other times they may want to strengthen a particular skill, such as expressing appreciation to a loved one. With some skills, they may also want to strike a more appropriate balance: for example, neither depending too much nor too little on others. People should eliminate some relationship skills weaknesses altogether: for instance, physical or sexual abuse. A person's repertoire of relationship skills comprises their strengths and weaknesses in each skills area.

## Coaching Relationship Skills

Flaherty writes, 'This may seem like an obvious point, but it's a vital one in coaching, because a coach is never able to begin coaching at the real beginning. The coach always begins in the middle' (1999: 25). Coaching in relationship skills always starts with people who have learned to relate in the skills in question for good or ill. Though they may have learned many good skills that need to be maintained and developed, they may also have learned poor ones, including sometimes an inability to see that they are insufficiently skilled in certain areas. Sometimes, people really know the skills in question and just require the coach to provide an enabling relationship in which they can show the skills they seemingly lack. The following illustrative sections assume that people also require a degree of assistance in knowing what the required skills are and how to enact them (Nelson-Jones, 2006b).

## *Skills for Listening and Showing Understanding*

Zeno of Citium said, 'The reason why we have two ears and only one mouth is that we may listen the more and talk the less.' Virtually everyone is not as good at listening as is desirable. Some people are in psychological pain and, until this is addressed, cannot release enough of themselves to listen to others properly. Many people have just not been brought up to listen properly and can be helped by coaching. Rewarding listening entails not only accurately understanding speakers' communications but showing and, where necessary, clarifying understanding.

Listening and showing understanding is a skill made up of many sub-skills. These include: possessing an attitude of respect and acceptance; understanding the speaker's internal viewpoint; sending good vocal and body messages; using opening remarks, small rewards and open-ended questions; paraphrasing and reflecting feelings. Since reflecting feelings is so important to listening, it is the skill on which I focus here.

In coaching the reflection of feelings, trainees must focus both on the receiver skills of picking up feelings words and phrases, and on the sender skills of showing their understanding. Skillful reflection of feelings words and phrases requires trainees to paying close attention to matters such as strength of feelings, and multiple and mixed feelings. Also sometimes trainees need to assist with the labelling of feelings. For instance, a male client might say 'I don't know quite how to express my feelings toward her, possibly angry … upset, no that's not quite it . . . .', to which the trainee adds, 'Hurt, anxious, confused … do any of these words strike a chord?' In addition, trainees may have to coach clients in paying more attention to speakers' vocal and body messages.

When trainees have helped clients decode others' feelings messages, they still need to coach clients in showing that they have accurately understood speakers. For instance, they can coach clients in how to reflect the crux of a message, keep responses simple, use vocal and body messages to add expressiveness to their verbal messages and, where appropriate, to reflect feelings and the reasons for them. Here is an example:

| | |
|---|---|
| *Penny:* | We used to have a really good relationship. Now I just despair about ever getting it back on track. I feel so down. |
| *Coaching trainee*: | You feel really low because you just do not see your way forward to retrieving the relationship. |

In addition, trainees must ensure that clients check their understanding. Sometimes messages are checked by slight voice inflections. On other occasions, clients can check by asking directly: for instance, 'Do I understand you properly?'

### Activity 10.1   Coaching a Client in Skills for Reflecting Feelings

Work with someone who acts as a client who needs to improve their listening skills in a particular situation, be it as a parent, as a partner, in a work or recreational setting, or in some other relationship.

1. For the following statement, identify the words Rafael has used to describe how he feels. *Rafael [to friend]:* 'I find being without a girlfriend depressing. Right now my prospects look bleak.'
   Rafael's feelings words:

   _____

   Your reflection of Rafael's feelings:

   _____

   _____

2. Work with the client in generating some statements from another person in a situation important to them, get her or him identifying the feelings words and then reflect on the feelings. Provide feedback as necessary.

3. Continue with task 2 but extend it to coaching the client in reflecting feelings and reasons.

### Skills for Choosing and Starting a Relationship

Coaches and trainees sometimes work with clients who want to start having a committed relationship. They can help some such people to develop systematic search-and-find skills to locate eligible partners. Search skills include reviewing existing networks, identifying gaps in them and brainstorming different ways to meet eligible partners. In addition, clients need to identify any ways that they might be putting off potential partners. Find skills include clients activating their networks, entertaining friends, spending less time or no time with some people, joining clubs and attending social events, taking advantage of chance encounters, accepting invitations and developing skills of being rewarding.

Where necessary, trainees can also help clients to develop 'getting to know you' skills. Some clients need to work on becoming better at disclosing themselves by increasing the breadth and depth of what they reveal.

Other getting to know you skills are to listen and understand well and to use good assertiveness skills, including resisting pressures to have unwanted sex.

Coaching trainees can focus on clients' mind skills for choosing a partner. Hamburg writes that 'the key to a happy marriage is picking the right person in the first place – someone with whom you are deeply compatible' (2000: 16). Hamburg's three dimensions for choosing a partner are the practical, sexual and wavelength dimensions. Though the initial saying 'yes' to another human being may be on first sight or meeting, it takes time to gather appropriate evidence to justify the initial choice. Trainees may need to help clients learn to make better decisions about potential partners and avoid rushing into commitment.

Clients can be helped to assess the influence of parental rules on their choosing a partner. They can also examine their rules about how people behave in close relationships, including their rules about sex roles. Trainees can also help clients to perceive themselves and potential partners accurately: for example, they may underestimate their own attractiveness and exaggerate that of another. In addition, trainees can work with clients on their self-talk in dating situations so that, if necessary, they calm themselves down and coach themselves though the tasks involved in getting to know another person. Trainees can help some clients, especially those with strong imaginations, use visualizing skills to gain information about potential partners (Lazarus, 1984, 2005). For instance, using time projection, clients can visualize how life together might be at some stage in the future. Trainees can also help clients to explain accurately what has happened in their past relationships and what is happening now. In addition, trainees can help clients to have realistic expectations both about the process of finding a partner and about life together.

## Skills for Managing Shyness

People do not need to be seriously disturbed to be shy. Zimbardo (1977) found that more than 80 per cent of respondents in his large-scale shyness survey reported that they were shy at some point in their lives. People can worry about social situations beforehand, be shy in them, and then think about them in recurrent and intrusive ways afterwards (Rachman, Gruter-Andrew and Shafran, 2000).

Coaches can help clients to develop more confident communication skills. One skill is that of introducing yourself. Trainees can help clients to give a brief greeting and clearly state who they are, for example, 'Hello, I'm Jane/John Smith.' If necessary, clients can be coached in speaking at a comfortable volume, clearly and fairly slowly so that others may hear them, as well as on smiling and looking the other person in the eye. Trainees can encourage clients to develop a repertoire of appropriate opening remarks and encourage others' attempts to make conversation with small rewards like 'really' and head nods.

Meeting new people involves searching for common ground. Clients can be coached to respect another's privacy when asking questions by not probing too deeply and when talking about themselves to match or even go slightly beyond the intimacy level of the speakers' disclosures. Shy people often have trouble ending conversations. Clients can be coached to break eye contact, start to edge away and make their body orientation less open, as body messages that they want to get away. They can also be made more conscious of the verbal messages that they give as signals for whether they want the relationship to continue or not: for instance, 'I hope we meet again' as contrasted with 'Well, that's about the sum of it.'

Coaching trainees can make clients aware that one of the main ways that they sustain their shyness is by thinking shy. For instance, unrealistic rules that contribute to people sustaining their shyness are, 'I must be liked by everyone I meet' and 'I must never make a mistake in social situations' (Ellis 2003, 2005; Ellis and Crawford, 2000). Coaching trainees can help clients to detect, dispute and restate irrational into rational rules. For instance, a restatement for 'I must never make a mistake in social situations' is 'To err is human. Though I would prefer not to make mistakes I can use them as learning experiences.' Trainees can also help shy clients to perceive more accurately. For instance, skills they can use to perceive themselves more accurately include owning their strengths and challenging their negative perceptions. In addition, they can use detecting, disputing and restating skills to perceive situations more accurately. Clients can also use calming and coaching self-talk to handle shyness situations better as well as using visual rehearsal to imagine performing competently. Coaching trainees can work with clients' explanations for shyness and help them take more responsibility for doing something about it. In addition, some clients are helped by changing their expectations to focus more on the gains than the risks of being more social.

## Skills for Developing Intimacy

Adjectives associated with the noun intimacy include private, personal, close and familiar. Beck (1988: 242) observes: 'Intimacy can range from discussing everyday details of your life, to confiding the most private feeling that you would not share with anybody else, to your sexual relationship'. Coaching trainees may need to help some clients become more intimate with themselves prior to becoming more intimate with others. For instance, if they are out of touch with their feelings, they are unlikely to experience another's feelings accurately. If such clients can be assisted to possess a more secure sense of their identity and accept themselves as independent yet fallible human beings, they are more likely to accept the full humanness of another.

Coaching trainees can help clients reach out to others by working with them on their ability to express feelings as they are identified and to change them as they understand better what they feel. Some clients require skills of letting themselves be known. Such skills include taking the initiative, requesting disclosure time, asserting themselves, taking calculated risks and reciprocating intimacy.

Trainees may also need to coach clients on receiving information to assist others in sharing very private information. For instance, clients may need to learn unconditional acceptance in which they accept another as a person independent of their specific behaviours. Other receiving intimacy skills are encouraging the experiencing and exploring of feelings, showing involvement and choosing whether or not to reciprocate.

Coaching trainees can assist clients in maintaining their interactive pattern of intimacy. An example of an unbalanced intimacy pattern is that of one partner, frequently the female, striving for greater emotional closeness, with the other partner, usually the male, preferring to keep emotionally distant (Christensen and Jacobson, 2000). Trainees can help clients to talk with their partners about how they relate. Egan calls this skill immediacy, or 'you–me' talk. He distinguishes between relationship immediacy ('Let's talk about how we've been relating to each other recently') and here-and-now immediacy ('Let's talk about what's going on between you and me right now as we're talking to each other') (Egan, 1977: 235). Skills for 'you-me' talk sessions include getting in touch with what you think and feel, sending 'I' messages, being specific and inviting rather than cutting off discussion of the points made. Trainees can also encourage clients to allocate sufficient time to maintain their relationships.

Trainees can work with clients' mind skills regarding intimacy. Clients can identify and challenge unrealistic rules concerning intimacy: for instance, 'I must have immediate and total affection', 'Others must always treat my feelings with great respect' and 'We must put career and other daily activities ahead of creating time to talk about our relationship.' Regarding creating perceptions, coaching trainees can help clients become more aware of and diminish defensive thinking. Clients can also be helped to perceive the other more accurately by collecting more information and avoiding jumping to conclusions. Clients can also use calming and coaching self-talk when revealing something sensitive about themselves or when receiving another's intimate disclosure. By using their imagination, clients can develop a better understanding of their partner's life experience. In addition, they can visually rehearse how to reach out to them. Regarding creating explanations, trainees can help clients explore and challenge reasons why they are less than successful in developing and maintaining intimacy in their relationships. Clients can also examine the gains as well as the risks of intimacy with themselves, reaching out, receiving another's intimacy, and developing and maintaining a good pattern of intimacy.

## Skills for Sexual Relationships

In its most basic form sexual relating is physical activity involving mutual genital contact for the purpose of procreating the species. Coaching trainees may discuss the purpose of sex with clients. Hamburg (2000) states that the sexual dimension in relationships has three components: comfort with sexuality, interest in sex and sexual style. Comfort with sex means how relaxed you and your partner are about doing all the various things that are connected with sex. Interest in sex means how preoccupied each partner is with sex and how often you want to do it. Sexual style is derived from your sense of what sex is primarily about – for instance, experiencing profound emotional connection or seeking pleasure. Sexual style also relates to the kind of identity or identities you want to take on during sex – for instance, masterful or passive. It is crucial that partners' sexual styles fit well enough so that each can enact and express their style freely.

In all cultures, males and females are subject to sex-role conditioning. However, in terms of their sexual functioning, men and women are 'incredibly and consistently similar' (Masters and Johnson, 1970: 38). Some clients may require assistance in behaving in ways that are sexually equal.

Coaching trainees may discuss kinds of sexual activity with clients: for instance, positions for sexual intercourse and ways of touching. In addition they may discuss with clients the conditions for sexual activity such as being in the mood, turn ons and turn offs, the surroundings, and timing and duration. Some clients may require knowledge about preventing conception and sexually transmitted diseases.

Clients may require coaching in communication skills for sexual relationships. Trainees may help them to express tenderness and affection and also to develop a comfortable language for sex talk as they disclose their own and tune into their partner's sexuality. With sexual equality, each partner has a right to express sexual likes and dislikes. Some clients may require help in becoming more assertive about sex, including having fun. Clients may also require assistance in discussing and negotiating issues connected with their sex life.

Masters and Johnson emphasize the point about inhibitions and guilt, performance anxiety, erotic boredom, and blind acceptance of sexual mis-information and myths accounting for most of the sexual dissatisfaction in American society (Masters, Johnson and Kolodny, 1986). Coaching trainees can work with clients' mind skills regarding sexual relationships. For example, they can work with clients to challenge unrealistic rules that interfere with sexual happiness. Such rules may concern body image, sex-roles, sexual feelings, sexual acts, sexual performance, power and control, and changing. Trainees may also help clients to challenge unrealistic per-ceptions about sex, such as 'sex is dirty', and to value their sexuality. Clients may be helped to get an adequate picture of themselves as sexual persons, including acknowledging and being able to communicate their unique sex-ual wishes. In addition, clients may be helped to obtain a fuller picture of how to pleasure their partner.

Trainees may need to work with clients' self-talk concerning sex. For instance, clients may require assistance in being calm and communicating clearly what they want. Some clients may require encouragement and assistance in sharing their sexual fantasies with their partners. Trainees can also impart visualizing skills to help clients perform more adequately. Lazarus (1984: 73) offers the basic rule: 'If you wish to accomplish some-thing in reality, first picture yourself achieving it in your imagination'. Some clients require assistance in creating more realistic explanations about their sex life, for instance avoiding blaming themselves or their partner and acknowledging that it is possible to improve their sex lives. Trainees can also work with clients' expectations about sex. Clients can systematically assess the realism of their expectations. For example, a client could ask herself or himself 'What are the gains of telling my part-ner what I want sexually?' as well as 'What are the risks of telling her or him?'

## Assertiveness Skills

Assertiveness is one of the most common areas of relationship skills coach-ing. Assertive behaviour, as contrasted with non-assertive and aggressive behaviour, entails responding flexibly and appropriately strongly in differ-ent situations. Alberti and Emmons define assertiveness as follows:

Assertive behavior promotes equality in human relationships, enabling us to act in our own best interests, to stand up for ourselves without undue anxiety, to express honest feelings comfortable, to exercise personal rights without denying the rights of others. (2001: 36)

In reality, a person's degree of assertiveness depends not only on the present situation but on one's genetic make-up, parental upbringing and the extent to which one has been victimized by peers (Gibb, Abramson and Alloy, 2004). When helping clients become more assertive, coaching trainees need to make sure to focus on vocal and body as well as verbal messages. Clients often require help in using the right amount of 'muscle' and with the timing of their assertive messages.

Coaching trainees sometimes need to work with clients on how to disagree assertively. Clients can soften their message by first reflecting the other person's message before stating their own: for example ,'You want us to go to dinner but I would rather eat at home.' They can also make statements like 'I beg to differ' and 'I'd prefer that we didn't.' Some clients require coaching on how to say 'no' assertively. Part of this is learning not to feel afraid or guilty about saying 'no'. Another part is actually saying 'no' backed up by vocal, body and, if necessary, taking action messages that show that you mean what you say.

Related to saying no, clients may require coaching on how to set limits on other people's behaviour. Trainees may also need to coach clients in how to request changes in behaviour, be it requesting a new behaviour, more of an existing behaviour or less or the cessation of an existing behaviour. For example, an assertive request to lessen an existing behaviour might be, 'When you're playing your compact disc so loudly, I cannot concentrate on revising for my exam tomorrow. Please turn the volume down?' Defensiveness is a common initial reaction to assertive messages, so clients may need to be coached in how to handle this too. Clients may also require coaching in how to encourage one another's assertion' for instance by providing openings and showing understanding.

Coaching clients to become more assertive also involves paying attention to their mind skills. Alberti and Emmons (2001: 81) observe: 'Right *thinking* about assertiveness is crucial. Thoughts, beliefs, attitudes and feelings set the stage for behavior'. Trainees can work to alter clients' unrealistic rules. The first step is to help clients become aware that they possess them. Next trainee and client can logically analyse how realistic they are and their positive and negative consequences. Then trainees can work with clients on restating unrealistic rules into flexible ones. For instance, the unrealistic rule 'I/my partner must never hurt each other' might be altered into the following realistic rule: 'While I prefer not to hurt my partner, I think it is important to confront significant issues between us.'

Trainees can help clients perceive being assertive more accurately. For instance, they can challenge female clients who consider assertiveness as 'unfeminine', 'bitchy' and 'castrating' (Butler, 1992). They can also work with clients' self-talk and get them to replace negative statements like 'I'm going to stuff it up' and 'What's the use?' with coping self-talk statements like 'calm down', followed by specific coaching self-talk statements. In addition, trainees can help clients use mental rehearsal that focuses on enacting competent verbal, vocal and body messages in specific situations.

Trainees may challenge clients' faulty explanations for not being assertive. For instance, clients may see themselves as lacking in confidence because of their nature or that they are a hapless victim of circumstance. Clients may also think that their partner should know what bothers them without being told. Such clients need to be helped to take responsibility for thinking, feeling and communicating assertively. In addition, clients may be excessively frightened of the negative consequences of being assertive and underestimate the positive consequences. If so, they can be challenged to appraise realistically the potential gains and losses from acting assertively.

## Skills for Anger Management

Anger or hostility can range from mild anger to extreme rage, be it short term or ranged over a long period of time, and can be acknowledged or denied in some measure. Research in the USA shows that men and women are angered by similar things, experience anger equally strongly and tend to express anger in similar ways (Deffenbacher, Oetting and DiGuiseppe, 2002). However, in close relationships, the expression of anger does not take place on a level playing field since men tend to be stronger and control more resources than women.

Coaching trainees can help clients to keep their tempers: for instance, by breathing slowly and regularly when feeling provoked, by counting to 10 or 100, or by taking 'time out'. Trainees can also coach clients to express anger assertively. Alberti and Emmons (2001: 143) observe: 'Remember that anger and aggression are not the same thing! Aggression is a style of behavior. Anger can be expressed assertively – aggression is not the only alternative'. Clients can learn to give specific feedback about what bothers them, state their feelings as 'I' messages and let another know what they want. Furthermore, they can accompany their assertive verbal messages with appropriate vocal and body messages.

Trainees can also help clients handle stress and relax themselves: for instance by muscular and visualized relaxation, by staying physically fit and by developing support networks. Trainees can coach clients in strategies for dealing with aggressive criticism. For example, they may learn to reflect it, give feedback about it, or back off now and react at a later date. Sometimes clients require assistance in apologizing and taking corrective action or, if the innocent party, in forgiving and moving on (Worthington and Scherer, 2004).

Trainees can work with clients' mind skills to help them become less angry. Clients can be helped to build the skills of identifying unrealistic rules, disputing them and replacing them with more realistic ones (Ellis, 2005). Sample unrealistic rules are 'I must always be right', 'My partner must never criticize me', 'Our relationship must never have conflict in it' and 'Life must be fair'. Anger-prone clients can also be coached in propositional thinking in which they treat their perceptions as hypotheses and then use scientific enquiry to generate and review evidence that confirms or negates their hypotheses. For instance, Maggie became angry because she thought that Pete's not being openly affectionate meant that he did not love her anymore. On further reflection she acknowledged that 'Pete has always been there for me' and that 'Pete comes from a family which is not openly affectionate and needs my help in becoming more expressive'.

Clients may also be coached in calming and coaching self-talk before, during and after anger-evoking situations. For instance, before they might say to themselves 'Remember, stick to the issues and avoid put-downs'; during, 'Stay cool … I'm not going to give her/him the satisfaction of getting to me'; and after, 'Even though the situation is unresolved, I'm glad I didn't come on strong.' Coaches may also help clients visually rehearse dealing with provocations, including visualizing restful scenes as part of the process. In addition, coaches can work with clients' tendencies to blame others by helping them to explain the cause of their anger more accurately. Some clients may require assistance in accurately predicting the consequences of their anger. For instance, they may come on too strong and insufficiently take into account the pain their behaviour causes and how it may escalate problems for them.

## Skills for Managing Relationship Problems

Coaches and coaching trainees can help clients to manage relationship problems better. Arguing is one of the activities most characteristic of marriage and more conflict is found in marriages than in any other kind of relationship (Argyle, 1991). Perhaps the critical consideration is how skilled clients are in managing their relationship problems, than whether they have them in the first place.

Trainees may work with clients on increasing their acceptance of another's behaviour and letting go of the struggle to change them. This is partly a matter of letting go of the premise that the differences in question are intolerable and also of the struggle to change a partner in terms of an idealized image of how they should be. Thinking, feeling and acting accepting is a process that may be very difficult in some cases and not desirable in others.

Trainees may help clients increase their exchange of rewarding behaviours with their partner. This assumes that the client's partner is willing to engage in this activity. Each partner makes an independent list of rewarding behaviours to offer the other partner and enacts items from their lists for an agreed upon period. Partners then hold a review session on what worked, with recipients having a chance to comment on and add to the giver's list. Then partners engage in a revised enactment of rewarding behaviours. This is followed by a another review of progress and making further agreements.

Trainees can also help clients to solve problems cooperatively with their partners using the CUDSA cooperative problem-solving model shown in Box 10.1. Skills for stage 1, confronting the problem, include keeping calm, picking a proper time and place, asserting that a problem exists and inviting cooperation in problem solving. Stage 2, understanding one another's perspective, involves each partner having uninterrupted 'air time' to state their perspective. Sender skills of understanding one another's perspective include brevity, discussing only one problem at a time and owning responsibility for your contribution. Receiver skills include using listening and showing understanding skills and admitting to and altering misperceptions.

---

### Box 10.2    A Cooperative Problem-Solving Model (CUDSA)

1. Confront the problem.
2. Understand one another's perspective.
3. Define the problem.
4. Search for and assess solutions.
5. Agree upon the preferred solution.

---

The task of stage 3, define the problem, is to try to arrive at a mutually acceptable definition of the problem. In stage three the sender and receiver roles that partners adopt are less clear than in stage two and consequently there is greater risk of destructive arguing. This risk can be lessened if partners use skills to avoid unfair fight tactics such as ascribing negative motives, and also use skills of identifying common ground. Stage 4, search for and address solutions, consists of two main elements: generating solutions and assessing solutions rationally. Stage 5, agree the preferred solution, involves skills such as making concessions and compromises and also stating agreements clearly.

Trainees can help clients to implement and review their agreements with partners. Frequently, some fine-tuning of initial agreements is necessary and sometimes more drastic changes must be made.

Trainees can also coach clients to make conflict less likely by staying in touch with their partners on a daily basis. Gottman and Silver (1999) recommend spending approximately five hours a week on partings at the start of a day, reunions at the end of the day, admiration and appreciation expressed every day, affection expressed daily and a weekly date in which partners talk with one another, update information, and, if necessary, work through issues in their relationship.

## Activity 10.2    Relationship Skills Coaching

Coach a partner as a client who wants to improve their performance in one of the following relationship skills areas:

* listening and showing understanding skills;
* choosing and starting relationships skills;
* managing shyness skills;
* developing intimacy skills;
* sexual relationship skills;
* assertiveness skills;
* managing anger skills; or
* managing relationship problem skills.

In the area in question, work with the client to agree on the mind skills and communication skills for improvement. Then help the client to develop and implement strategies for achieving goals and improving relevant mind skills and communication skills. Afterwards, discuss and reverse roles.

# 11
# Occupation Skills Coaching

This chapter introduces the reader to three areas of occupation skills coaching: namely, study skills, career choice and career performance coaching.

## Study Skills Coaching

Though study skills coaching may seem as though that it is only for students, many of the skills are useful outside of educational institutions as well. All people need to learn to study efficiently and arguably few study and work to their full potential. Box 11.1 shows some study skills that coaches and coaching trainees can help clients to improve.

---

### Box 11.1    Some Study Skills

- Choosing what to study skills.
- Goal-setting skills.
- Time management skills.
- Reading skills.
- Writing skills.
- Note-taking skills.
- Test-taking skills.
- Handling procrastination skills.
- Handling anxiety about mathematics and statistics.
- Public speaking skills.

---

### *Choosing What to Study Skills*

Some people have study problems because they are studying a subject that is of little or no interest to them. Coaching trainees can check with clients how interested they are in their subject. If they are disinterested, it is a matter of checking further whether it is because of the way the subject is being presented or that the client is studying the wrong subject. Trainees can help clients assess what they really want to get out of both studying and life. Some clients need assistance in being systematic about collecting and reviewing academic and career information. In many instances, trainees can work with clients' mind skills. For instance, regarding creating rules, clients may be studying subjects that are more in tune with parental rules than with their own wishes. Regarding creating perceptions, some clients choose subjects based on their perceptions that they lead to high status careers rather than because they are interested in them. Regarding creating explanations, clients need to be accurate in explaining the reasons for not doing well; a reason may be that they are studying the wrong subject, for example.

### *Goal-Setting Skills*

Clients who are studying always have to set themselves short-term, medium-term and long-term goals. Some clients could improve the way they do this. Regarding action skills, trainees can assist clients to set themselves goals that are, as far as possible, specific, measurable, attractive, realistic and time-framed, the first letter of each attribute making the word SMART (Grant and Greene, 2001). Goals should be specific, because vague goals lead to half-hearted attempts to achieve them; measurable, so that clients can evaluate their progress; attractive, to encourage putting in a sustained effort; realistic, so that they are capable of being achieved; and time-framed, so that an appropriate time frame is in mind.

Trainees can work with clients' mind skills when setting goals. For instance, clients can be helped to dispute and reformulate demanding and perfectionist rules concerning achievement. They can be helped to perceive realistically both what is wanted academically and their attempts to attain this. Clients can also be taught calming and coaching self-talk in regard to achieving their goals. They can use visualization to imagine themselves both in process of achieving their goals and also, at some stage in future, having successfully achieved them. Trainees can work with clients to create accurate explanations concerning why they should set goals and correct errors in them. They can also help clients to be realistic about their expectations in regard to achieving the goals that they are considering.

## Time Management Skills

Coaches and coaching trainees can build clients' time management skills. An important way to do this is to coach timetabling activities skills. Clients can be helped to timetable study and other activities, minimum study goals and homework assignments. Trainees may need to explain the value of timetabling and the negative consequences of failure to timetable. Trainees may initially provide timetables but they should aim to get clients to be doing this themselves. The idea is for trainees to help clients to develop their own timetabling and time management skills so that they can gradually step back from assisting them. Trainees need to be sensitive to clients' anxieties about timetabling and to be prepared to refer vulnerable clients for counselling. Even when coaching ordinary clients, it is possible to get them to spend too much time scheduling activities and too little time carrying them out. Trainees should check with clients on their progress in adhering to timetabled activities and find out about any difficulties experienced. Often non-adherence to timetabled activities shows that clients have one or more poor mind skills, for instance perfectionist rules about achievement. If so, trainees should help clients learn better mind skills.

## Reading Skills

Few people read as fast or with as much comprehension as they might. Assuming you have the skills yourself, you can coach clients in the skills of effective reading and, if necessary, recommend speed-reading courses to them. Clients can be coached in previewing material to see how thoroughly it needs to be read, in reading blocks of words rather than each line from beginning to end, and in reviewing material to ensure that they retain what they need. Clients' mind skills can also be addressed. For instance, most clients can fruitfully have the perception that their reading skills are very good challenged. Clients can also be helped to dispute and replace demanding rules that interfere with reading well, for instance rules about perfection. If necessary, clients can also be trained in self-talk to calm themselves down when reading and to coach themselves in how to read quickly and accurately.

## Writing Skills

The term writing skills will be used also to cover preparing material on computers. Coaching trainees can help some clients to prepare and write material better. An important skill is for clients to learn to make sure that they are clear as to what is required. Trainees may need to get some clients spending more time collecting material before they write, whereas others need to get going. Clients can be encouraged to outline their work, do it bit-by-bit, check and, if necessary, change parts of it. They should not expect always to get it right the first time. Some clients may need to improve their use of English skills, such as improving the brevity and clarity of their expression.

Trainees may need to coach clients' mind skills connected with writing. For instance, clients need to possess realistic rules concerning the feedback they get, neither paying too little attention to it nor being overwhelmed by it. Trainees can help clients to perceive their skills accurately and to seek to improve them if needed. Clients can be taught calming self-talk if anxious about writing. They can also be taught to coach themselves in the skills of being creative and organized. Some clients may be helped to visualize themselves engaging in the various tasks of writing. Clients may require help in creating accurate explanations for their writing successes and failures. They can also be coached to possess more realistic expectations about the processes and outcomes of their writing.

## Note-Taking Skills

Some clients require assistance in taking good notes. They may be disorganized, take down everything or not make enough notes. Clients need to be helped to systematically think through the amount and kind of notes they need for each subject. They need to be clear about why they are taking notes: for instance, are they taking notes just to pass a test or will the material be useful later on in life? Clients also need to think through how they are going to store their notes and for what purpose.

Clients mind skills are relevant to note-taking, only some of which are mentioned here. Trainees may need to help some clients dispute demanding rules that lead to taking down too much material and replace them with realistic rules that allow flexibility in the amount and kind of notes. They need to help clients accurately perceive the notes they require and their ability to take them. Clients can also learn to use self-talk, possibly accompanied by visualization, to coach themselves through the steps of taking notes effectively.

## Test-Taking Skills

People's problems taking tests and examinations can cause them a range of difficulties including anything from mild to severe anxiety and lowered performance. Coaching trainees may need to help clients prepare better by developing skills such as being clear about what is worth revising and how to spend time appropriately. They can also assist clients to become more mindful of good skills to use during tests, such as reading questions carefully, allocating and keeping to time, and checking what they have written.

Trainees may need to focus on clients' mind skills. For instance, unrealistic perfectionist rules about performance are a common cause of test anxiety. In such instances clients need assistance in challenging unrealistic rules and arriving at more realistic ones. Trainees can also work with clients' perceptions. For instance, they can correct black and white thinking by helping clients, rather than looking at tests as an all-or-nothing experience, see that, though they may not do as well as they would like, they can still do alright. Furthermore, even if they fail, they may be able to retake the test. In addition, trainees may train clients in calming and coaching self-talk in regard to both revising for and taking tests.

## Handling Procrastination Skills

Many people procrastinate a little when it comes to doing work such as writing essays, and some procrastinate a lot. Furthermore, people have different degrees of awareness regarding their procrastination. Once coaching trainees get clients to admit that they are procrastinators, there are many things that they can do. Clients need to clear a space, keep it tidy and probably only use it for studying. Clients may need to become better at setting goals, both for what work to do first and how to do specific tasks. Working on timetabling skills may help in regard to setting goals for which jobs to do when. Helping clients break specific tasks down into manageable parts may contribute to their getting started on projects. Clients may also procrastinate less when they set themselves time for breaks as well as for work.

Trainees can help clients create realistic rules concerning what they will achieve and how hard they will work. They can also help clients have more realistic perceptions. For instance, perceptions like 'I'm lazy', 'I'm no good', 'I'm a procrastinator' and 'The project is too difficult' can each be examined, challenged and made more realistic. Clients can also be taught self-talk to calm themselves down when starting work and to coach themselves in skills like breaking projects down, beginning with a small task, and congratulating themselves as they progress. Trainees may also get clients using visualizing skills to imagine carrying out tasks successfully. Clients can be helped to assume responsibility for doing something about their procrastination and avoid explanations like 'It's my nature' or 'I've got so used to it, I don't imagine I can change.' Trainees may also challenge clients' expectations that 'I'm going to procrastinate' and help them to change them to 'I'm going to make steady progress'.

### *Handling Anxiety about Mathematics and Statistics*

Trainees may need to coach some clients not to allow themselves to be overcome by fears about mathematics and statistics. Getting clients started on manageable tasks before attempting more difficult ones is one way to build confidence. However, most anxiety about mathematic and statistics is probably due to clients using poor mind skills. Clients can be helped to challenge perceptions that 'I'm no good at maths' and 'I'll never be any good at statistics', and learn to alter them to more realistic perceptions like 'I can learn maths even though I may have some difficulty at times' and 'I can be quite adequate at statistics.' Trainees may need to work with clients' self-talk: for instance, telling themselves to 'stay calm' when doing problems and coaching themselves through the necessary steps, possibly accompanied by visualizing doing this. Coaching trainees can also help clients to alter explanations about why they find difficulty doing mathematics and/or statistics, to make them less rigid. 'It's my nature' can become 'It's my upbringing and now I can change,' for example. Creating the expectation that change is possible helps clients to achieve what they previously feared.

### *Public Speaking Skills*

Coaching trainees can help clients to speak well in public in many ways. Clients may need to work on preparing the content of talks so that their material lends itself easily to verbal presentation. They would be well advised to put the talk in note form on a number of prompt cards. Trainees can then coach clients on the verbal, vocal and body message aspects of their talk. Clients can give mini-talks in the office or even on the phone. Trainees may also be able to coach clients giving talks in real situations.

Even when they have done much public speaking, some people still suffer from anxiety about doing it. Clients may have created unrealistic rules about giving the perfect talk with no mistakes, however unused to public speaking they may be. Trainees need to help clients dispute and reformulate such rules into realistic ones: for instance, 'I'm learning to speak in public and I can improve at it but I will never be perfect.' Trainees can also work with clients' perceptions both about themselves, for example they may exaggerate how badly they speak, and about their audience's reactions, such as assuming the worst rather than accurately getting feedback.

Clients can also be coached in calming self-talk to help manage anxiety and in coaching skills so that they pay attention to giving important verbal, vocal and body messages. When practising on their own, clients may also use visualizing skills, both to imagine themselves speaking competently and also to imagine the audience's reactions. Trainees can help clients be accurate in explaining the causes of success and failure as speakers. In addition, they can help clients create expectations about performing adequately and give up expectations about being overcome with anxiety and speaking poorly. Though in this section I have focused on trainees helping clients to give talks, they can use many of the same skills when participating in academic and other groups.

## Activity 11.1 Study Skills Coaching

Coach a partner who has a study skills area that she/he wants to improve. The study skills areas include choosing what to study, goal setting, time management, reading, writing, note-taking, test-taking, handling procrastination, handling anxiety about mathematics and statistics and public speaking skills. Inasmuch as possible,

- facilitate client disclosure;
- agree on a shared analysis of how to achieve the client's goals;
- intervene; and
- end coaching.

Afterwards, discuss and reverse roles.

# Career Choice Coaching

Nowadays many people no longer have the same permanency in careers and jobs as previously. Thus career choice coaching is not just about initial career choice but can give people skills that they can use for later career changes. Usually even the initial choice of career tends to be a process that takes place over a period of time.

## Communication/Action Skills

Assuming that clients have little idea of what they want to do or what is available, coaches and coaching trainees need help them to develop skills for gathering information and assessing information. Trainees can assist clients to explore and identify their interests and aptitudes. They can provide conditions of safety where clients can get in touch with what they truly think and feel. In addition, where appropriate, trainees can administer interest inventories and aptitude tests. When feeding back the results of such measures, trainees should be careful to get clients participating and not to over-interpret the results. In addition, trainees may suggest to certain clients that they try out different careers: for instance, it may be possible to shadow a mentor actually on the job. Often, at the very least, clients can spend time talking to people in the occupations in which they might be interested.

Trainees or coaches can help clients search out and assess written educational and occupational information relevant to choosing a career. For example, trainees can get clients to access occupational information libraries that may be either in the form of actual written material or on the Internet. Clients can also get information in other ways, such as by contacting professional associations, companies and educational institutions. Trainees can also assist clients to build their assessing information skills. Some of this assessment will be to do with the relevance of the information and some with its quality.

Trainees may need to help some clients with specific communication skills concerning choosing a career. Some clients may need to develop their listening skills, both to others and to themselves. Many clients may require assistance in being assertive in going after the information they want and not getting put off when they find some people unhelpful. Clients may also need help in articulating their ideas and wishes more clearly and developing this as a skill for the future. Since trying out jobs may be part of the process of choosing a career, clients may also require coaching in work skills, for instance in communicating with bosses, peers and sometimes customers.

## Mind Skills

Coaching trainees can help clients to develop skills of thinking realistically when choosing careers. For example, trainees can work with clients who have demanding and perfectionist rules concerning themselves or about specific careers and jobs. Some clients may need assistance in overcoming demanding rules about the career-choosing process. They can be helped to realize that it may take time and include trial and error, rather than assuming that all will happen quickly and easily. Trainees can also assist clients to develop skills of perceiving their interests, aptitudes, strengths and weaknesses accurately. Under-confident clients can be helped to clarify and own their strengths, and not to give up on any career they want too easily. Over-confident clients may need assistance in adjusting their evaluations of their abilities and desirability to become more in line with their qualifications and what different careers require. All clients need to view the information they collect and the different careers accurately, and some may require coaching in building such skills.

Some clients get anxious when thinking about what they might do and their suitability for the job market. Trainees can coach such clients in calming self-talk. They can also help clients acquire coaching self-talk concerning taking rational steps in the career-choosing process. Furthermore, they can assist clients in how to talk themselves through setbacks in what is often a fairly long process of choosing a career. Clients may also use visualizing skills; they can visualize as best as they can what certain careers entail, for instance. In addition, they can visualize themselves going through a rational career-choosing process as well as the dangers of being irrational.

Trainees may need to help some clients explain the success and failure of their attempts to choose a career. Trainees should always encourage clients to assume responsibility for trying hard. Clients may require assistance in having more realistic expectations, both about what they have to offer as well as what different careers require. Where necessary, trainees can help clients challenge their expectations about specific careers and about the career-choosing process, and replace them with more realistic ones.

## Concluding Comments

As mentioned at the beginning of this section, nowadays many people have to adjust to changes in the career and job market, often owing to the increasing rapidity of technological development. Consequently, trainees have to help clients to acquire the skills of coaching themselves now and of self-coaching for later on. In addition, trainees can help clients learn skills of monitoring themselves and, where appropriate, of initiating changes in their career or job rather than being forced by others or by circumstances to change. Some clients may still need further career choice coaching at some stage in their futures and others may be coached for the first time during rather than at the start of their careers.

## Activity 11.2    Career Choice Coaching

Coach a partner who assumes the position of being in process of choosing a career for the first time. Inasmuch as possible, coach her/him not only with regard to her/his current situation but also help her/him acquire self-coaching skills for later on. Take the following steps:

- facilitate client disclosure;
- agree on a shared analysis of how to achieve the client's goals;
- intervene as best you can in the time available; and
- end coaching.

Afterwards, discuss and reverse roles.

# Career Performance Coaching

This is a general introduction to career performance coaching, which is often conducted by coaches specializing in it. Some career performance skills overlap with those already covered in study skills coaching, for instance goal setting, time management and public speaking. Goleman (1998) claims that there are two main reasons for career fizzle: rigidity and poor relationships. The following section looks at some communication skills and mind skills that clients can focus on and improve.

## Communication Skills

Clients may seek coaching to improve numerous communication skills relevant to their careers and work. Some clients can improve their skills for getting acquainted: for instance, on the verbal, vocal and body messages connected with greeting someone positively and on not waiting for others to make the first move. Trainees can coach many clients on assertiveness skills; clients may need assistance on presenting themselves and their ideas positively, for example. Some clients may require help in saying no to others or in suggesting different ways of handling situations. Trainees can also coach clients on their skills for attending meetings, such as when and how to speak out and when to remain silent.

Some clients need help with the skills of cooperating with others rather than dominating or being dominated by them. Trainees may also coach clients in how to deal with difficult people, be they above them, at the same level or below them. For instance, clients with aggressive bosses can gain the skills and confidence to present their ideas calmly and not allow themselves to feel overpowered. Clients may themselves need coaching in leadership skills.

Sometimes it is helpful if they can receive 360-degree feedback from a range of people in relationships all around them (Rogers, 2004). Client permission needs to be granted to get this kind of feedback that may really point out some of the areas on which they need to work. Ways in which trainees can collect such feedback include interviewing selected people in person or by phone and also by sending out questionnaires. When coaching clients for receiving others' feedback, trainees should always facilitate them in discussing their reactions to it and in developing their own ideas in light of what others see. Often the changes required will concern not overusing strengths rather than actual weaknesses.

Some clients require assistance in handling performance assessments. They may need to become calmer and more focused when receiving the assessment. In addition, they may require assistance in evaluating the assessment and making the necessary changes in their behaviour. Interviews are another area for which clients may require coaching, be it for promotion or for a new job. Trainees can role-play interviews with clients both to find out their skills weaknesses and to develop their strengths. Coaches can also help clients to develop entrepreneurial skills, though possibly this is an area best left to experienced coaches rather than trainees since the costs of making mistakes can be very high.

Coaches and trainees can work with women regarding career performance since many women feel unsure of themselves in a predominantly male business world. For example, trainees can help female clients evaluate their physical appearance and image to make sure that it fits their career goals. Trainees can also assess with clients and provide feedback to them on their ways of communicating and behaving. Sometimes, such assessments can involve others. Some women require coaching regarding which areas of work to specialize in. Trainees can encourage upwardly mobile women to consider moving outside of traditional areas, such as human resources, and to develop skills in areas like finance and strategic planning. Women may not be sufficiently assertive in letting their career development needs be known and so risk being overlooked. Peltier (2001: 204) observes that 'Coaches can help female clients communicate their career aspirations to those who 'count' in their organizations'. Sometimes this may need to be done repeatedly with several key people in an organization.

## Mind Skills

Usually in combination with communication skills, coaches and trainees can work with clients' mind skills to enhance their career performance. Clients may have one or more of numerous irrational rules: for instance, 'I must be top', 'I must make much money' and 'I must work perfectly.' Coaching trainees can help clients to discover rules that get in their way, dispute them and alter them into rational or realistic rules. For instance, 'I must work perfectly' can be changed to 'I want to work as well as I can and also have sufficient time for my private life.' Trainees can also assist clients to develop more accurate perceptions of themselves and of others. Under-confident clients can be assisted in looking for and acknowledging their successes. Clients can be coached in how to evaluate others and perceive their work strengths as well as areas they need to improve.

Clients may need to learn to use calming and coaching self-talk so that they handle many work situations better. For example, clients facing difficult clients of their own need to stay calm and to remind themselves of appropriate verbal, vocal and body messages. They can also prepare for such situations by visualizing staying calm as they use their skills to manage the situation successfully. In addition, clients can also be coached in using visualizing skills to imagine their futures, say three months or five years from now.

Trainees may also work to improve clients' skills of creating explanations. Clients can be coached in how to assess their career performance and to explain accurately the reasons for their successes and failures. They can also be coached in using these skills in specific situations, for instance getting or losing a sale. Coaches and trainees may assist clients to create more realistic expectations both about themselves and others. For instance, they may help pessimistic clients to overcome focusing overly on negative circumstances and possibilities. A degree of exaggerated optimism may be beneficial in business, but basically clients need to be realistic about the chances of positive outcomes from their endeavours.

## *Activity 11.3   Career Performance Coaching*

Coach a partner who has a career performance area on which they want to focus. Inasmuch as possible coach her/him not only with her/his current situation but also help her/him acquire self-coaching skills for later on. Take the following steps:

- facilitate client disclosure;
- agree on a shared analysis of how to achieve the client's goals;
- intervene as best you can in the time available; and
- end coaching.

Afterwards, discuss and reverse roles.

# 12
# Health Skills Coaching

The area of health skills coaching is very wide. Here I focus on managing stress, managing weight and managing alcohol.

## Managing Stress

Here are two examples of clients who seek coaching to overcome problems of stress:

> Katie is a high-pressure real estate salesperson. She is always on the go professionally and personally. She lives on her nerves and burns the candle at both ends and in the middle. When things go wrong, she gets tense and irritable. She is like a tightly stretched rubber band close to breaking.

> Stu has recently been promoted at work and now has to supervise 15 people. While pleased to get the promotion, he still needs to develop the skills of being a good supervisor. He feels under a lot of pressure, does not sleep well and his appetite is poorer than usual.

Stress can come both from within and outside. Everyone has an optimal stress level or a particular level of stimulation at which they feel most comfortable. At this level they experience stress without distress (Selye, 1974). Beneath this level, they may be insufficiently stimulated or bored. Above this level, they are likely to experience physiological and psychological distress. Body reactions include proneness to ulcers and heart attacks. Feelings of distress include anxiety, tiredness, frustration and disorientation.

If the heightened stress is prolonged or perceived as extremely severe, they may feel in a state of excessive stress or crisis. Also, some clients may feel burned out. Freudenberger (1980: 17) defines burnout: 'To deplete oneself. To exhaust one's physical and mental resources. To wear oneself out by excessively striving to reach some unrealistic expectation imposed by one's self or by the values of society'.

To some extent the skills of managing stress are peculiar to specific situations; as Stu from the example develops supervisory skills, he is likely to feel less under stress, for instance. Other skills are more general and it is with these communication/action skills and mind skills that coaches and trainees can help clients.

## Communication/Action Skills

The previous two chapters on relationship skills coaching and occupational skills coaching provided some ways that coaches and trainees can help clients to manage stress. By dealing with relationship and occupational situations better, clients are likely to reduce the amount of stress they feel. Here I focus on some additional skills of managing stress.

### Limiting Activities

Trainees can help clients develop skills of reviewing their activities and of curtailing or dropping some that are not essential from the points of view of working or leisure. Clients may need assistance in learning to say 'no' assertively to requests and expectations to do things. They may also require assistance to follow through on this message and to develop setting limits and creating boundaries as long-term skills.

### Being Efficient

Trainees can assist clients to examine how efficient they are at work and in their personal lives. Clients may find ways of doing things faster and better, with the result that they feel less stressed.

### Relaxation

Trainees can teach clients both muscular and visual relaxation methods. Clients should learn that success in learning relaxation, just like success in learning any other skill, requires practise and that relaxation homework will be required. One relaxation method is progressive muscular relaxation that is based on a five-point focus-tense-hold-release-relax cycle (Bernstein and Borkovec, 1973). Trainees can take clients through 16 muscle groups in the body, demonstrating them as necessary. Once clients have learned how to tense the various muscle groups, they are instructed to keep their eyes closed during relaxation training and practise.

Trainees can either make up cassettes of relaxation instructions that clients can take away for homework purposes or recommend existing relaxation training cassettes. Often clients visualize restful scenes at the end of progressive muscular relaxation. Such a scene might be 'lying in a lush, green meadow on a warm, sunny day, feeling a gentle breeze, watching the clouds'. Clients can also be taught brief relaxation procedures. For example, they can learn to instruct themselves to 'Take a deep breath and tense all my muscles … hold for five seconds … now release and relax as quickly and deeply as I can.'

## Meditation

Meditation is both a communication/action skill and a mind skill. Trainees may coach some clients in meditation to help them handle stress better. Meditation falls into two main categories: mindfulness of breathing, or breath meditation, and awareness or insight meditation. All meditation approaches require practise, with perseverance increasing the likelihood of better results. Meditation can be significantly enhanced by attending retreats in which clients engage in continuous meditation practise for days or weeks. Breathing meditation consists of relaxed concentration on the flow of your breathing, on the in-breaths and on the out-breaths. Breathing meditation may be performed sitting, standing, walking or reclining. For interested readers, Buddhist insight meditations include calmly becoming aware of the impermanence of whatever experiences and sensations arise and meditations that cultivate the four divine abodes of mind – loving kindness, compassion, sympathy and equanimity (Thitavanno, 2002).

## Developing Adequate Recreational Outlets

Trainees can help clients to know the value of recreation and to practise self-care by regularly engaging in recreational activities. For some clients this may be a matter of finding new hobbies to engage in: for instance, gardening, painting, music, getting in touch with nature or sports. For other clients, it may be a matter of time management to free time for activities that sustain them as human beings rather than just work activities. In addition, trainees may assist some clients to spend time on short and annual vacations, and to acknowledge their importance.

## Staying Physically Fit

Coaching trainees can help some clients to acknowledge that they feel better when they are physically fit. Clients can be assisted in finding ways of taking exercise and in developing such activities on an ongoing basis.

## Developing a Support Network

Stressed people often isolate themselves from others. Clients may require assistance in identifying and building relationships with supportive people. Trainees can help clients develop skills of asking for and giving support to family, friends and acquaintances.

## Mind Skills

Clients may feel stressed because they have little direction in their lives. Trainees can help clients set clear goals for themselves and plan for the future. They can assist clients to design strategies for achieving their goals and plans. The following are some other ways that coaching trainees can work with stressed clients' mind skills.

## Creating Rules

Frequently, stressed clients have unrealistic rules that contribute to their distress. For example, clients may have demanding rules about performing perfectly themselves, others performing perfectly, making a lot of money and being quickly and highly successful. Trainees can help such clients see the negative effects of such rules, dispute them and reform them into more realistic rules. Trainees can also help clients to acquire unconditional self-acceptance (USA), unconditional other-acceptance (UOA) and unconditional life-acceptance (ULA) (Ellis, 2001). Unconditional self-acceptance involves clients making a decision to accept themselves independently of their performances. With unconditional other-acceptance, just as clients rate their own thinking, feeling and behaving but do not give a global rating to themselves, so they can rate the behaviours of other people but not their total selves or being. Unconditional life-acceptance means that clients learn to accept conditions that they cannot change, despite not liking them.

## Creating Perceptions

Coaching trainees can work to make stressed clients perceive more realistically. Clients may need to focus on altering their perceptions of themselves. There are many distortions that trainees can help them to correct (Beck and Weishaar, 2005). For instance, clients may stress themselves by thinking dichotomously, such as 'Unless I do extremely well on this exam, I am a total failure.' They may also magnify events, such as 'If I appear the least bit nervous when doing this task it will mean disaster.' In addition, they may need to alter their perceptions of others: for example, the perception that others are judging them all the time negatively or that others are much more able than they really are. Clients may also feel stressed because they overestimate the probability and severity of threats; magnify the negative consequences (catastrophizing); underestimate their resources for dealing with threats; and insufficiently take into account the presence of support factors, for instance the presence of others who may help. Trainees can help such clients by coaching them in how to elicit and identify automatic thoughts, reality-test and correct automatic thoughts, and identify and modify underlying beliefs. Clients can be coached in Socratic questioning to expand and evaluate how they think. Typical questions are: 'Where is the evidence?', 'Are there other ways of perceiving the situation?' and 'What would be the worst thing that could happen?'

## Creating Self-Talk

Trainees can coach clients in how to create coping self-talk to manage stressful situations. Clients can learn calming self-talk such as 'calm down', 'take it easy' and 'relax'. Trainees can also assist clients to identify and practise the self-talk statements that will help them before, during and after specific stressful situations. For example, clients anxious about public speaking can be taught to coach themselves through the steps of preparing, giving and having finished giving a talk. Trainees should coach clients in how to create self-talk not just to cope with immediate situations but also to have it as a skill to help them in the future.

## *Creating Visual Images*

Trainees can coach clients in how to use their imaginations to help them to manage stress. When thinking about stressful situations, clients can learn to accompany calming self-talk with calming visual images. Such visual images might either be acting calmly in the situation or may involve a distracting visual image like lying on a beach on a warm, sunny day. Clients can also use visual images as they coach themselves through the steps of stress-inducing tasks. In addition, they can imagine completing tasks successfully and feeling good about this.

## *Creating Explanations*

Trainees and coaches may need to coach clients in how to explain their feelings of stress accurately. Some clients may also require assistance in acknowledging their stress levels accurately. Clients may also require help in learning how to take responsibility for feeling stressed and, where possible, acting appropriately in situations. Furthermore, they need to be careful about not making false explanations. For instance, some unemployed clients have to beware not to wrongly think 'It was my fault' when numerous external factors may have contributed to their current feelings of stress, such as recessions, takeovers, downsizing and technological change. Other unemployed clients may wrongly think of another that 'It was their fault', when they may have some poor personal or work-related skills that increased the chances of their losing their jobs and of not finding another. They are only likely to feel less stressed when they start taking responsibility for improving their skills.

## *Creating Expectations*

Trainees can also coach some clients to manage stress better by creating more realistic expectations. For example, clients may predict risk and reward inaccurately. For instance, clients who overestimate bad consequences are likely to stress themselves unnecessarily. Probably the same is true for clients who underestimate good consequences. On the other hand, clients who underestimate bad consequences and overestimate good consequences may each end up feeling unnecessarily stressed. Trainees can assist clients to assess probability better by encouraging them to ask each time, 'What rational basis do I have for creating expectations about this event?' and 'What irrational considerations might interfere with the accuracy of my expectations?'

Time projection, which entails imaginary mind-tripping into the future, is a useful visualizing skill that clients can use to create more accurate expectations (Lazarus, 1984). Clients can both visualize how the present might look from the vantage point of the future and also visualize looking into the future. Furthermore, they can visually project how to deal with worst-case scenarios.

## Activity 12.1   Managing Stress

Coach a partner who either wants to improve her/his own skills or role-plays a client who wants to improve her/his skills at managing stress. Inasmuch as possible:

- facilitate client disclosure;
- agree on a shared analysis of how to achieve the client's goals;
- intervene by focusing on at least one mind skill and one communication/ action skill; and
- end coaching.

Afterwards, discuss and reverse roles.

# Managing Weight

Many people have problems keeping their body in shape and remaining fit and healthy. Probably far more are too fat rather than too thin. This section focuses on coaching people who have not got to the stage of needing therapy to manage their weight. Since motivation is extremely important, coaches and trainees may have to work with clients to sharpen their goals before they can get them focusing on changing the specific communication/action skills and mind skills that contribute to their being overweight. As part of this process, coaching trainees can help clients to learn what is their most healthy weight range. Sometimes clients eat too much because they are not dealing well with other problems and stresses. The following section does not cover such clients directly, though it is still relevant to many of them.

## Communication/Action Skills

Coaching trainees and clients can choose which of the following skills are likely to be useful in managing weight for the client's particular situation.

## *Being Open about One's Goals*

Clients may be more likely to stick to weight goals that are not only realistic but are public as well. This means telling at least one significant person about their goals and probably others as well. Going public indicates a degree of commitment on their part. Furthermore, it may serve to gain the support of others in helping them to achieve their goals.

## *Managing the Presence of Food*

When purchasing food, clients need to know what is nutritious, healthy and not fattening. Trainees may need to help them to acquire and act on such knowledge. Trainees can also help clients think of ways of storing food at home that do not unnecessarily reinforce the temptation to eat. This may range from simple things like putting food out of sight when it is neither being prepared nor eaten, to locking it up when not officially wanted.

## *Developing Good Eating Habits*

When working to avoid over-eating, clients need to monitor how much, what and where they are eating. Clients can learn to eat regularly and moderately and to avoid such activities as snacking and eating junk food. As part of this monitoring process, they may need to log what they eat, where and when until they get control over their eating.

## *Assertiveness Skills*

Trainees may need to coach some clients in how to become more assertive when it comes to attaining and maintaining their eating goals. The first person they need to learn to say no to is themselves. Trainees can help clients to understand why they have given in to eating in the past, as a basis for not doing so in future. Sometimes clients need to become more assertive with others in saying no to eating too much and not joining in events where overeating is the norm. In being assertive they need pay attention to sending good vocal and body messages as well as good verbal messages. If necessary, clients may have to choose some different friends and colleagues or at least alter some of the activities they engage in together.

## Getting Reinforcement

Trainees can help clients to reward themselves for keeping their weight control goals. Clients can weigh themselves regularly and keep a record of their weight. For many, maintaining their goals is likely to be rewarding enough in itself. Some clients may also verbally reward themselves for attaining weight goals. Another form of reward is for clients to buy or do something that they want as a condition of meeting their goals: for instance, purchasing a neat fitting dress that emphasizes their new figure. Clients can also ask significant others to notice and reward them when they attain and maintain weight control goals.

## Physical Exercise

Coaching trainees can review with clients whether they are engaging in sufficient physical exercise and if not, why not. Clients may need assistance in seeing the value of being and staying physically fit. Trainees can then help them choose appropriate methods of physical exercise, allocate time to carry them out and deal with any problems that occur. Trainees may also need to help some clients reduce or give up some activities, such as sitting and watching TV for hours and not getting sufficient sleep.

## Seeking Professional Assistance

Though this section has been written for those who are not seriously overweight, nevertheless there may be occasions when professional assistance is useful. Some clients may need to check with doctors to ensure that there is no medical contribution to their being overweight and, if there is, to get help in dealing with it. Either by reading about nutrition or meeting a nutritionist, clients can also be assisted to decide what foods they can both enjoy and eat. In addition, clients can read cooking books and take cooking courses to make sure that they eat as well as possible.

## Mind Skills

The following are some ways relevant to managing weight that coaches and trainees can work with clients' mind skills.

### Creating Rules

Trainees can help to make clients more aware of underlying demanding rules they may have in regard to eating. Examples of such rules are: 'I must eat what I want now', 'I must always have the food that I especially like rather than the food that is good for me' and 'Others must approve of me regardless of my weight and looks.' Once identified, such rules can be disputed and reformulated: for instance, 'I must eat what I want now' can be altered to 'I eat at regular times.'

### Creating Perceptions

Trainees can help clients to examine the realism of the perceptions that they have about themselves and others. For example, clients may think 'I can eat junk food and still look okay', 'My being overweight does not affect my health' and 'When something goes wrong, I can handle it by eating a lot.' Perceptions they may have of others include 'Others do not notice my weight.' Clients can be assisted to see that there may be many other ways of viewing their situations and choose the most realistic perception in each case; for instance, 'Others do not notice my weight' can be changed to 'Though others may not notice my weight, some people do and, anyway, I notice it and want to change.'

### Creating Self-Talk

Trainees and coaches can coach clients in self-talk that helps them reduce their weight or stay at their appropriate weight. They can be taught calming self-talk when they are near food or difficult situations. Trainees can also work with clients to discover the coaching self-talk statements that work best for them. All of these statements are likely to emphasize choice: example, 'I can say no', 'I want to lose weight', 'I choose to stick to my diet' and 'I can be social without eating too much'. Clients can also remind themselves of the negative consequences of eating too much, such as 'I will not look so good' and 'I will not be so healthy.' Some clients may find affirming self-talk useful; saying 'well done' when they eat moderately, for example.

### Creating Visual Images

Some clients find visualizing a useful skill when watching their weight. Trainees may help overweight clients' motivation by getting them to visualize how they look now. This can motivate them in two ways: increasing dissatisfaction with how they look to themselves and becoming more aware of how they look to others. Trainees can coach clients in visualizing positive images: for example, how their bodies would be if they lost weight or seeing themselves wearing smart clothes. Clients can also imagine the negative consequences of eating too much, such as seeing themselves staying fat.

Trainees may also use covert sensitization (Cautela, 1967) to help clients control their weight. Here they administer, and ultimately get clients to administer to themselves, aversive consequences in their imagination: imagining the sight, touch sensations and smell of vomiting all over themselves when they eat a piece of chocolate cake, for example.

## Creating Explanations

Trainees may need to help some overweight clients to change their explanations, which can include helping clients who think 'I can't change' move to 'I can choose to change – it's my responsibility.' Clients may require assistance in acknowledging personal responsibility for their weight, eating habits, looks, health and to some extent for others' reactions to their looks. Some clients eat when they feel confused about problems. Here trainees can help clients to deal with the problems directly and learn not to eat as a way of handling stress.

## Creating Expectations

Trainees can assist clients to have realistic expectations about the negative consequences of staying overweight such as the effects on their health and possibly their relationships. Trainees can also help clients to develop clear expectations about the gains of losing weight – that they will feel and look better. When tempted to overeat, clients can be coached to predict 'Eating too much will create problems rather than solve them'.

Trainees and clients need to collaborate to identify the specific mind skills and communication skills that clients need to work on if they are to overcome weight problems. Activity 12.2 provides the opportunity to practise helping a client.

### Activity 12.2   Managing Weight

Coach a partner who either wants to manage her/his weight better or role-plays a client who wants to improve her/his skills at managing weight. Inasmuch as possible:

- facilitate client disclosure;
- agree on a shared analysis of how to achieve the client's goals;
- intervene by focusing on at least on mind skill; and one communication/action skill; and
- end coaching.

Afterwards, discuss and reverse roles.

# Managing Alcohol

Coaches and trainees can also help clients to manage alcohol. This section is not about coaching alcoholics but about helping those for whom drinking is or could be a problem (but is not yet out of control). Some clients may regularly drink too much, others may from time to time engage in binge drinking, some will do both. Clients also vary in the length of time they have been drinking too much and the extent to which they acknowledge this. The following are some approaches that coaching trainees can take, though they will need to tailor the chosen approaches to particular clients.

## Communication/Action Skills

Communication/action skills that coaching trainees may use to help clients manage alcohol include the following:

### Monitoring and Regulating Skills

Clients need to know what their alcohol consumption is and what they consider to be a reasonable level of drinking. Trainees may start by getting them to monitor their drinking, including such dimensions as when, where, what, how much and with whom. Together clients and trainees can work out plans to regulate the clients' drinking. Such plans include working out a method for clients to record their drinking. Clients then need to monitor systematically their progress in attaining goals. Trainees can work with clients during this process both by ensuring that they acknowledge their successes and helping them when they lapse and do not reach their targets.

## Placing Alcohol in the Home

Trainees may help some clients decide where to place alcohol at home. Previously clients may have had drinks far too visible and available; clients may face less temptation once alcohol gets stored discretely at home.

## Assertion Skills

Some clients' motivation for drinking too much may be less because they like to drink and more because they do not like being the odd one out. Such clients may require coaching in saying no, either to going to events where they are likely to drink too much or to requests to drink when attending such events. Clients can be helped to understand the reasons why they say yes, as well as the consequences. They can also become clearer as to the advantages of saying no to drinking too much. Clients need to practise the vocal and body messages attached to saying no as well as the verbal message.

## Skills for Choosing Friends

Depending on how friends react to clients who wish to drink less, clients can decide whether to keep them as friends or not to see so much (or anything) of them. Trainees may help some clients make decisions about whether to keep some people as friends. Furthermore, they may need to help clients develop the skills of ending friendships and, possibly, of choosing different friends.

## Getting Support Skills

Clients who want to change their drinking habits can consider whether they will be more likely to achieve their goals if they gain support. For instance, girlfriends, boyfriends and spouses may be valuable sources of support for clients in their endeavours. Sometimes, both partners have a problem with drinking too much. If so, partners may support each other as they change but this is unfortunately not always the case.

## Mind Skills

The following are some ways that coaches and trainees can assist clients to address their mind skills in regard to managing alcohol.

## Creating Rules

Trainees can help clients identify one or more of numerous rules that may induce and sustain drinking: for instance, 'I must have a drink', 'I must go down to the pub', 'I must be one of the boys/girls' and 'I must be manly'. In addition, clients may have rules focused on others, such as 'Others must approve of me.' Trainees can assist clients to develop skills of disputing unrealistic rules and replacing them with realistic ones – 'I must have a drink' can become 'I can choose whether or not to have a drink and will do so in moderation.'

## Creating Perceptions

Trainees can help clients address cognitive distortions that help them to keep drinking too much: changing black-and-white thinking from 'Unless I drink a lot, no one will have any time for me' to 'I will still have friends and can find some more even though I am drinking less', for example. Trainees can assist clients to identify unhelpful perceptions of themselves attached to drinking, such as 'I am weak if I don't drink', 'I am strong if I drink' and 'I'm not being sociable unless I drink a lot.' They can also get clients to challenge the reality of perceptions like 'It's okay to drink a lot' and 'No one minds my heavy drinking.' In addition, where appropriate, trainees can get clients to challenge perceptions that contribute to anxiety, depression and distressed couple relationships that, in turn, contribute to clients' drinking. Trainees can conduct Socratic dialogues to get clients to expand and evaluate how they think: for instance, in regard to the perception 'I am weak if I don't drink?' they can get clients asking, 'Where's the evidence?' and 'Are there any other ways of perceiving the situation?'

## Creating Self-Talk

Trainees can coach clients in how to use calming self-talk when they are about to drink too much. In addition, clients can use coaching self-talk: for instance, 'Watch it. I'm going to stick to my contract', 'I'm going to regulate my drinking from the start this time' and 'I can save money if I don't drink excessively.' Clients can also be taught affirming self-talk like 'I'm glad that I did not get drunk' and 'I feel better about myself when I don't drink too much.'

## Creating Visual Images

Trainees and coaches can ask clients to visualize the negative effects of drinking too much. If realistic negative images are insufficient, clients can undergo covert sensitization in which they imagine exaggerated negative images (Cautela, 1967). For instance, as with overeating, vomiting all over themselves as they drink too much. Clients can also be coached in visualizing positive behaviour, such as drinking in moderation and saying no, firmly but politely, when they have drunk enough. They can visualize themselves receiving rewards for their positive behaviour – themselves and others feeling better and having a relationship maintained rather than put under strain, for example.

## Creating Explanations

Trainees can coach clients in how to assume responsibility for themselves and their alcohol intake. Clients can become aware of the excuses they use for continuing to drink too much ('It's their fault', 'I can't help it', 'It's my genes' or 'Other people pressure me to drink'). Trainees can help clients to learn that they are always responsible for how much alcohol they consume and that, based on this understanding, it is their choice as to what they do about it. In those instances where clients are drinking as a way of dealing with problems, trainees can encourage them to explain and deal with the problems directly.

## Creating Expectations

Coaching trainees can work to make clients' expectations more realistic in regard to their drinking behaviour. Clients can be assisted to see the negative consequences both for themselves and for others if they continue drinking too much. If necessary, trainees can get clients to imagine the negative effects of continuing to drink a lot and of possibly losing control over their drinking. On the positive side, trainees may help clients to strengthen their expectations from controlling their drinking in terms of better relationships, health, self-respect and possibly income.

## Activity 12.3   Managing Alcohol

Coach a partner who either wants to manage alcohol better or role-plays a client who wants to improve her/his skills at managing alcohol. Inasmuch as possible:

- facilitate client disclosure;
- agree on a shared analysis of how to achieve the client's goals;
- intervene by focusing on at least one mind skill and one communication/ action skill; and
- end coaching.

Afterwards, discuss and reverse roles.

# 13
# Ethics in Practice and Training

Life coaching, being a relatively new development in Britain and Australia, is still evolving into professional associations, which in turn will promulgate codes of ethics. In the USA, the International Coach Federation has *The ICT Standards of Ethical Conduct*, which is divided into four areas: professional conduct at large; professional conduct with clients; confidentiality/privacy; and conflicts of interest (ICT, 2005). The development and promulgation of professional codes of ethics is important for coaching trainees as they develop personal systems of ethics for their coaching practice. Such codes can provide a starting point for a process of ethical decision-making since they lay out what is generally considered acceptable behaviour in the profession. Since they may influence coaches to behave ethically, codes of conduct help to protect the public from potentially unethical coaches, and such coaches from themselves. Furthermore, in cases of unethical behaviour, codes of practice can form part of the process of hearing complaints against coaches, something that would be difficult to do in their absence. Where coaches and trainees have behaved ethically, adherence to an accepted professional code can help to protect them against charges of malpractice. Readers of this book are advised to look out for the development of ethical codes that are relevant to their coaching practice.

There is some question of the extent to which ethical codes actually do foster ethical awareness and behaviour. One reason is that they may turn out to be boring documents emphasizing 'don'ts' rather than 'do's'. Another reason is that some coaches and trainees may consider such guidelines are for other ethically vulnerable practitioners rather than for themselves. They may deceive themselves into a false sense of practising ethically.

A further reason is that ethical codes may engender passivity and even apathy. Such codes may be used as prescriptions that do coaching trainees' thinking for them and 'do little to support the active independent critical judgment and discernment that should be associated with true moral responsibility, and indeed, good professionalism' (Pattison, 1999: 375). Furthermore, even where ethical codes exist, there are always dilemmas that are left to practitioners to decide as best as possible.

## Ethical Issues and Dilemmas in Coaching Practice

Ethical issues and dilemmas permeate coaching practice. To use legal language, coaches and trainees always have a duty of care to their clients. Virtually everything coaching trainees do can be performed ethically or unethically. In Box 13.1 the ethical issues and dilemmas connected with enacting this duty of care are divided into six areas, which may overlap: coach competence, client autonomy, confidentiality, client protection, conflicts of interest, and professional monitoring and development.

---

### Box 13.1   Ethical Issues and Dilemmas in Coaching Practice

#### Coach Competence

- Relationship competence.
- Technical competence.
- Readiness to practise.
- Fitness to practise.
- Recognizing limitations and making referrals.

#### Client Autonomy

- Respect for client self-determination.
- Accuracy in pre-coaching information.

*(Continued)*

---

## Box 13.1   (Continued)

- Accuracy in statements about professional competence.
- Honest statements about coaching processes and outcomes.
- A clear contract negotiated in advance.
- Informed consent to interventions.
- Informing the client of data collected about her/him.
- Respecting the client's right to terminate coaching.
- Respect for diverse values.

## Confidentiality

- Communication of any limitations in advance.
- Consent for communication with third parties.
- Issues of disclosure to save life or to prevent serious harm to others.
- Permission to record sessions.
- Permission and anonymity in research projects.
- Security of all client records.

## Client Protection

- Maintaining clear boundaries to the coaching relationship.
- Avoidance of financial exploitation.
- Avoidance of emotional and sexual exploitation.
- Protection of clients' physical safety.
- Adequate indemnity insurance.
- Knowledge of relevant law.

## Conflicts of Interest

- Avoided if possible.
- Openly discussed with client.
- Resolved with clients' best interests in mind.

## Professional Monitoring and Development

- Recognition of personal issues that may interfere with coaching performance.
- Regular and ongoing supervision/consultative support.
- Continuing professional development.
- Keeping abreast of research and other relevant literature.

## Coach Competence

How competently are coaches and trainees performing? With many different approaches to coaching, the issue arises as to what constitutes competence. In Box 13.1 I distinguish between relationship competence, offering a good coaching relationship, and technical competence, the ability to assess clients and to deliver interventions. There is far greater agreement between the different coaching approaches on the ingredients of relationship competence, such as respect and support for clients as persons and accurately listening to and understanding their worldviews, than there is for technical competence. Suffice it for now to say that technical competence is what leading practitioners in a given approach would agree to be competent performance of the technical aspects of that approach. Some coaches and trainees may fall below acceptable levels of either relationship competence or technical competence, or very possibly both. If so, this is a challenge to the coaching profession to raise its standards of selection, training and practise.

Readiness to practise means that coaches and trainees require appropriate training and practise before they are ready to see clients and to use their coaching skills competently. Fitness to practise assumes that coaches and trainees have satisfactory coaching skills in their repertoires and an ethical problem only arises when they are precluded in some way from using these skills competently. An example of readiness to practise as an ethical problem is when trainees take on cases, for example clients with certain health problems, who are beyond their level of training and competence. An example of fitness to practise as an ethical problem is that of a trainee who drinks at work and so fails to maintain competence. Trainees can avoid ethical issues concerning readiness to practise if they are prepared to refer certain clients to others more qualified to help them. Furthermore, where trainees do not possess the requisite competence to help some categories of clients, they can discourage colleagues from referring such people to them.

## Client Autonomy

Respect for the client's right to make the choices that work best for them in their lives is the principle underlying client self-determination. Coaching trainees should seek to support clients' control over and ability to assume personal responsibility for their lives. When, for example, trainees provide inaccurate pre-coaching information or make false statements about their professional qualifications and competencies, they are stopping potential and actual clients from making informed choices about whether to commence and/or continue in coaching with them.

Most often it is unnecessary and unrealistic for coaching trainees to provide lengthy explanations to clients about what they do. Nevertheless, before and during coaching, they can make accurate statements concerning the coaching process and about the their respective roles. Furthermore, trainees can answer clients' queries about coaching honestly and with respect. Since coaching tends to be short term and structured, it lends itself to clients being given clear written contracts. Information in such contracts can include: the qualifications of the coach; the nature of the services available; limitations, boundaries and perspectives of the coach; a statement of the client's rights; and the terms of the contract, such as times, frequency, methods of communication and fees for the coaching service (Whitworth, Kimsey-House and Sandahl, 1998).

Coaching trainees should make realistic statements about the outcomes of coaching and avoid making claims that might be disputed both outside and inside of court. Throughout coaching, clients should be treated as intelligent participants who have a right to explanations about why trainees suggest interventions and what is entailed in implementing them.

Sometimes in coaching clients agree to data being collected from a number of sources to help them understand how they function better. However positive or negative the findings from such data collection turn out to be, the client has a right to receive it accurately. Another client right is the right to to terminate coaching. Where possible, trainees should find the reasons for such decisions and, if appropriate, refer clients on to those who may be better equipped to deal with them.

An issue of client autonomy is where the values and backgrounds of clients may differ from those of their coaches, for instance as a result of cultural or religious influences. Coaching trainees should not impose their values on clients and, where appropriate, should be prepared to refer clients on to others who may more readily understand their concerns. It is highly unethical for trainees to assess and treat clients as having problems on the basis of judgments determined by culture, race, sex or sexual orientation, among other characteristics.

## Confidentiality

There may be reasons connected with matters such as agency policy and sometimes the law why coaching trainees cannot guarantee confidentiality. Rogers (2004: 168) writes: 'The coaching relationship is not privileged under law and clients need to be told that this is so'. Coaching trainees should endeavour to communicate pertinent limitations on confidentiality to clients in advance. In cases where third parties are funding the coaching, recipients of the coaching can decide what they will allow to be disclosed to a funding sponsor – therefore, coaches should refrain from doing so without the client's explicit consent. Other than in exceptional circumstances, trainees should seek clients' permission for any communication to third parties. Sometimes, especially when the coaching is focused on building strengths, clients will be happy for others to know that they are being or have been coached. Some satisfied clients allow and sometimes even encourage coaches to quote them in advertising their services. On other occasions, the issue of whether or not to disclose to third parties can provide major ethical dilemmas for coaching trainees, for instance assessing whether to disclose to another party threats of suicide, or threatened or actual serious aggression.

Confidentiality assumes that clients have the right to control the disclosure of their personal information. Clients' records, whether they are case notes, tapes or research information, need to be held securely at all times. In instances where coaching trainees require tapes for supervision purposes, they should refrain from putting pressure on clients to be recorded. Most clients will understand the request and, provided they are assured of the security of the tapes, will give their permission. In cases where clients have reservations, they are often reassured if told that they may stop the recording any time they wish. In instances where trainees want clients to participate in research projects, not only should their permission be sought but when reporting findings clients' wishes for anonymity must be protected.

## Client Protection

The category of client protection encompasses looking after clients as persons. Coaching trainees require sufficient professional detachment to act in clients' best interests. Dual relationships are those where, in addition to the coaching relationship, coaches or trainees may already be in, considering entering, or entering other kinds of relationships with clients: for instance as friend, lover, colleague, trainer or supervisor, among others. Whether a dual coach–client relationship is ethical, unethical or presents an ethical dilemma depends on the circumstances of the relationship. In some work settings, coaches may meet clients at functions that both are expected to attend. Sexual contact with clients is always unethical.

Instead of or as well as sexual exploitation, clients may also be subject to emotional and financial exploitation. Emotional exploitation can take many forms, but has the underlying theme of using clients in some way for the coach's personal agendas; for example encouraging dependent and admiring clients rather than fostering autonomy. Financial exploitation can also take many forms, including coaches charging for services they are unqualified to provide, overcharging and prolonging coaching unnecessarily.

Coaching trainees need to ensure that all reasonable precautions are taken to ensure clients' physical safety. In addition, coaches and coach training organizations should consider protecting their clients and themselves by carrying adequate indemnity insurance covering such matters as professional indemnity (malpractice, errors and omissions) and public liability (including occupier's liability). Coaches and trainees may also be better placed to protect their clients, and sometimes themselves too, if they have adequate knowledge of pertinent aspects of the law.

## Conflicts of Interest

Conflicts of interest should be avoided if possible. Rogers (2004) observes that when organizations ask her for progress reports on clients as a condition of the work, she will refuse the work. A major reason for doing so is that it would be impossible to create trust if the client believes that coaching is about assessment. Rogers also does not work with direct competitor organizations simultaneously because of the likelihood of commercially sensitive information being part of the coaching. While she can keep such secrets, she is concerned about clients' possible reservations about confidentiality.

In those instances where any actual conflict of interest or the potential for a conflict of interest arises, coaching trainees should openly disclose it, fully discuss it with the client and look for a fair resolution. Though possibly more an issue for later than when training, where coaches have relationships with third parties concerning referrals or advice, they should disclose them.

## Professional Monitoring and Development

Coaching trainees have a responsibility to current and future clients to keep monitoring their performance and developing their skills. Trainees need to evaluate and reflect upon what they do, receive either supervision or consultative support to gain insights into good skills and pinpoint other skills that they can improve, and be prepared to engage in a range of activities that expand their knowledge and understanding of how to perform better. In addition, they should manage their own issues so that they do not intrude into the coaching relationship (Rogers, 2004). Furthermore, trainees have an ethical responsibility to keep abreast of relevant literature, both about coaching processes and outcomes and also about social, professional and ethical issues that can impact on their clients and themselves.

### Activity 13.1   Ethical Issues and Dilemmas in Coaching Practice

1. Critically discuss how each of the areas in Box 13.1 contains important ethical issues, and possibly dilemmas, for coaches.
2. In which areas do you consider yourself most at risk of acting unethically when you coach?
3. What can you do to protect yourself and your clients from your potential to act unethically in the areas you have identified?

## Ethical Issues and Dilemmas in Coach Training

Inasmuch as trainees are seeing clients on placements, coach training involves the ethical issues and dilemmas associated with coaching practice. Furthermore, there are additional ethical issues and dilemmas attached to training. Individual trainees and staff tend to see coach training from their own perspectives but in reality there are numerous parties with varying interests in the conduct of training, and hence in how ethical issues and dilemmas are addressed. As well as trainees and trainers, these interested parties can include supervisors, placement agencies, future clients, academic departments, academic institutions and professional associations.

### Competence and Performing Multiple Roles

A theme throughout this section on ethics in coach training is that staff members and trainees are each vulnerable to ethical issues and dilemmas, some similar and others differing according to their roles. For example, both staff and trainees face inevitable role conflicts that create ethical dilemmas if they are to give sufficient time to teaching and to learning essential coaching skills. The basic role of any academic staff member includes teaching, research and administration. In addition, coaching course staff members need to arrange and monitor trainee placements. Furthermore, they should be maintaining and developing their own coaching skills by continuing to see clients. On top of this, some will be playing important roles in their professional associations. In addition, staff members have private lives that ideally provide nourishment for performing strongly in their professional lives.

Coaching course staff can allow the ethical dilemmas involved in juggling multiple roles to become ethical lapses when they allow insufficient time and energy to perform their training and supervision duties competently. For example, staff members may be earning extra income from private practice and consulting activities and, hence, be insufficiently prepared for their training duties or less than desirably available to trainees. Another example of an ethical lapse is that of staff members who allow their research interests and promotion ambitions to dominate their time at the expense of trainees. However, with the increasing demands on staff members in higher educational institutions, there is also an increasing risk that fully responsible training can no longer either be offered or expected since trainers need immense dedication and exceptional physical and mental energy to perform their roles well.

Most trainees learning coaching skills are mature. Many courses are part-time or evening courses. All professional courses require supervised placements and attendance at supervisions in addition to regular academic and practical requirements. Where academic requirements involve learning statistical, computing and research design skills, and then conducting a detailed research project, trainees can find that the competing demands of academic and practical work create a particularly difficult ethical dilemma in relation to time management. In addition, all trainees have private lives, some have children to look after and many are in part-time or full-time employment.

When coaching trainees commit themselves to embarking on coaching courses, they are also committing themselves to spending sufficient time to learn the skills and to coach clients on placements properly. Unless there are exceptional mitigating circumstances, it is an inexcusable ethical lapse for trainees to devote insufficient time and attention to developing competence in the required coaching skills. By so doing such negligent trainees sacrifice the interests of all the other parties mentioned in the introduction to this section, including their own interests. Usually trainees' ethical lapses in regard to giving sufficient time to developing skills represent shades of grey, rather than being black-and-white matters.

## Confidentiality

On coaching courses, trainers and supervisors can build and reinforce trainees' awareness of the need for confidentiality. By participating in skills training groups, trainees should be aware of such issues as not putting pressure on others to disclose more than they are comfortable with, protecting one another's secrets, seeking permission to reveal information to third parties, and safe storage of any written and taped records.

Before commencing their placements trainees need to familiarize themselves with any limitations on confidentiality that the agency or institution requires, so that then they can communicate these limitations to clients in advance. Often new clients have been informed when being referred that they are seeing coaching trainees who are required to discuss their work with supervisors both to provide a better service and as part of their training. In those cases where trainees are required to audio-record or videotape sessions for supervision, clients often also already know that this is part of the process. Nevertheless, trainees should still check with clients that they have permission to record sessions and, if required, obtain a signed release to do so. Furthermore, trainees can inform clients of how any cassettes or tapes of sessions will be kept and when they will be erased.

Trainees may face ethical dilemmas concerning confidentiality in instances of conflicting requirements between ethical codes and agency policies. Most, if not all, of the ethical dilemmas concerning confidentiality with which coaches in practice wrestle, trainees on placement may encounter too: for example, risk to third parties and risk to the client. It is essential that trainees bring to the attention of and discuss with their supervisors any such ethical dilemmas and most trainees are only too happy to do so. Failure to discuss ethical dilemmas concerning confidentiality is a serious ethical lapse in itself, since both supervisors and sponsoring agencies have assumed responsibility for the quality of the trainee's work and for protecting the clients they coach.

## Dual Relationships and Sexual Contact

Dual relationships are those where the participants engage in a relationship that has a different agenda to their professional relationship. In coach training there are two main types of dual relationships that can take place: those between trainees on placement and their clients, and those between trainees and staff. Though there are a variety of other agendas that may take place in dual relationships, such as business or social, here my emphasis is on intimate emotional and sexual relationships.

A case in which a trainee on placement develops a 'hidden' sexual relationship with a client contains numerous breaches of trust. Foremost, the client may be damaged by the relationship. Sexual relationships with clients can also have serious legal ramifications for coaches. The trainee has also breached trust with his supervisor, the placement agency, his coach training course and with any professional association accrediting the course. Trainees on placements who find themselves sexually attracted to clients can protect all concerned if they raise such issues with their supervisors. Their sexual feelings are not wrong in themselves and, during their careers, many coaches experience sexual attraction to one or more of their clients. It is how these sexual feelings are handled that can lead to serious ethical misconduct. Supervisors also have a clear ethical responsibility to keep the supervisory relationship as a professional one. The damage of inappropriate staff–trainee relationships can spread well beyond coach training courses into trainees' subsequent professional practise.

Especially since most trainees are of mature age, they have a responsibility not to engage in staff–trainee relationships that may have negative consequences for their fellow trainees, the staff and for themselves. In most instances, trainees who receive messages from staff members that the training relationship might be accompanied by an emotional or sexual one should use assertion skills to nip such advances in the bud. In rare instances, they might suggest to the staff member that any possibility of a personal relationship should be put on hold, pending the end of their course. If sexually harassed, coaching trainees of both sexes can go to people like heads of departments, students' rights officers or counselling services and consider using institutional sexual harassment procedures, assuming they exist. Coaching course staff also may need to take appropriate action in instances where trainees sexually harass them.

## Ethics and staff–trainee relations

On coaching courses, it is preferable if staff and trainees can develop a set of ethical group norms regarding how they treat one another and clients. When it comes to ethical decision-making it is undesirable to have an 'us-versus-them' tussle, either explicit or implicit, in staff–trainee relationships. Both parties have a responsibility to act ethically, to treat one another with respect and to assume responsibility for the maintenance of ethical standards on the course. For example, if a trainee shirks their responsibilities to learn coaching skills properly by not attending some sessions for no legitimate reason, the trainer deserves support from other course members in explaining why it is neither in the trainee's nor the course's best interests that this situation continue.

Trainees also need to be mindful that coach training, with its practical as well as academic components, is resource intensive while most academic budgets are being squeezed. In the pressure cooker of coach training, trainees individually and collectively need to be very careful about playing the victim, casting one or more staff members as persecutors and then seeking support from third parties. Just as coaching course staff have a duty of care to act ethically towards trainees, so trainees have a similar duty to act ethically towards them.

### Activity 13.2    *Ethical Issues and Dilemmas in Coach Training*

1.  Critically discuss the ethical issues and dilemmas for trainees on coach training courses in each of the following areas:

    *   competence and performing multiple roles;
    *   confidentiality;
    *   dual relationships and sexual contact; and
    *   staff–trainee relations.

2.  What other areas for ethical issues and dilemmas are important in coach training and why?

## Making Decisions about Ethical Issues and Dilemmas

Coaches require both ethical awareness and the skills of ethical decision-making. Bond (2000) states that he has become increasingly aware of the need to encourage ethical mindfulness rather than an unquestioning adherence to ethical principles. Though Bond writes in regard to counsellors, his remarks apply equally to coaches. Being ethically mindful consists of both wrestling with the issues involved in ethical decisions and dilemmas in a systematic and considered way and assuming personal responsibility for acting ethically. Possessing a systematic step-by-step way of approaching difficult ethical dilemmas can increase coaches' chances of making sound ethical decisions. Box 13.2 presents Bond's ethical problem-solving model.

---

### Box 13.2    *Bond's ethical problem-solving model*

1.  Produce a brief description of the problem or dilemma.
2.  Decide 'Whose dilemma is it anyway?'
3.  Consider all available ethical principles and guidelines.
4.  Identify all possible courses of action.
5.  Select the best possible course of action.
6.  Evaluate the outcome.

---

In light of the emphasis of this book on good and poor mind skills, the Bond model is rather too optimistic in implying that ethical decision-making is a rational process. As the saying goes 'Who ever said that humans were rational?' Coaching trainees tend to bring different decision-making styles to ethical decisions: for example, some avoid making them for as long as possible, others rush into making them, still others worry over every detail. In addition, even when trainees make decisions, they differ in their commitment to them and in their abilities to implement them skillfully.

Coaching trainees should always be alert for how they may be turning what is outwardly a rational decision-making process into one that is less than completely rational because of their own needs and anxieties. Furthermore, the more they can successfully work on their own mental development, both as persons and as coaches, the more likely they are to work their way rationally through the ethical dilemmas that inevitably arise in coaching.

## Activity 13.3    Making Decisions about Ethical Issues and Dilemmas

1.  Critically discuss the strengths and weaknesses of Bond's ethical problem-solving model.
2.  What can you do now to improve your ability to make decisions wisely when faced with ethical issues and dilemmas as a coach in future?

# 14
# Developing
# Self-Coaching Skills

Though some approaches take the position that it is ongoing and can last for life (Williams and Davis, 2002), life coaching conducted by coaches or coaching trainees is more commonly viewed as something that is performed either once or as needed. Even where life coaching lasts for life, clients still need to develop self-coaching skills. To some extent the life coaching model introduced in Chapter 3 has the development of self-coaching skills taking place in the agreeing on a shared analysis of how to achieve the client's life goals phase of Stage 2 (Understanding) and the intervening phase of Stage 3 (Changing). This process continues further in the ending phase of Stage 3 and the maintenance and improvement phase of Stage 4 (Client self-coaching). Using self-coaching skills well is the major objective of the self-directed growth phase of Stage 4.

The very idea of a skills model of life coaching has the development of self-coaching skills implicit in it. Coaches and trainees work with clients in such a way that they understand the mind skills and communication/action skills that will help them to achieve their objectives. Though life coaching can differ in the amount of attention paid to self-coaching for afterwards, the fact that skills are identified and worked on, including by homework, means that self-coaching always takes place. Coaching trainees can build clients' skills of monitoring their performance after as well as during coaching. Furthermore, you can assist clients to develop skills for improving their behaviour, if necessary, when on their own.

# Self-Directed Coaching

Especially in longer-term life coaching, coaches and trainees can coach clients in how to coach themselves afterwards not only in the skills addressed already but also in new or different skills they need to confront issues and problems in their lives. Luciani (2004: 212) writes: 'The key to launching your Self-Coaching success is to have some early victories. And for this you need to begin at the beginning, looking for small, less risky challenges'. However, even before this, clients can be trained in self-coaching.

## The CASIE Model of Self-Coaching

Because of limited exposure, clients in brief coaching are unlikely to learn how to apply the life coaching model to future problems. Clients in longer-term coaching will acquire some knowledge of the model as they and their coaches or coaching trainees work with the skills that they need to address. Consequently, longer-term clients have a start in knowing where to look when assessing future problems. The life coaching model presented in Chapter 3 can be adapted into a simpler model that clients can use to coach themselves. This model can be called CASIE when used for client self-helping purposes:

**C** *Confront* and clarify the area for change.
**A** *Assess* and restate the area into skills to improve.
**S** *Select* self-helping interventions.
**I** *Intervene*.
**E** *Evaluate* the consequences self-helping interventions.

Trainees can coach clients in being prepared to confront areas in which they need to improve and to clarify them into manageable units. Clients then require coaching in how to assess the area or problem and to restate it into at least one communication/action skill and one mind skill. Since clients will probably be learning the self-coaching model towards the end of coaching, trainees can use the areas and problems on which they have already worked as examples of how to break problems down. Trainees may still need to coach clients to understand the specific mind skills and communication/action skills they can use to state areas in skills terms. When training clients in mind skills, a little goes a long way. Trainees should make sure that clients understand at least one mind skill thoroughly before going on to another. Clients should also be clear about breaking communication/action areas down into their verbal, vocal, body and taking action dimensions.

When clients intervene on their own, they should know about not trying anything too difficult too soon. Instead trainees should help them to learn, where possible, to build their skills gradually. Readers are referred to the planning sub-goals and sequencing graded tasks section of Chapter 8. Clients should also be helped to observe closely both what they do and its results so that they can adjust their skills as necessary. When working on their own, clients need to be careful not to give up but rather to analyse accurately the reasons why they may not be succeeding.

---

### Box 14.1    Example of Self-Coaching

Jon, 32, a previous life coaching client was having trouble with his older sister Fiona, 33, with whom he ran the family printing business. He had been putting off having a real discussion with her for some time. Jon remembered the CASIE self-helping framework and decided to put it into practice. He confronted the fact that he needed to have a frank discussion with Fiona. He assessed his situation and decided he needed to focus on the mind skills of creating rules, perceptions and self-talk. The demanding rule that he decided to work on was 'I must always agree with my sister'. The unrealistic perceptions were about himself, 'I do not have the strength to stand up to Fiona', and about Fiona, 'She is never going to listen to me.' He also needed to focus on his self-talk to calm himself down before discussing the problem with her and to coach himself: for instance, 'Do not raise my voice and stick to the point'. The communication skills he decided to focus on were the verbal, vocal and body messages for handling conflict assertively.

Jon worked on his mind skills. For example, he challenged his demanding rule 'I must always agree with my sister' and restated it as 'While I want to get on with my sister, some differences between us are inevitable and we can try to work through them together.' Jon looked for evidence to support his perceptions ('I do not have the strength to stand up to Fiona' and 'She is never going to listen to me') and decided that he was almost certainly wrong on both counts and that he would never know unless he tried to discuss his differences with her. He also practised using calming and coaching self-talk that would help him deal with Fiona. In addition, Jon focused on the communication skills of what he could say to Fiona to create the conditions whereby they both could start rebuilding trust and discussing their differences honestly. He practised vocal and body as well as verbal messages. Then Jon found a mutually good time to have a talk with Fiona and used the mind and communication skills he had decided on. He evaluated the discussion as being the start of having a more honest relationship with Fiona and realized that he needed to keep working on and improving his skills in future.

---

## Remember Positive Consequences

Whether the results of coaching by another or of self-directed coaching, coaching trainees can remind clients to look out for the positive consequences of changes in behaviour. Former clients are more likely to repeat behaviours perceived as rewarding than those perceived otherwise. Sometimes the rewards are obvious, such as when a problem with another person was cleared up. Sometimes the rewards are subtler, such as the gradual growth of trust in a relationship. On other occasions the rewards may come from minimizing negative consequences: for instance, ending a relationship with minimal damage to the self-respect of both parties.

> Kurt was the manager in a photography shop with seven employees. He decided to work on his tendency to get aggressive with his staff but in doing so felt he was losing some of his authority. However, when he listed the positive consequences of treating his staff with more respect and moderation, he realized the importance of continuing to curb his temper and develop his anger management skills.

## Co-Coach

Trainees can also tell clients the value of working with a partner once formal coaching ends. Grant and Greene (2001: 154) observe that 'Co-coaching is a formalized agreement between two or more people to support, motivate and facilitate change'. Though not suitable for everyone, some former clients gain much from working with another who could be a spouse, friend or workmate. Co-coaching may be performed either face-to-face or on the telephone.

Former clients must know that co-coaching requires written and clearly defined boundaries regarding such matters as how long co-coaching will continue, how often partners will meet or speak, what skills each is going to focus on and how the coaching sessions will be structured. One option for structuring the session is to allow one partner to speak for 10 minutes, followed by 5 minutes' discussion and then the process gets repeated for focusing on the other partner. Partners in co-coaching need to use good listening skills and to allow each other the freedom to solve their own problems. They also require good questioning skills: for instance, 'How might you have acted differently?' or 'How can you work on changing the beliefs that are unhelpful?'

### *Use Mind Skills*

Coaches and trainees can coach clients in mind skills that are relevant to self-directed coaching.

### *Creating Rules*

Former clients are more likely to keep using improved mind skills and communication/action skills if they can challenge any demanding rules that may weaken their resolve and then restate them into preferential rules. In particular, those clients who have worked on demanding rules during coaching are in a strong position to do so. Box 14.2 provides examples of restating demanding into preferential rules.

---

### Box 14.2    Creating Preferential Rules about Maintaining Improved Skills

| | |
|---|---|
| **Demanding rule** | Maintaining my improved skills must be easy. |
| **Preferential rule** | There is no such thing as a cure. I need to keep practising my improved skills so that using them may then become easier. |
| **Demanding rule** | After terminating coaching, I must never go backwards. |
| **Preferential rule** | Maintaining any skill can involve mistakes, uncertainty, and setbacks. All I can do is to learn from and retrieve mistakes and cope with setbacks as best as possible. |
| **Demanding rule** | Others must support and approve of my efforts to improve my skills. |
| **Preferential rule** | Though I might prefer to have others' approval, what is important is that I keep my skills development goals in mind and work hard to attain them. |

---

### *Creating Perceptions*

Former clients should strive to perceive their good and poor skills accurately. They can discourage themselves if they pay disproportionate attention to setbacks rather than to successes. When lapses occur, former clients should try to avoid the perceiving error of over-generalizing them into relapses: 'Since I have gone back to my old behaviour once, I have permanently relapsed and can do nothing about it.' Lapses should stimulate using retrieval or 'getting back on the track' skills rather than giving up.

## Creating Self-Talk

Former clients can use coping self-talk to deal both with situations they have worked on in coaching and new situations that arise. They can tell themselves to 'Stop ... think ... calm down' and then instruct themselves in what to do. When former clients do have lapses they can say to themselves: 'Now is the time for me to use my retrieval skills'. For instance, a former client of mine, who became extremely anxious about performing his golf downswing correctly, learned to replace his anxiety-engendering self-talk when his golf ball ended up in awkward situations by telling himself 'No upheaval, just retrieval.' Former clients can also use affirming self-talk to maintain their improved skills. They can encourage themselves with internal rewards like 'Well done', 'I hung in there and made it' and 'I'm happy that I'm maintaining my skills.'

## Creating Visual Images

Former clients can visualize anticipated high-risk situations and develop strategies for coping with them. They can also visualize themselves getting the rewards of appropriate behaviour. In addition, they can visualize the negative consequences of engaging in or relapsing back to unwanted behaviours. Some former clients may need to exaggerate the negative consequences to strengthen their willpower (Cautela, 1967; Lazarus, 1984).

## Creating Explanations

Former clients require accuracy in explaining the causes of positive and negative events as they implement and maintain their improved skills. For instance, where justified, they can attribute the cause of their successes to factors such as effort, willingness to take reasonable risks and use of targeted skills

Successful former clients assume personal responsibility for their lives. When in difficulty, looking at the adequacy of their own thinking, communicating and use of targeted skills is the best place to start. They ask themselves questions like 'What are my goals and how is my behaviour blocking me from attaining them?', 'What are my characteristic poor mind and communication/action skills in relation to this problem?' and 'How well am I using the skills I have learned and how can I improve?'

## *Creating Expectations*

Creating realistic expectations can assist former clients to maintain skills in a number of ways. Those able to predict high-risk situations that present a greater than usual temptation to lapse into unwanted behaviour can develop strategies to deal with them. Characteristics of high-risk situations include feeling emotionally upset, being under considerable stress, feeling lonely, social pressure from others and losing control under the influence of alcohol.

Former clients can strengthen their resolve to maintain their improved skills if they are able to predict the benefits of continuing to use them and the costs of giving them up. Furthermore, former clients can maintain skills in specific situations where realistic risk-taking is desirable if they focus on the gains of action as well as on potential losses. By so doing, they challenge and counterbalance their excessive expectations of danger.

## *Develop a Support Network*

Trainees can encourage clients, where appropriate, to develop their support networks. People, as individuals and as couples, exist in support networks of varying degrees of adequacy: family, friends, work colleagues, clubs, church and so on. In addition, former clients can have access to voluntary or professional helpers. Former clients can develop a support network that contains people who use and reward the skills that they wish to maintain and develop. Specific networking skills include identifying suitable people and organizations to partake in the support network, knowing how best to access them, using them when necessary and being prepared to contribute so that the flow of support is in both direction.

Former clients may also choose to meet on a regular basis with a group of other people to work on their skills. Being in a support group has the advantage of enabling them to practise their skills, observe others' skills and obtain feedback.

## *Practise Daily*

Trainees can remind clients that there is no such thing as not using skills. All the time they are practising using skills, whether they like it or not. The old saying 'practise makes perfect' is unrealistic. Better to say 'practise makes competent'. By practising their skills conscientiously, not just in crises but all of the time, former clients are more likely to improve them. Furthermore, they can become more confident and flexible in applying skills. Often there is a very important gap between learning a skill and putting it into practise. Psychologists call overcoming this gap 'transfer of training'. However, transfer of training can go beyond maintaining a skill to improving it with continued practise.

## Attend Workshops and Training Courses

No hard-and-fast distinctions exist between training courses and workshops. However, if anything, training courses are spread over a longer period, say a month or more, whereas workshops are ordinarily relatively intense experiences lasting from a day to a week. Means whereby former clients can find out about skills workshops and training courses include seeking information from coaches and trainees; professional associations in psychology, business and health; and looking in newspapers, relevant journals and newsletters. In all instances they should look before they leap. Since acquiring good skills requires much work and practise, courses and workshops offering miracle cures are to be avoided. Box 14.3 provides a checklist for assessing training courses and workshops.

---

### Box 14.3    Checklist for Assessing Training Courses and Workshops

1.  What are the course's or workshop's goals?
2.  What are the training methods that may be employed during the course or workshop?
3.  What is the pertinent training and experience of the trainer or trainers?
4.  What is the size of the course or workshop and is there a screening process prior to entry?
5.  When does the course or workshop start? How long is each session? Over what period will the course or workshop continue? Where will it be held? Are the facilities adequate?
6.  What, if any, is the fee for the course or workshop and are there any additional expenses that may be incurred?

---

## Activity 14.1    Developing Self-Coaching Skills

Work with a partner and discuss the following ways that as coaches you could encourage clients to engage in self-coaching:

- using the CASIE model of self-coaching;
- remembering positive consequences;
- co-coaching;
- using mind skills
  - creating rules
  - creating perceptions
  - creating self-talk
  - creating visual images
  - creating explanations
  - creating expectations;
- developing a support network;
- practising daily; and
- attending workshops and training courses.

# References

Alberti, R.E. and Emmons, M.L. (2001) *Your Perfect Right: Assertiveness and Equality in Your Life and Relationships* (8th edn). Atascadero, AC: Impact.

Argyle, M. (1991) *Cooperation: The Basis of Sociability.* London: Routledge.

Argyle, M. (1999) *The Psychology of Interpersonal Behaviour* (5th edn). London: Penguin Books.

Auerbach, J.E. (2001) *Personal and Executive Coaching: The Complete Guide for Mental Health Professionals.* Ventura, CA: Executive College Press.

Bandura, A. (1977) *Social Learning Theory.* Englewood Cliffs, NJ: Prentice-Hall.

Bandura, A. (1986) *Social Foundations of Thought and Action: A Social Cognitive Theory.* Englewood Cliffs, NJ: Prentice-Hall.

Beck, A.T. (1976) *Cognitive Therapy and the Emotional Disorders.* New York: New American Library.

Beck, A.T. (1988) *Love is Never Enough: How Couples can Overcome Misunderstandings, Resolve Conflicts, and Solve Relationship Problems through Cognitive Therapy.* New York: Harper and Row.

Beck, A.T. and Weishaar, M.E. (2005) 'Cognitive therapy', in R. Corsini and D. Wedding (eds), *Current Psychotherapies* (7th edn). Belmont, CA: Thomson Brooks/Cole. pp. 238–68.

Bernstein, D.A. and Borkovec, T.D. (1973) *Progressive Relaxation Training: A Manual for the Helping Professions.* Champaign, IL: Research Press.

Blatner, A. (2005) 'Psychodrama', in Corsini and Wedding (eds), *Current Psycho-therapies*, pp. 405–38.

Bond, T. (2000) *Standards and Ethics for Counselling in Practice* (2nd edn). London: Sage.

Butler, P.E. (1992) *Self-Assertion for Women* (rev. edn). San Francisco: Harper Collins.

Cautela, J. (1967) 'Covert sensitization'. *Psychological Reports,* 20: 459–68.

Christensen, A. and Jacobson, N.S. (2000) *Reconcilable Differences.* New York: Guilford.

Cormier, S. and Nurius, P.S. (2002) *Interviewing and Change Strategies for Helpers: Fundamental Skills and Cognitive-Behavioral Interventions.* Belmont, CA: Thomson Brooks/Cole.

Corsini, R. and Wedding, D. (eds) (2005) *Current Psychotherapies* (7th edn). Belmont, CA: Thomson Brooks/Cole.

Deffenbacher, J.L., Oetting, E.R. and DiGuiseppe, R.A. (2002) 'Principles of empirically supported interventions applied to anger management', *The Counseling Psychologist,* 30: 282–80.

Downey, M. (2003) *Effective Coaching: Lessons from the Coach's Coach* (2nd edn). New York: Texere.

Dryden, W. and Feltham, C. (1992) *Brief Counselling: A Practical Guide for Beginning Practitioners.* Buckingham: Open University Press.

Egan, G. (1977) *You and Me: The Skills of Communicating and Relating to Others.* Monterey, CA: Thomson Brooks/Cole.

Egan, G. (2002) *The Skilled Helper: A Problem-Management and Opportunity-Development Approach to Helping* (7th edn). Pacific Grove, CA: Thomson Brooks/Cole.

Ekman, P., Friesen, W.V. and Ellsworth, P. (1972) *Emotions in the Human Face.* New York: Pergamon Press.

Ellis, A. (1987) 'The impossibility of achieving consistently good mental health', *American Psychologist,* 42: 364–75.

Ellis, A (1999) *How to Make Yourself Happy and Remarkably Less Disturbable.* Atascadero, CA: Impact.

Ellis, A. (2001) *Feeling Better, Getting Better, Staying Better: Profound Self-Help Therapy for Your Emotions.* Atascadero, CA: Impact.

Ellis, A. (2003) *Ask Albert Ellis? Straight Answers and Sound Advice from America's Best-Known Psychologist.* Atascadero, CA: Impact.

Ellis, A. (2005) 'Rational emotive behavior therapy', in Corsini Wedding (eds), *Current Psychotherapies,* pp. 166–201.

Ellis, A. and Crawford, T. (2000) *Making Intimate Connections: 7 Guidelines for Great Relationships and Better Communication.* Atascadero, CA: Impact.

Flaherty, J. (1999) *Coaching: Evoking Excellence in Others.* Boston: Butterworth-Heinmann.

Freudenberger, H.J. (1980) *Burnout: The High Cost of High Achievement.* London: Arrow Books.

Gazda, G.M. (1989) *Group Counseling: A Developmental Approach* (4th edn). Boston: Allyn & Bacon.

Gibb, B.E., Abramson, L. and Alloy, L.B. (2004) 'Emotional maltreatment from parents, verbal peer victimization, and cognitive vulnerability to depression', *Cognitive Therapy and Research,* 28: 1–21.

Goleman, D. (1998) *Working with Emotional Intelligence.* New York: Bantam.

Gordon, T. (1970) *Parent Effectiveness Training: The Tested New Way to Raise Responsible Children*. New York: Wyden.

Gottman, J.M. and Silver, N. (1999) *The Seven Principles for Making Marriage Work*. New York: Three Rivers Press.

Grant, A.M. and Greene, J. (2001) *Coach Yourself: Make Real Change in Your Life*. Cambridge, MA: Perseus Publishing.

Grant, A.M. and Palmer, S. (2002) 'Coaching psychology', meeting held at the annual conference of the Division of Counselling Psychology, British Psychological Society, Torquay, 18 May.

Greenberger, D. and Padesky, C.A. (1995) *Mind Over Mood: Change How You Feel by Changing the Way You Think*. New York: Guilford Press.

Hall, E.T. (1966) *The Hidden Dimension*. New York: Doubleday.

Hamburg, S.R. (2000) *Will Our Love Last?: A Couple's Road Map*. New York: Scribner.

Holland, J.L. (1987) *Self-Directed Search: 1987 Manual Supplement*. Odessa, FL: Psychological Assessment Resources.

Hudson, F. (1999) *The Handbook of Coaching: A Comprehensive Resource Guide for Managers, Executives, Consultants, and Human Resource Professionals*. San Francisco: Jossey-Bass.

Interest Group Coaching Psychology (2005) 'Coaching psychology'. Australian Psychological Society. Available at www.psychology.org.au/units/interest%5Fgroups/coaching/

International Coach Federation (2005) *The ICF Code of Ethics*. Available at www.coach-federation.org/ethics/code_ethics.asp

Ivey, A.E. and Ivey, M.B. (2003) *Intentional Interviewing and Counseling: Facilitating Client Development in a Multicultural Society* (5th edn). Belmont, CA: Thomson Brooks/Cole.

Kazdin, A.E. (1976) 'Developing assertive behaviors through covert modeling', in J.D. Krumboltz and C.E. Thorsen (eds), *Counseling Methods*. New York: Holt, Rinehart & Winston. pp. 475–86.

Lazarus, A.A. (1984) *In the Mind's Eye: The Power of Imagery for Personal Enrichment*. New York: Guilford.

Lazarus, A.A. (2005) 'Multimodal therapy', in Corsini Wedding (eds), *Current Psychotherapies*, pp. 337–71.

Luciani, J.J. (2004) *The Power of Self-Coaching: The Five Essential Steps to Creating the Life You Want*. New York: Wiley.

Masters, W.H. and Johnson, V.E. (1970) *The Pleasure Bond*. New York: Bantam Books.

Masters, W.H., Johnson, V.E. and Kolodny, R.C. (1986) *Masters and Johnson on Sex and Human Loving*. London: Pan MacMillan.

Meichenbaum, D.H. (1985) *Stress Inoculation Training*. NewYork: Pergamon Press.

Meichenbaum, D.H. and Deffenbacher, J.L. (1988) 'Stress inoculation training', *The Counseling Psychologist*, 16: 69–90.

Moreno, Z.T. (1959) 'A survey of psychodramatic techniques', *Group Psycho-therapy*, 12: 5–14.

Mulligan, E. (1999) *Life Coaching: Change Your Life in 7 Days*. London: Piatkus.

Neenan, M. and Dryden, W. (2002) *Life Coaching: A Cognitive-Behavioural Approach*. Hove: Brunner-Routledge.

Nelson-Jones, R. (2006a) *Theory and Practice of Counselling and Therapy* (4th edn). London: Sage.

Nelson-Jones, R. (2006b) *Human Relationship Skills: Coaching and Self-Coaching*. London: Brunner Routledge.

Pattison, S. (1999) 'Are professional codes ethical?', *Counselling*, 10: 374–80.

Peltier, B. (2001) *The Psychology of Executive Coaching: Theory and Application*. New York: Brunner-Routledge.

Prior, D.M. (2003) 'Professional coaching language for greater public under-standing', david@getacoach.com

Rachman, S., Gruter-Andrew, J. and Shafran, R. (2000) 'Post-event processing in social anxiety', *Behaviour Research and Therapy*, 38: 611–17.

Rogers, J. (2004) *Coaching Skills: A Handbook*. Maidenhead: Open University Press.

Selye, H. (1974) *Stress Without Distress*. Sevenoaks: Hodder & Stoughton.

Thitavanno, P. (2002) *A Buddhist Way of Mental Training* (2nd edn). Bangkok: Chuan Printing Press.

Thorsen, C.E. and Mahoney, M.J. (1974) *Behavioral Self-Control*. New York: Holt Rinehart & Winston.

Whitworth, L., Kimsey-House, H. and Sandahl, P. (1998) *Co-Active Coaching: New Skills for Coaching People Toward Success in Work and Life*. Mountain View, CA: Davies-Black.

Wigman, A. (2005) *The Pathways and Pitfalls of Personal Coaching*. Available at www.associationforcoaching.com

Williams, P. and Davis, D.C. (2002) *Therapist as Life Coach: Transforming Your Practice*. New York: Norton.

Williams, P. and Thomas, L.J. (2005) *Total Life Coaching: A Compendium of Resources*. New York: Norton.

Woods, E.A. (1997) *Training a Tiger: A Father's Guide to Raising a Winner in Both Golf and Life*. New York: Harper Perennial.

Worthington, E.L. and Scherer, M. (2004) 'Forgiveness is an emotion-focused coping strategy that can reduce health risks and promote health resilience: theory, review and hypotheses', *Psychology and Health*, 19: 385–405.

Yalom, I.D. (1995) *The Theory and Practice of Group Psychotherapy*. New York: Basic Books.

Zimbardo, P.G. (1977) *Shyness: What It Is, What to Do About It*. Reading, MA: Addison-Wesley.

# Name Index

# Subject Index

acceptance, 44
active listening, 43–4
agreeing on a shared analysis, 35–7
assertiveness skills, 164–6, 189, 194
assessment and goal setting skills, 59–76
Association for Coaching, 1
audiovisual aids, 81–3, 99–100, 106–8
Australian Psychological Society
    Interest Group Coaching
        Psychology, 1, 2

behaviour rating forms, 69–70
bodily communication skills, 14–16, 85
British Psychological Society
    Coaching Psychology Section, 1

career choice coaching
    communication/action skills, 176–7
    mind skills, 177–8
career performance skills
    communication skills, 179–80
    mind skills, 180–1
CASIE model of self-directed
    coaching, 212–13
changing stage, 37–40
choosing and starting relationships
    skills, 159–60
client self-coaching stage, 40–1
clientele for, 4
coaching relationship, 8, 43–58
co-coaching, 214
communication and action skills
    bodily communication, 12
    taking action communication, 12
    touch communication, 12
    verbal communication, 12
    vocal communication, 12

consolidation skills
    assist clients to deliver
        self-reward, 129–30
    assist clients to experiment, 119–22
    encouraging monitoring, 127–9
    facilitate learning by doing, 113
    negotiate homework, 130–4
    plan sub-goals and sequence graded
        tasks, 114–16
    provide feedback, 122–7
    rehearse and role-play, 116–19
cooperative problem-solving (CUDSA)
    model, 168–9
creating expectations, 23–4, 56, 178, 181,
    187–8, 192, 196–7, 217
creating explanations, 21–2, 55–6, 178, 181,
    187, 192, 196, 216–17
creating perceptions, 18–20, 54, 87–9, 177,
    180, 186, 192, 196, 215–16
creating realistic decision-making, 25
creating realistic goals, 24–5
creating rules, 17–18, 54, 86–7, 104–6, 177,
    180, 185–6, 191, 195, 215
creating self-talk, 20–1, 55, 89–91, 109–11,
    177–8, 180–1, 186, 191, 196, 216
creating visual images, 21, 55, 178. 181, 187,
    191–2, 196, 216

delivery skills, 83–5
demonstration skills
    of communication/action skills,
        98–102, 109–11
    considerations in, 95–8
    goals of, 93–4
    methods of, 95–7
    of mind skills, 103–9
developing intimacy skills, 161